LONE DRUID:
CHRONICLES OF A RELUCTANT WILDERNESS ACTIVIST

LONE DRUID
CHRONICLES OF A RELUCTANT WILDERNESS ACTIVIST

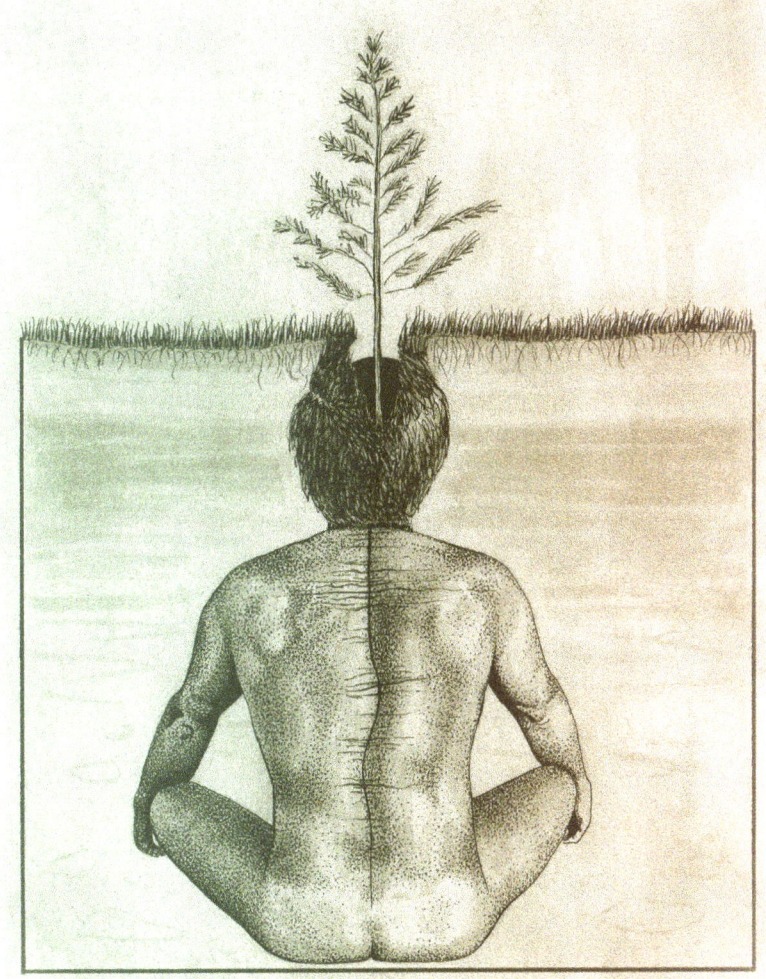

RIC BAILEY

Wake-Robin Press
2024

Lone Druid:
Chronicles of a Reluctant Wilderness Activist
by Ric Bailey

Copyright © 2024 by Ric Bailey

All rights reserved.

Views and opinions expressed in this book are solely those of the author and do not necessarily reflect the views and/or opinions of the publisher. The author in no way represents any company, corporation, organization, or brand mentioned herein, or that might otherwise benefit from the publication of this book.

Printed in the United States of America

First Edition: April 22, 2024
ISBN 978-1-946970-18-3
Library of Congress Control Number: 2024905265

Published by

Wake-Robin Press
An imprint of redbat books
La Grande, OR 97850
www.wakerobinpress.com

Text set in Adobe Jensen Pro and Frente H1

Unless otherwise noted,
Photographs by
David Jensen

Cover Art by
Annie Williams

Cover Design & Book Layout by
redbat design | www.redbatdesign.com

CONTENTS

CHAPTER 1: Revelations of Youth 1
CHAPTER 2: The Geography of Self 9
CHAPTER 3: The "Eco-Psyche" Fuels a Rural Migration 17
CHAPTER 4: Autumn's Dour Refuge 25
CHAPTER 5: Flying to the Mountains and Landing in 1880 33
CHAPTER 6: The Forsaken Recreation Area 39
CHAPTER 7: The Onset of Activism 47
CHAPTER 8: A Radical Digression 53
CHAPTER 9: Managing an Unpaid "Career" 59
CHAPTER 10: A Complicated Identity 65
CHAPTER 11: Scheming a Legislative Solution 71
CHAPTER 12: Splinters of Desperation 79
CHAPTER 13: The Mauling of the Packwood Bill 85
CHAPTER 14: Litigation and a Disturbing Revelation 91
CHAPTER 15: Birth of the
    Hells Canyon–Chief Joseph Campaign 99
CHAPTER 16: Two Canyons and a Linchpin 109
CHAPTER 17: The Unanticipated Rise of HCPC 119
CHAPTER 18: The Delight of Unforeseen Changes 127
CHAPTER 19: "Yeah, Sure. We Can *Do* Recreation!" 133
CHAPTER 20: The Jet-Boat War 139
CHAPTER 21: Crying Wolf 151
CHAPTER 22: A Recipe for Salmon, Beef, and Mutton 159

CHAPTER 23: Mining, Ski Areas,
  Truck Drivers, and Concerts..169

CHAPTER 24: Kill Bills 177

CHAPTER 25: A Shocking Portent:
  A Positive HCNRA Management Plan..183

CHAPTER 26: A Few Months in "The Life"..191

CHAPTER 27: The "Salt Creek Massacre" and Yellow Ink 199

CHAPTER 28: Speaking of Semantics 209

CHAPTER 29: Departure, Phase One..217

CHAPTER 30: The Scourge of Quid Pro Quo Wilderness 227

CHAPTER 31: Departure, Phase Two..235

CHAPTER 32: Of Collaboration..241

CHAPTER 33: The Limits of Compromise 251

CHAPTER 34: The Organization Versus the Cause? 259

CHAPTER 35: You Can Never Go Home 271

CHAPTER 36: Honoring Life...279

ABOUT THE AUTHOR:
  Ric Bailey: Worker and Activist 291

For Tim~

No Retreat,
No Surrender

> Politics makes liars of us all.
>
> —UNKNOWN

* * *

> You are a strange species, not like any other. And you'd be surprised how many there are—intelligent but savage. Shall I tell you what I find beautiful about you? You are at your very best when things are worst.
>
> —JEFF BRIDGES' ALIEN CHARACTER FROM THE FILM *STARMAN*

CHAPTER 1
REVELATIONS OF YOUTH

One enticing autumn day in 2012, I mounted my bicycle and pedaled up to Hurricane Creek Trailhead for a walk to Slickrock Creek. One of my favorite places, the Hurricane Creek canyon materialized like an apparition from the Wallowa Valley. Above it were the knees of Chief Joseph Mountain, an imposing spectacle of dark cliffs that typified the Wallowa Mountains of Northeast Oregon.

The cottonwoods and larches were retiring to singing gold among the thickets of Douglas fir and ponderosa pine trees. The creek alternately roared and whispered with its familiar granite voice. It was one of those moments of mirth when a feeling of undying love for my home country reverberated through me.

What sublime fortune it was that brought me to this place of refuge. To inhale luscious mountain air and sip cool water straight from the stream. To behold sheer, smooth gray cliffs standing as guardians, cradling and inspiring.

My senses quenched after the hike, I pedaled back on the rough road toward home in Joseph, Oregon, eventually coasting fast down a straight, paved section a half mile below the trailhead. Rocketing down the grade, the next corner about a hundred yards away, I heard a vehicle approaching, a powerful engine growling above the sound of the creek. I slowed and headed to the right shoulder of the narrow road.

As it came to within about fifty feet, the beige Ford three-quarter-ton pickup slowed. It featured wide tires, lots of chrome, and a roll bar. That's all I noticed before it sped up and veered toward my side of the road.

I stood my ground. But the rig kept coming, the increasing pitch of its guttural diesel engine filling the canyon. I waved my arms at the driver. At about fifteen feet from collision, I bailed, dumping the bike on its right side and launching myself into the trees.

As I skidded through the rough brush, the truck passed, somehow avoiding the bicycle. The driver yelled, "Asshole!" out his window, but I didn't get a look at his face. As he sped up the hill, I saw through the back window he had a passenger.

My right shoulder and side had absorbed most of the impact. With blood boiling in my head, I rose shakily from the ground. My bike was rideable, but I remained at the place of near-impact and prepared to confront the idiot driver, who had performed his deed while heading up a road that dead-ends at the trailhead.

I tried to maintain self-control by going through the process of rational confrontation—perform a citizen's arrest, and be calm. Of course, given the driver's intent to do serious bodily harm with his jacked-up truck, I could be risking an unfair fight, outnumbered and with a disabled right arm, or face one-sided gun play. I've never carried a weapon and know little about guns.

I stood beside a large fir tree that provided a solid barrier should the driver decide to try and run me over again. I resolved that, when he came back, I'd stand on the edge of the road and wave him down.

After about fifteen minutes of trepidation, I heard a diesel-powered vehicle approaching, coming down from the trailhead. It was just beyond a bend in the road, out of my line of sight. But before coming into view, it apparently veered off onto the primitive dirt road that goes to the abandoned Hurricane Creek Campground extension. This parallel side road is tank-trapped with mounded rock piles, but they would be no match for the mini monster truck. The spur rejoins the main road maybe three-quarters of a mile down.

I boarded my bike and headed toward the lower junction to intercept my prospective assassin. But he apparently beat me to it. The truck was nowhere to be seen. Maybe he'd stopped somewhere along the side road above me? With my shoulder on fire, I abandoned confrontation and instead painfully rode the three miles home and tended to my injuries. The scratches from the rough vegetation would disappear within a couple of weeks. But my already-arthritic shoulder became nearly immobile for several days and soon was a lingering condition. Four years later, I would capitulate to shoulder-replacement surgery.

Did the driver know who he had run off the road, or did he do that to every bicycle he encountered? Did he mistake me for someone else he knew and despised? Or was he just a belligerent road hog emboldened by his compensation vehicle? The answer was obvious. He knew who he was attacking.

In the days following the assault, my thoughts often returned to my youth. I wondered how an inherent, lifelong love of nature could have led me to become the pariah of Wallowa County.

* * *

In 1960, two months before my seventh birthday, our family moved into a new home in Lake Oswego, Oregon. One year later, Hallinan Heights, our neighborhood, was invaded. I walked from our house to the site of the incursion and stared down the iron beast face-to-face: mechanical monster versus child. Upon its bent grille a welded plate read ALLIS CHALMERS. I dared Al to charge. My jaw quivered slightly, even though the beast was without pilot at the moment, its master having departed the work site.

Al was huge. The top of my head didn't reach the bottom of his engine compartment. His scraper trailer was as captivating to me as to any kid inherently fascinated by big machines. His linked body was like the head and thorax of a gigantic insect.

Al's task was to gouge deep ruts in the land, removing soil, vegetation, and stones without discrimination. His scowling face glared at me. And mine back at him. What he was doing angered me.

Two blocks from my childhood home, the earthmover I called Al was scraping a road up the steep hill behind our neighborhood. Before he came, I'd played pioneer in the mass of tangled vegetation, ferns, banana slugs, and straight, slender fir trees despite contracting multiple poison oak rashes. The calm woods where I explored and climbed trees, the places in which I hid from the world the first time I ran away from home, were being violated. In one sense, I wanted to watch Al, the giant beast, in motion. In another, I wished he were somewhere else.

I left the machine to wait in stewing silence for its driver to return in the morning and unleash its ferocious voice. Walking into our house, I asked my dad, "Why are they digging up the forest?"

He responded, "They're going to build some homes up on the hill." I didn't know how to answer, as my realtor father seemed to see it as something positive, but I sensed a bit of hesitation in his voice.

As time passed, a deep sting of sadness that my little tract of serenity had been so rudely attacked persisted. I'd never conceived of it being defaced, and wondered what the entire hill had looked like before our subdivision was built.

I didn't know what survey stakes were, only that they had some association with the invasion of my woods. Their bright-orange ribbons were disturbingly out of place. So I pulled them all up, took them home, put them in our burn barrel, and torched them. But soon, there was a wide, muddy rut of road where the stakes once stood.

Up to that point, my patch of woods had survived the 1950s building boom that was devouring all such woods in the greater Portland, Oregon area. The physical beauty and spiritual presence of that forest had captivated me. My refuge's demise triggered a mental rush of anxiety. I considered the loss of something I sensed could not be replaced. Where would I go now?

It was a simple conclusion that someday there may be no more such places left. No more natural forests, no more silence and solitude, no more beauty. I was not yet old enough to reason what this loss might mean in the long term and the progression of civilization, but as I grew up, the meaning became clear.

* * *

I feel fortunate to have grown up in Northwest Oregon, in the midst of the Pacific Northwest's idyllic forests. I became inextricably attached to them, as much through innate adoration as familiarization. Although my folks weren't campers or hikers, they still exposed me to the forests on excursions to the Oregon Coast and Mount Hood. Most of my outdoor acumen came from my father's parents, who took me camping and fishing.

I was seven when my parents first drove my brother and me east to Madras, the tiny Central Oregon desert town on the east side of the Cascade Mountain crest, where my cousins lived. There, I got my first taste of rural life and loved it. The wide-open spaces, the ramshackle town, the working-class ambiance exhibited by local farmers and ranchers was by far preferable to the mechanisms of the suburbs.

Once we drove beyond the Cascade passes toward Madras, all the northern and central Oregon Cascade peaks were revealed in full splendor. Due to a trick of geology, they're often hidden to those on the west side in the Willamette Valley. From the higher-elevation east side, one can see all the stately peaks lined up like beacons of joy.

The stratovolcanoes of the Cascades are fascinatingly distinct individuals, unique in their symmetry, with their own personalities. Gargantuan, stocky Mount Rainier, the lord of the bunch, rises almost ten thousand feet above the surrounding forested foothills.

I needed to know the mountains' names. I was driven to go to them, to enter their sacred realm and bond with them, to discover reality in far-off enclaves of fantasy. The mountains and forests were so beautiful! I could not explain why, they just were. I anxiously asked my parents whether people could actually go into those forests and walk amid the bold peaks. I counted each day until I could.

In 1962, the real estate company my father worked for built an A-frame cabin on the banks of the Zigzag River near Rhododendron, Oregon. The familiar stratovolcano called Mount Hood, visible from the Portland area, loomed like an apparition of glory above us. As a child tentatively piercing the outer edges of untouched forests around the mountain, I felt an intoxication that wasn't just sensory, it was emotional.

That cabin on Mile Bridge 35 Road became a hallowed place. I remember wondering if it was possible to permanently live in a forest like the one that embraced the cabin. Each time we visited, I would leap from our big Oldsmobile Delta 88, stop at the doorstep to take in the rich forest air, walk in and toss my overnight bag onto the bed, then charge outside, bound for exploration.

As she was unpacking, I'd tell my mom, "I'm going to look for the Mile Bridge!" I never did find it, but that was inconsequential. Mom was always noticeably nervous allowing a preteen to wander alone through the deep, dark woods. But she knew I'd sneak out anyway and relented. "Don't go far, and stay out of the river!"

And thus, I stalked the giant Douglas firs, western hemlocks, and red cedars. The radiant green blanket of trees—the aura of their bright-hued needles against a clean blue sky—defined color. My feet were surrounded by a tiny community of life, with reddish-orange mushrooms, gangs of colorful insects, and small rodents bustling in a perpetual motion that was as peculiar in its intricacy as the trees were distinctive in their immensity.

In the high Cascades, I perceived a glorious, unbroken panoply of deep, rich life. The seemingly indomitable forest, its tough roots intertwined with the volcanic soil, rose from valley floors and, with a heraldry of gods, reached its patient tendrils up toward the glaciers.

Before Europeans came, the largest Douglas fir trees rose to heights equal to the tallest redwoods; some of the largest were reputedly over four hundred feet tall and sixty feet in circumference, with perfectly upright, cylindrical trunks. These elders are branchless for over a hundred feet from the soil, then bedecked with majestically splayed limbs. It took a long time before I associated mortality with such a wondrous presentation of enduring life.

In those woods, I absorbed the scent of earthly detritus, the bold odor of pitch and loam, that delicious organic smell—the vaguely musical whispering of primeval life. It was intoxicating even to a kid.

My first extensive hike through a wild wood was at Cascade Head on the Oregon coast. I was eight years old. At our Neskowin Beach hotel room, my father said suddenly, "Tomorrow, we're going on a hike!" Excited, I assumed we were going to play football. As it turned out, one of dad's acquaintances knew of a nearby woodland trail.

The next morning, my father, my brother and I, and a few other adults with some kids older than me set forth on our walk. We strode along Neskowin Beach and then left the ocean's roar and walked uphill. We broke into a gully where the disturbing stumps of a clearcut dominated. I've always hated clearcuts, a logging technique where all the saleable trees are removed, the big trees are hauled to the sawmill, and all the other vegetation unfit for the sawmill is left to rot, or piled and burned. What's left are stumps squatting solemnly, poking out like festering zits from the soil. Hundreds of years of living forest is eliminated in a week.

But soon, we entered a new world—a damp, enthralling, primeval silence. Those massive Sitka spruce and western hemlock trees hit me in the heart like goddesses of raw allure. None of the adults on the hike knew the names of the various tree species, but I marveled at the distinctions between them. Their bark, branches, needles, and towering trunks spoke of fascinatingly diverse personalities.

I've always felt applying names to every living thing constricts the interconnectivity of the world by placing it into discriminatory categories, yet from the inevitability of naming, one reaches an understanding that each plant and animal contributes to the integrity of the whole.

* * *

When I entered my teens, I came to recognize the distinctions between natural forests and tree farms, where the original forest is removed and seedlings are artificially planted. Something about the artificial forests was immediately disconcerting. The big trees and the diversity were gone. So was all the life that used to buzz around in the soil and underbrush. Mortality reared its ugly head.

Today, science understands the marked distinction between biodiversity-rich natural forests and sterile tree farms, where the forest is treated like a crop of corn. No giant trees, no diversity of species, just dour sticks to be mowed down in forty years.

I hungered for more of the wild woods. My mind hummed as it contrived new ways to evade school and inhale the forest scent, greet those crystal streams, and revel in untouched beauty. Despite my parents' wrath, I occasionally skipped school and found refuge in many of the wild forests around Mount Hood.

Driven like a magnet to the woods, I began to break free of my parents' reign even before I was old enough to get a driver's license. I would commandeer my mom's 1960 Volkswagen Bug, load up a friend or two, and head toward the mountains, intent on finding new forests, peaks, and streams to explore.

During summer break from high school in 1969, I joined my pals Gary, Calvin, and Jim and headed out to the Clackamas River. We managed to get hold of a map and plotted a route up the river beginning at the town of Estacada.

We tied some fat inner tubes to the roof of Jim's father's fang-adorned 1956 Buick—without valid driver's licenses, to the best of my recollection—and headed toward aqueous bliss. From there, we ventured upriver as far as the road condition would reasonably allow. We left the Buick with little concern for how we'd get back to it, and plopped our inner tubes into the river.

Thus, my river-running days began. My pals and I ran those Class III Clackamas rapids in our trusty inner tubes—without life jackets. We were like children in a new world, babysat by bastions of huge trees and joyous whitewater.

When we reached a Forest Service ranger station, we stopped and cast our weary, thoroughly doused bodies onto the side of the Clackamas River Road. We waited only a few minutes before Jim caught a ride up to the Buick and brought it down, whereafter we cruised back to Lake Oswego and miraculously managed to escape parental wrath.

The magical, far-off places I had dreamed of visiting at age six—back when Elvis topped the charts and the Soviet Union was contemplating placing nuclear arms in Cuba—had become real. As the summers of my youth flew by, my walks evolved into treks that went deeper and deeper into backcountry.

CHAPTER 2
THE GEOGRAPHY OF SELF

I managed to ignore worldly events until it became impossible. The world beyond wilderness was sneaking up on me, though I continued to try and bat it away from my mind. After all, I was in love, and the object of my affection was a range of mountains seven hundred miles long.

At age eighteen I became eligible for the military draft lottery, as per Richard Nixon. The only interest I had in Vietnam was thinking about what it might be like to explore its tropical forests. But of course, that was not what they would send me there for—it was to burn down the forests and kill the native people. It turned my stomach.

I was not an anti-war fanatic, but I was also not a subscriber to "my country, right or wrong." Despite my revulsion toward the war, I faced the possibility of getting drafted among the first 160 birth dates picked for duty. Unsure how the draft lottery worked, I was relieved when the first date picked was September 14. Having been born on September 13, if the lottery was chronological, I'd be number 365. But I later learned it was a random selection, not chronological, and checked the list of dates.

I wound up being number 229, but it turned out not to matter anyway. Due to concussions suffered playing football, I was classified 4F. I didn't know exactly what that meant, but a call to the local recruiting office revealed that I was deemed "unfit for combat duty." Without my knowledge, my mother had written a letter to the draft board and enclosed the diagnosis from our family doctor. I was spared the task, due to the brain injury.

The prospect of going to Vietnam had laid upon me a greater fear than fighting in a war I didn't believe in. I feared not being able to be alone. It was a mysterious sensation, but one I didn't see as a recurring and expanding event until I was well into adult life. Eventually, the specter of depression manifested from the desire to be alone, and expanded as I aged. Besides, the thought of being constantly barked at by a dictatorial sergeant with bad breath just didn't wash.

As adolescence melded into adulthood, I most often headed out into wild country by myself. But I didn't completely understand my reclusive nature until many years later. I was relieved when high school ended because I had more freedom to be alone in the woods.

* * *

I had wandered nonchalantly through high school. Pleas from my parents to focus and get good grades were swatted away like persistent mosquitoes. Mom always threatened that if I didn't start applying myself in school, I'd wind up being a ditch digger. I proved her right, but it wasn't at all objectionable. I like dirt. Besides, languishing in some sterile office would be tantamount to the slow extraction of fingernails.

Though my family was firmly middle class, I grew up in upper-crust Lake Oswego, the wealthiest per-capita town in Oregon. There, I nervously dated the daughters of doctors, lawyers, and business executives. I never tried to fit in with any of the high school cliques, and had only a handful of what I would call close friends. I avoided group activities like the Boy Scouts, and cringed at religion-based social forums like Young Life, very popular at Lake Oswego High.

The Lake Oswego affluence was uncomfortable, and in that shark-pond school of budding business enterprisers, I gave no concern to being a straight-D student. Maybe mild dyslexia and ADHD had something to do with that, but the reality was, I had no interest in learning what they were teaching. Nary a class had anything to do with nature, not even the science classes. I favored visits to secluded fishing holes over sitting in the classroom.

After escaping high school, I conceded to parental wishes and simultaneously pursued a football pipe dream by heading to Chabot College in Hayward, California. Concussions had prevented football from being a regular activity in high school, but now I was free to give it another go.

After again being cranially damaged at Chabot, and completely repulsed by the big city, I ran gleefully home to the Pacific Northwest. I went straightaway to the Coweeman River in Southwest Washington, to a spot amid a cherished forest where my grandparents had taken me steelhead fishing several years prior.

What I found shocked me to the core. The once-crystal stream was fouled. What used to be a two-mile trail to the fishing hole was now a rutted, muddy incision of road that gouged its cursed way another three miles past the hole. The giant trees were gone: a once-idyllic avenue of firs was a defeated stump land. Tears of wrath streamed down my face, and a new level of anger was kindled.

* * *

I returned to Portland, and at first bounced from one outdoor job to another, despising the nine-to-five routine and the chains of artificial time. I missed the randomness of life's chances, moments that evolved in their own sweet time. The only time I had worn a watch was when my parents bought me one for Christmas—I think in 1964. I wore it for two days, then it mysteriously stopped. I haven't worn a watch since.

Having my life and dreams shoved into predetermined conformity made me feel like a machine, a mechanism for the annihilation of randomness, for the suicide of spontaneity. I despised being imprisoned in preplanned periods of work and play.

I never thought of life in terms of the conventional pursuits, like college, career, getting married, and having kids. I instinctively set my priorities straight—I needed to be able to find aloneness in the wildlands.

I hopped from one "relationship" to another, with a complete lack of perspective on commitment. I casually brushed off implications of exclusivity as if the concept didn't exist. I wasn't aware of the underlying reasons for being noncommittal, I only knew I needed to have the freedom to be solitary.

My only plan for the future was to seek out those forests that had never been logged, places where no roads intruded, where there were only foot trails. I was happy to focus my outdoor pursuits on the Pacific Northwest. I figured there were more than enough wildlands in my home territory to satisfy my lust, and my attraction to the local mountains was obsessive.

Yes, my home territory! I had become proud to be a native of the Pacific Northwest, and a defensiveness grew from it. I felt an urgent need to protect my home, and I often wondered if the places I was discovering were in danger of being destroyed, like the woods close to my childhood home and the fishing hole on the Coweeman.

At the same time, I diligently honed my outdoor skills, and often thought of retiring from society and living in the woods full-time. Once I went to a presentation by Willi Unsoeld, one of the world's most famous mountaineers. After his talk, I approached him. "Could you recommend an outdoor school where I could learn advanced survival skills?" His answer? "Just go outside." It made perfect sense.

I became addicted to my solo backpacking excursions. My Kelty Serac pack was my most prized possession. Alone in the wild country, I felt revelations of life so simple, yet so profound, trying to carry on a life completely entangled in society's web felt like self-betrayal. I endeavored to live in the woods, close to high mountains.

Irresponsible? Unmotivated? Self-serving? Naw. Just unconventional priorities.

I took any outdoor work I could find, buying time to do my mountain work—the tasks of scaling peaks and finding the deepest forest enclaves.

Being pretty much a complete failure in the classroom, and having no interest in any kind of indoor job, I was relegated by default to labor. Not that I minded. I dug a lot of ditches by hand, drove dump trucks, and piloted excavators.

I was a working man, and proud of it. It felt good to walk in the footsteps of my proud carpenter/mason grandfather, Les Bailey. I shared that pride with my workmates. We deplored being looked down upon by many of the wealthy white collars. I became a strong union supporter and joined the Teamsters.

In 1973, I got what turned out to be the closest thing I'd come across that resembled a long-term job. I was hired at $4.75 an hour at a roll-form steel-stud manufacturing plant called Sea-Port Distributing. It was a small operation: husband-and-wife owners and three of us out in the mill and warehouse. We manufactured the metal equivalent of two-by-fours and two-by-twelves used to frame homes, but our metal studs were for office buildings.

At the steel-stud plant, I mostly worked next to a huge, shrill, screaming machine. I drove a forklift and bundled steel studs as they came out of the shaping machine. I really looked forward to the times I was called upon to drive the semi-truck to Seattle, Denver, or Salt Lake City to deliver our product.

The trucking experience was a trial by fire. My only training was one trip to Salt Lake City with an experienced driver who had no interest in teaching me how to drive a tractor trailer. On my next trip, I drove solo. I was self-taught in the particulars of how to shift gears with no clutch and hook up a flatbed trailer to the old Mack truck.

In 1974 I left Sea-Port so I could move out of Portland into the mountains. I had a pocket full of money, as I'd continued to live dirt cheap—I never bought much of anything. I landed in the village of Rhododendron, a few miles from the Mile Bridge cabin of my youth, and worked at Timberline Lodge, grooming ski trails in a snowcat and loading skiers onto chairlifts.

Timberline became a burden: being constantly surrounded by skiers with their banana-yellow ski boots and haughty attitudes was nauseating.

In that cabin on the Zigzag River, I continued my excursions to find new backcountry. On one occasion, I embarked on a refreshing hike into what is now the Bull of the Woods and Opal Creek Wilderness areas between Mount Hood and Mount Jefferson. Afterward, I wound up in a tavern in the tiny town of Eagle Creek. The guy at the table next to mine offered some conversation, and eventually a tip about a job at a logging operation. He presented it as a rare opportunity, so I bit.

At the time, I wasn't fully educated on the impact on wilderness from logging on federal land. As it turned out, the logging operation I was about to join was on private land. I hated clearcutting, but I wasn't at all averse to cutting wood. In fact, it was—and still is—stimulating for some reason. Plus, this seemed like an ideal outdoor job, hard work at a good pay rate. Being close to exhausting all the stray one- and five-dollar bills stuffed in various pants pockets, taking a good-paying job seemed the smart thing to do.

The logging company was C-H Enterprises, a ragtag outfit with ancient equipment that the company mechanic constantly fussed over and bitched about. I often wondered if it was a legit company. The owners were absent. The only people of authority I ever met were the foreman who hired me and the warehouse manager.

I got the job after a hasty interview, and at 4:30 the next morning, I was setting chokers in a full-scale cable-yarding logging operation. I was eventually elevated from choker setter to timber faller. It seemed the company's three primary fallers had bailed out in a dispute over being paid by the hour versus by piecework based on the timber volume they cut.

Luckily, the project I was working on involved very few trees over twenty-five inches in diameter and 120 feet tall. That was an easy entry for one who was not fully educated in felling large trees. I had used chainsaws to cut firewood, and I learned the basics by watching the fallers, who had allowed me to take down a few trees from time to time.

After C-H became an off-and-on employer—mostly off—I bounced from one temporary outdoor job to another, and in between jobs, covered as much ground upon the trails and trail-less regions of the public land in Oregon and Washington as I could.

My alpine pursuits eventually moved north to the huge, icy monolith that is Mount Adams, "Klickitat" to the natives, and the second-highest peak in Washington. I maintain a special bond with that mountain because, due to a number of geologic confoundments, and despite its massive 12,300-foot-high bulk, it's difficult to see from almost anywhere farther than thirty miles away. I had caught luscious glimpses of it from the ridges of the Columbia River Gorge and eagerly anticipated climbing it.

One of those times at the gorge, from atop Nesmith Point, I had gazed at Mount St. Helens (pre-1980 eruption) and Mount Adams, humbled by their regal presence. A vibrant energy emanated from them that stung my consciousness with unspeakable power in the purest, simplest form. I recognized that my entire existence was a response to the vulnerability of the forests that embraced these mountain icons.

The revelation atop Nesmith inspired an honest assessment of civilization. And in that hour, my recognition that humanity was chewing away at the edges of those living mountain realms was graphic and terrifying. I visualized unrestrained industrial advancement into backcountry as a giant metallic rat, gnawing away at the diminishing edges of a sacred home, threatening its poignant harmony. "Progress" became a jaded word, and eventually a question with a hideous answer—progression toward what? The consumption of every tree, stream, and stone?

I saw the industrial juggernaut as devouring refuges all across the planet, places where peace and freedom are physical and where the planetary business of sacred life as it originally came to be still existed. I recognized such places are unguarded from society's self-perpetuating, directionless socio-economic surge, driven by the impossibility of perpetual "growth."

After I finally solo climbed Adams, I was initially proud of myself, as anyone who has conquered a mountain would be. But when I objectively contemplated the idea of "conquering" a mountain, my musings led to utterly rejecting that concept. To think that I had somehow defied the mountain or was at odds with it was incongruous. The cardiovascular challenge of getting to the top was absolutely necessary to experience the fulfillment. The breathtaking view, I concluded, is only truly afforded those who have the breath to *give* to the journey up.

As I absorbed the view from Mount Adams's summit, I couldn't squelch the desire to head farther north in Washington, to hulking Mount Rainier and the North Cascades, the latter a deliciously vast wilderness of more than two and a half million acres. They include some of the most magnificent ancient conifer forests in the world and rows of jagged peaks that pose a different presence than the stratovolcanoes to the south.

Leaving the Cascade foot trails to seek secluded meadows, towering lookouts, and crystalline swimming and fishing holes became an art form. I could say that my soul was nourished by the Cascades, but I would more aptly describe their effect as a soothing salve for the dark places that overwhelmed my brain. I rarely crossed paths with other people on those trails.

As I got to know them intimately, the mountains and their domains became much more than pretty places to explore. They were alive with a strange and magical consciousness, imbued with spiritual presence, yet exposed in a paradoxical vulnerability.

The line had to be drawn. Here I would stand. No more untouched forests would be logged. I tried to figure out what I could do to protect them. Something had to be done, *now*, before the last road-free, unlogged vestige was ripped from the bosom of those noble mountains.

CHAPTER 3
THE "ECO-PSYCHE" FUELS A RURAL MIGRATION

I was insatiably hungry for more backcountry to explore. I wasn't a kid in a candy store nor a hog in the fat house, more of an aspiring druid exploring living chapels.

In the days after that dreadful experience at the Coweeman River, I developed a self-employment task—learning about land management policy. I needed to know who was responsible for the dead-end acts of annihilating what little was left of wild forests, and how the vandals could be stopped.

Time in the back woods became much more than spiritual refreshment and retreats to solitude. The gratification of exploration made way for the intense post-hike examination of maps to see where logging and logging roads were intruding—and where wild forests needed protection.

It was from US Forest Service maps that the tenets of who owns plots, and how they are managed and protected, came into focus. I was aware of the human propensity for dividing land up into convenient rectangular plats, but who owned and controlled which parcels wasn't clear.

I learned that there are public lands, federal, state, and municipal, that aren't private property. They belong to everyone and are managed by the respective government agencies. That was reassuring, though the details of federal land management determinations were hazy.

It came as a delightful shock when I found there are wilderness areas where people couldn't build a road or fell a tree. Wow! At the revelation of a law—the Wilderness Act, passed in 1964—that would protect backcountry, hope was kindled. On some of my previous hikes, I had seen signs saying I was entering a wilderness area, but I thought that just meant the area had only trails.

As my understanding expanded, I got plugged into organized efforts to protect wilderness. In the mid-1970s, newspapers contained reports of the Endangered American Wilderness Act and places called French

Pete and the Kalmiopsis. These federal public lands in Oregon were untouched by industrial exploitation.

I tracked down the oft-quoted Oregon Wilderness Coalition (OWC) and spoke to some of its leaders. I was surprised to find there were actually people paid to protect wilderness. But that was later tempered by the discovery that the salaries of OWC employees were less than I'd made driving a dump truck.

It was during discussions with OWC people that I first learned the national forests were being heavily logged. It infuriated me. I had assumed the national forests were the same as national parks, and all the logging I saw was on private land.

Encouraged by OWC, I wrote letters to the editor of whatever newspaper would print them, and to members of Congress. But I yearned to do more: to help designate more wilderness, stop industrial incursions into the wild places I'd discovered, and hold accountable the people who were responsible for puncturing them with road incisions and invasive clearcuts.

Flirtation with activism advanced, but association with other activists was infrequent at best, primarily due to my chronic wanderlust and remote residences. I rarely even had a reliable telephone number.

At the time of my first contact with OWC in 1976, I was living in that moldy old cabin beside the Zigzag River. Soon, I felt the need to be farther than forty-five miles from the expanding metropolis of Portland. So I moved to Bend, Oregon, at the behest of a lucrative job—ditch digging at high Davis–Bacon Act wages, $8.25 an hour, far more than I'd made at any previous job. After that job was completed, I joined a local company installing pipelines on the Paiute Indian reservation near Burns, Oregon, also at Davis–Bacon wages.

The move to Bend provided opportunities to explore new wild country, particularly the Three Sisters Wilderness and other semiarid ponderosa pine forests of the Deschutes River territory. But the move was more than a good job and exposure to new wild places, it was the continuation and expansion of my rural migration.

I remained in touch with OWC when I moved to Bend. There, I met Tim Lillebo. He was the organization's only eastern Oregon employee, an organizer, lobbying genius, and inspirer of both politicians and fledgling activists. Tim was a fellow blue collar. He'd worked on bridge construction crews with his father and had done some timber felling. We clicked at once.

Tim eventually became my closest friend, and I wasn't alone in recognizing him as the most effective and heroic activist central and eastern Oregon ever had. In close conversations, we often spoke about our shared instinctive love of nature. Our love of wilderness was not taught, nor particularly inspired by exposure to backcountry. It was involuntary, and that reality was mutually fascinating.

We could speak about wilderness in the sense of feelings rather than just observations. Impressed and elated that someone else felt as I did, I gave this untutored instinct for loving wild places a name. I called Tim's and my instincts the *eco-psyche*. In his book, *Confessions of an Eco-Warrior*, late wilderness advocate Dave Foreman refers to what I call the *eco-psyche* as "the wilderness gene." This was the only other reference I'd heard to an innate love of wilderness.

Tim and I fantasized about going back to 1801, the year before Lewis and Clark headed west, and exploring the Pacific Northwest before chainsaws or bulldozers existed.

I often wondered aloud about the polar opposite of love for wilderness. Even after speaking to people who despise protecting wilderness and have a burning desire to destroy it, I refuse to believe that point of view is driven by instinct—it must be learned.

I theorized that the biggest disadvantage lovers of wilderness have in protecting their interest—and by extension, the greater interest in protecting biodiversity, wildlife, and ecosystems—is that we must pass laws to do so. Consuming resources and "developing" land are inherent human traits. Yet once it is destroyed, wilderness is lost forever. And as long as it exists, it will be in jeopardy: laws like the Wilderness Act can be erased.

The realization that so many people don't understand or appreciate nature saddened and angered me. I knew there would always be orc-like people endeavoring to inject bulldozers into nature's last untouched vestiges for profit, and I'd forever be at war with them.

* * *

In Bend I took my first serious stab at activism beyond letter writing. With Tim's help, in 1978 I tried to rejuvenate the dormant local wilderness advocacy group, East Cascades Action Committee. I pretty much failed due to my limited "people skills."

After a couple of years in Bend, the gnawing urge to be living in an even more rural locale took hold. Bend was beginning a giant growth spurt that wound up being perpetual. I decided to leave the protection of the Central Oregon Cascades to Tim.

I'd been living in a tepee twelve miles west of Bend with a small group of friends while working a third excavation job. Again, I had a pocket full of money. When the work was exhausted and I was laid off, I decided it was time to begin a vision quest. I got the idea to explore what I felt was one of the most enticing wilderness enclaves anywhere—the Canadian Rockies. I loaded up my expedition backpack and used my thumb to travel north.

During the hitchhike, a ride landed me in the Wallowa Valley late on a summer evening. I'd considered refusing the lift because the guy who picked me up said he was headed far off the beaten path. I might wind up somewhere where there were no rides to get me to Canada. But what the hell, I figured, it would be fun to get acquainted with new country.

The next morning found me in a grove of cottonwoods bordering a hay field in the valley. As I peeked out of my sleeping bag, my gaze excitedly fixed on some grand mountains dominating the southward viewshed, barely two miles away. I postponed Canada exploration for several days as my eager legs powered me up into the tall, shining Wallowa Mountains, a range I'd never even heard of. I hiked for four days in the Wallowas before resuming my planned journey. It was a memorable jaunt through steep, bisected canyons up to verdant mountain meadows sprinkled with wildflowers, and the best of high-alpine terrain.

That northward hitchhike/backpack excursion took me to dozens of idyllic places, from Banff and Jasper National Parks up into the Yukon. I feasted on some breathtaking wildland experiences on barely maintained trails.

I began the trip with $480 in my pocket. After two months, I was running low on funds, missed Oregon, and couldn't stop thinking about the Wallowas.

I didn't want to leave the Cascades, but the urge to be in a more rural locale won out. I went back to Bend, bought an old pickup truck, said some goodbyes, and headed toward the Wallowa Valley town of Joseph. My initial residence there was my backpacking tent, nestled near Hurricane Creek Campground. When November brought more snow than my tent could handle, I found a one-room cabin for $90 per month, where I got the respite of a hermit's tranquility during the sub-zero winter.

I had no idea what the Wallowa territory was like socially or economically. But I couldn't have cared less. It was a remote mountain town, as geographically isolated as any place I'd seen—far from the rat maze of the urban jungle. The mountains tugged vigorously at my psyche, begging me to explore their reaches. My seemingly directionless life had been steered toward this wild, idyllic region.

From that meager Joseph abode, I contemplated my zigzagging course since that fateful confrontation with Allis Chalmers eighteen years prior. I wondered how my drive to protect wild places would fit into this new place. I soon found that my anger at the demise of wilderness had plenty of fodder in the Wallowa Valley, and would shape my activism for the next thirty-six years.

EAST FORK LOSTINE RIVER, EAGLE CAP WILDERNESS
IN THE WALLOWA MOUNTAINS

CHAPTER 4
AUTUMN'S DOUR REFUGE

The Wallowa territory hit me like a revelation of rock. At first, my treks focused on the bold Wallowa Mountains. In his book *Lasso the Wind*, author Timothy Egan describes them as "peaks of such heart-stopping beauty that you feel like tipping them after taking their picture."

But it wasn't long before I was drawn to another nearby icon—not a protrusion like the mountains, but an erosion—Hells Canyon.

The accolades of Hells Canyon, the Wallowas' sister geological wonder immediately to the east, had occasionally teased me in recent years. I recalled hearing it billed as the deepest canyon on Earth. I was enticed by the exploration potential of this paradise of severe topography.

On a dreary autumn day in 1979, I made my first excursion to the ten-mile-wide abyss that is in fact nearly two thousand feet deeper than the Grand Canyon. The chill in the Wallowa Valley and the four inches of new snow that reached down to the base of the mountains, maybe a couple of miles from the front door of my rental cabin, shoved me east to more arid canyon floors.

I ventured to the tiny village of Imnaha, defined by two buildings and a boxlike post office, a thirty-mile downhill trip from Joseph. It was a revealing drive. Joseph is at the head of the Wallowa Valley's gentle gradient. The granitic Wallowa Mountains rise directly from the valley like a humongous, ragged scoop of petrified ice cream plopped on the valley floor.

Heading east, the change in topography is drastic. Six miles from Joseph, I began a long descent down Little Sheep Creek. The alpine ambiance yielded immediately to a patiently eroded, peculiarly terraced basalt canyon.

When I arrived at the lonely Imnaha Store, nestled in the picturesque depths of a precipitous canyon, I thought I was in Hells Canyon. In fact, it was Imnaha Canyon, a beautiful, shapely arroyo, defined by layer upon layer of volcanic flows, each equal in depth. On one side the top is a plateau, on the other a knife-edged ridge. Each side rises nearly four thousand feet above the Imnaha River. It is decorated with "stringers" of ponderosa pine forest running vertically upslope.

From the village of Imnaha, I could choose from three roads—turn right and head upriver toward the east end of the Wallowa Mountains; go straight and climb a 20-percent grade onto massive Lord Flat, whereafter the road would eventually take me to the west rim of Hells Canyon; or turn left, downriver toward entry into Hells Canyon's depths. I went left.

I found Dug Bar Road to be one of the most sublimely lonely and visually stunning roads one could dream. I sampled panoramas of sculpted canyons—Cow, Lightning, and Horse Creeks. They rose gently at first from flat, bunchgrass-covered benches, then climbed precipitously to Grizzly, Haas, Windy, and Summit Ridges.

From some of the higher viewpoints along the road, the dark, decaying teeth of the Seven Devils Mountains—the east rim of Hells Canyon—loomed like a rising subterranean portent: it appeared the peaks had been abruptly shoved upward through the top of Lord Flat, even though they are separated from it by the gaping abyss of Hells Canyon, which at the moment remained hidden from view.

Dug Bar Road appeared to be nothing more than a random track. I found no campsites, trailheads, or other signs of recreation accommodations, but that was fine by me. I found that once you get past the first six miles, there is only one habitation the road serves—the McClaran Ranch—still occupied by the original family owners. Their narrow private tract is enclosed on all sides by national forest.

At a point where the road rose above the Imnaha River, I left my truck and climbed to the headwall of a ridge that resembled the high prow of a ship. As I gazed at the Imnaha Canyon and the vast and peculiar wild country that frames it, I wished the road wasn't there. It bisects a huge tract of otherwise roadless, undisturbed backcountry with deep valleys: an incredible low-elevation wilderness.

I had never even seen photos of such a place. "*Habitat!*" I shouted to myself, surprisingly, because I knew little of the biological sciences. I later learned that rare mammals like Canada lynx, wolverine, and marten find a hospitable refuge in the expanse of the Imnaha territory, apart from a larger world that has not been respectful of their needs. Salmon and steelhead run the gauntlet of the seven high dams blocking the

Snake and Columbia Rivers to find biological nirvana in the vast spawning grounds of the Imnaha River.

The stringers of timber mingled with open, grassy expanses and were beautifully predictable—rising only on the north-facing undulations within longitudinal gulches. Steep, bunchgrass-covered inclines flecked with occasional lonely pines and drier soils dominated the south-facing sides. From above, the vegetative composition resembled the color scheme of a tiger's coat.

The road beckoned me toward Hells Canyon, so I rejoined my truck. From the moment I left the Imnaha Store, I saw neither a vehicle nor a person the entire day.

As the road began its ascent up Summit Ridge, which divides the Imnaha River from the Snake River, it twisted from north to east and hit a short saddle. From there, one could hang glide maybe 3,500 vertical feet down to join the Snake River's sortie through Hells Canyon, but the river remained hidden from view.

I stopped at the saddle, reveling in this new place in the restless air. As the wind hit me, I felt like a tiny cell in the midst of vastness.

From there, I walked north up the slope, where threads of strung-out gray clouds hung like colorless yet intricate tapestries. The sharp wind rose and fell, bending the scant patches of bunchgrass like feathers in a headdress. A musky scent lingered in the air. "Elk," I excitedly informed myself. Yet as I scanned the beige slopes, none could be seen.

Suddenly, a discrepancy in shape froze my glance. A peculiar circular form peeked out from the rectangular rocks at the top of the ridge. Focusing, I identified a full-curl bighorn ram. If I crept around the eastern edge of the ridge, could I sneak up on the shy sheep? Downwind, could I lurk behind a boulder and see him up close?

Movements around the ram quickly changed the image—there were ewes, as should have been expected. They meandered randomly around the reclining ram, grazing nonchalantly. I wanted to be among my fellow mammals.

The sheep seemed attuned to vibrations. I tried to put myself in their minds: intruding personalities bring movements and scents that trigger reactions. The aura of the pursuer emits energies detected by keen defensive receptors.

I cautiously maneuvered out of their view. Then, moving quickly, angled across the slope and strode up. Approaching the crest of the ridge,

I rose, inch by inch, until I was peering over a parapet of stone. But by the time I caught sight of them again, the sheep had retreated across a narrow draw.

I watched them from a distance of about two hundred feet. The ram seemed inclined to disrupt any direct line of sight between him and me. If I moved, he'd relocate behind a boulder or tuck behind the lee side of the ridge.

Whenever he stood up, I could admire the ram's shape. He was impressively stocky, and his hide was a darker gray than the ewes. Those thick, spiraled horns were the raw, bony accoutrements of pride. After about an hour and a half of playing visual tag, the ram and his flock casually bounced down a steep, rocky slope I would never have tried without a rope and solid belay.

After that enriching encounter, my day involved seeking viewpoints that afforded prize views. I was wowed by the consistent inconvenience of the topography as Hells Canyon was at last revealed. Contrary to popular belief, the most harmonic phrase in the English language is not "cellar door." It's "columnar basalt."

I beheld the latter, occasional presentations of raw stone, perfectly vertical anomalies composed of hexagonal slices that resembled a cartoonish, long-toothed grin. Above them were steep, soil-clad slopes teeming with clumps of bunchgrass, coincidentally resembling a whisker-pocked face. During my excursion, I communed with circling peregrine falcons, two golden eagles, and a huge centipede—all living expressions of the dynamic ecosystem.

My rewarding vistas were paid for with steep, twisting climbs up trail-less slopes, one of Hells Canyon's glorious attributes—if you don't mind going off-trail in mostly open country, you can bushwhack to see views few others have enjoyed.

Looking upstream toward Deep Creek, Hells Canyon is wide and U-shaped. Looking downriver, it morphs into a deep, narrow slot of stark black cliffs, all smoothed by the river's wash of desert varnish.

All day, I wished everyone could feel the magic I felt, to glory in the scene with the pure wind in their hair amid silence; to be charmed by the mystical symmetry and see creatures living as they had for eons.

Suddenly, as I sat at the foot of a cliff, sadness gripped me. Most people will never see such glory or learn to appreciate its importance. I dismissed the encroaching darkness by gazing up to the tops of Hells

Canyon's exposed ridges, covered by a clean blanket of fresh snow. The snow line was distinct, as if the canyon gods had laid a giant tarp that ran at an exact horizontal elevation.

That analogy recast into a vision of being in a great womb. I felt at once protected and exposed, old and yet reborn, and unconditionally embraced.

The black night fell slowly, like a soaring hawk's patient descent. The slice of waxing moon had long since vanished behind the highlands of Summit Ridge to the southwest when the first snippet of sleep found me. But I awoke often, fighting with a mysterious feeling of dread.

Intermittent dreams merged with waking. Finally, light began to encroach. The stars dimmed, but remained the luminous orbs of outback heaven, untainted by any artificial light. The sky was clean. The wind was gone. I felt elated by the discovery of a deliciously inspiring new place, yet haunted by an inexplicable gloom.

I glanced across the river, where one group of columnar basalt pillars presented a distinctive grin. One broken tooth leaned drunkenly against its stout kin. What marvelous art! Random and involuntary, yet symmetrical to the human eye.

I jousted with the gloom. The wilderness—inhale it! I drew strength from the sensory intoxication of inexplicably evolved harmony and became an instinctive animal, a unit of perception in the bastion of nature's originality. I found balance in the extremes within which we all seek balance.

Our moods reflect the moods of the world. We are devices through which the universe constantly observes itself; interconnected, like the ecosystems within this miraculously prodigious planet. "The darkness is a passing thing," I tried to convince myself. "Go back to sleep."

THE LOWER IMNAHA RIVER CANYON IN THE HELLS CANYON NATIONAL RECREATION AREA

CHAPTER 5

FLYING TO THE MOUNTAINS AND LANDING IN 1880

I adore rural enclaves because of their antithesis of city life, with mom-and-pop restaurants and ramshackle log pubs featuring old dogs curled up next to the wood stove. Where folks grow and shoot their own food, and where *trading* is as much a monetary rule as money.

Yet Wallowa County culture hit me like a revelation of the Wild West. As much as I loathed my urban upbringing, nothing I knew about rural culture had prepared me for the prevailing provincial, anthropocentric mindset. I had no information about local sympathy for conservation, but I quickly learned that its few allies were deeply in the minority. A pro-resource-consumption—or more pointedly, *anti-environment*—philosophy was the dominant local attitude, based on a "We don't want outsiders telling us what to do" mindset.

I was tickled by one particular articulation of how shallow this provincial attitude was. At a well-attended public meeting to discuss a new plan for managing federal land in the Columbia River Basin, I sat next to Louie Dick Jr., of Nez Perce and Wanapum ancestry. We listened as a rancher growled that his family had been in Wallowa County "for four generations, and we know the land and how to manage it," federal policy and public interest be cursed.

"For what it's worth," Louie laughingly responded, "I've got him beat by a few hundred generations."

The ancestry of every person of European descent who lived there had come from somewhere far away over, at most, the past few generations. Logging-at-any-cost County Commissioner Pat Wortman's family hailed from Missouri, and one of my most outspoken detractors, Dave Shriner, was from California. The only people who could legitimately claim possession would be Louie and the other Native Americans. The Nez Perce Tribe had been exiled in 1877 after being cheated out of the 1855 treaty that gave them what's now Wallowa County as part of their reservation.

As for us Europeans, I was a native Oregonian. Two of my grandparents were born within a hundred miles of the Wallowa Valley, in Lewiston, Idaho, and Walla Walla, Washington. Did that convey any entitlements? No. I learned that being a local had more to do with your point of view than your residential duration. Besides, the tenuous territorial lines that defined being a "local" moved around like a migrating bathtub ring depending on who one was speaking to.

The rancor with which the wilderness haters propounded their rhetoric, and the scorn with which they branded the supporters of wilderness, was just as vehement among Wallowa County leaders as it was among the most vociferous rustics. County commissioners were often among the most radical.

Wallowa County government aggressively proselytized policies that favored taking all the best timber first and leaving the crap; belligerently advocated for reducing native ungulate herds to reserve more forage for their Asian-spawned cattle and invasive sheep; extirpated wolves and haughtily opposed their reintroduction; and supported plugging local rivers with concrete. Wallowa County welcomed every robber baron that craved its resources, from timber to water, lignite to grass, without reservation or condition, and kissed the barons' asses to degrading lengths.

Despite my appreciation of isolation, I utterly rejected the narrow-minded, unlimited industrial exploitation mantra. So, I endeavored to adapt without conforming. All the same, I once told the Wallowa County commissioners if they were going to apply the "ancestral privilege" argument, they'd be ceding Wallowa County back to the Nez Perce.

I couldn't help but parallel my arrival to Wallowa County with tropes of the Old West. Indeed, this place felt strangely familiar, reckoning back to my childhood days watching *Gunsmoke* and *Bonanza* on TV: combative ranchers occupying large spreads, and timber speculators treating the place as a frontier resource colony.

As for those self-anointed monarchs of dubious ownership, if the Nez Perce rose up and cast the Wallowa County claim jumpers on their ten-gallon heads, I wouldn't complain. By the monarch's standard, if the British or Chinese invaded Wallowa County and took over, they'd be justified. Those who live by the double standard should die by it.

After my arrival, I initially kept a low profile and was slow to make the few close friends I eventually had. There was a small, scattered clique of progressive-minded locals, but fitting into cliques had never been one of my priority endeavors. Therefore, I never did cotton to that subculture.

Still, I eventually developed a social attachment to Wallowa County. For example, the colorful distinctions born of geographic isolation, such as local sayings that enliven the ears in a folksy vein. As in many other isolated communities, it had its own (swiftly vanishing) accent and colloquialisms, like "I'm goin' down to bag some steelhead on Imnaha" (rather than going "to the Imnaha"), where the "on Imnaha" part dips off into a subtly nasal baritone. "Got high-centered in Stockman's" translates to "Stayed too long at the bar and got wasted." And in Wallowa County, you didn't *wash* your pick-em- up truck, you *worsh* it.

Social considerations aside, I was heartened by the sizable wilderness areas within county lines. In addition to the Hells Canyon Wilderness, there are the Wenaha-Tucannon and Eagle Cap, the latter encompassing most of the high Wallowa Mountains—all certainly a curious testament to someone's appreciation for the wildness of the territory, contradicting local sentiment.

But local support for protecting public land came at a price. The Wallowa County status quo would shun businesses that might show even a hint of support for protecting land. This can be economically fatal in rural towns, which partly explains the hesitation of local sympathizers toward supporting the wilderness cause. Even noting their membership in an environmental advocacy organization could plant the scathing brand of "enemy" on the face of an employee or a small-business owner. Personal attacks in the less-than-objective local newspaper, the *Wallowa County Chieftain*, were often slanderous.

Paul Grow, the owner of a local bike shop, was once attacked by the timber forces because one of the antagonists had read of a "Paul's Bike Shop" as being a supporter of an environmental group. Actually, that Paul's Bike Shop was 450 miles away in Eugene.

"Extract and consume" was the dominant local mantra, wielded like a battle axe, and the very concept of public lands was despised. Why do people live here, I wondered, if they want it to be like everyplace else?

During my ventures into the backcountry, it was impossible not to notice the expansive logging operations. My explorations had me tracing the lines on maps to determine what the land designations were in the places where the logs were being removed.

This became somewhat of an unpaid "job," as I thoroughly investigated land designations and ownerships, and tried to discover what was happening on each, and who was responsible for newly incised roads and the big pine stumps.

As for paid work, I took on low-paying, part-time jobs. I joined a tree-planting crew, made sandwiches at the local bakery, and supplemented my income by cutting and selling firewood. My sturdy Ford pickup and my chainsaw were all I needed for that endeavor. I enjoyed cutting wood, and saw no harm in taking dead trees from already-logged areas.

In the spring of 1980, I landed a seasonal job on a US Forest Service fire-suppression crew. It was a perfect summer job—working outdoors and fighting wildfires.

When fire season ended with the autumn rain and snow, I got picked up by the Forest Service's ever-busy timber-marking crew. This allowed me another three months of work. I helped lay out timber sales and marked trees for removal. The timber sales were being laid out so quickly, we rode snowmobiles into December to mark sales. I loathed the work, and after that experience, declined to accept the extended work season on the timber crew.

I recall district silviculturist Dave Little convening a pow-wow with the timber-marking crew. "Mark heavier!" he implored us, pointing to some of the four-foot-diameter ponderosa pines along Peavine Creek in the Forest Service's Wallowa Valley Ranger District that had thus far escaped our blue "mark to cut" paint.

Ken Bronec, as conscientious a Forest Service employee as I'd ever met, innocently asked Little about the wildlife protection provisions mandated for the area we were marking. "Your first concern is volume," Little responded. "We have output targets to meet."

The thought of the local national forests being incised with more logging roads, and seeing more majestic ponderosa pine trees eliminated, seemed like a terrible waste and an ecological injustice. Notwithstanding all the other considerations, I couldn't grasp the economic-based support for removing all the ecologically and commercially most valuable trees as quickly as possible. It didn't seem conducive to sustainable, long-term jobs and industry.

With job security a concern due to my occasional outspokenness, my gettin'-to-know-ya exploration of the Wallowa Valley populace timidly advanced. As it did, I had to be careful to whom I dropped the word *wilderness*. The vehement opposition to leaving anything alone was overwhelming, and knew no distinctions via age, hairstyle, or culture.

I'm not big on caveats, but in reality there were many fine people in Wallowa County, wearing diverse political stripes and sporting colorful philosophies. There were folks on both sides of various issues who could accept disagreements and react without threats and intimidation. I did find a few of them but the ecologically challenged majority held sway, and the more tolerant mindset was not inclined to publicly contradict them.

I was surprised to find there wasn't a more enlightened approach to economic survival in Wallowa County. Seeing the one-dimensional local leadership giving the out-of-state owners of local sawmills virtually everything they wanted, I often wondered who the local economic pundits really served.

Besides, aren't the wildness of the land and the isolation of the community among the reasons people live here? It seemed I'd landed in a manifest destiny holdout of the Wild West, a time-warp community beset by unplanned, boom/bust industrial growth under the asinine assumption that the resources are infinite, and any industry is good industry.

As I witnessed more and more logging trucks hauling out giant ponderosa pines, I began to forget the original reason I'd moved to the Wallowa territory: to embrace a simple, peaceful life in a mountain town and enjoy the trails and wild rivers.

That life was in my grasp; but I quickly abandoned it. Yet prior to realizing my fate as an embattled activist, I reveled in the simple life of the local working class. One cherished memory has me at the baseball field on the Enterprise town fairground. A troupe of young women, twenty-somethings whose boyfriends and husbands were mostly loggers and millworkers, were preparing for a softball game. My then-girlfriend was among them. They were dancing and singing "Put me in, coach," from the song "Centerfield" written by rock legend John Fogerty, who owned property twenty miles to the north. The vivid romanticism of that memory still conjures naked sentimentality. I was embraced by the simple lifestyle and honest simplicity of the culture.

Some of the women were new moms. Some worked at the local clinic, some were waitresses, some ran nurseries. They were living in paradise. They were wonderful, honest people dancing beneath beautiful mountains in the loving arms of an isolated dreamscape where time seemed frozen and the world outside the Valley was far away, and mute.

I assumed some of those young women and their mates believed the wild land was an integral aspect of their culture, and their identity. But to what degree would they accept leaving some of the land alone when all they were told was how protecting any of it would cost jobs?

The notion of people living in harmony within a landscape of fantasy and simplicity captivates and invigorates me. But there was a dichotomy between that vision of bliss and my anger over the destruction of the land. It became an emotional tug-of-war that fueled the polarity in my head.

Tiny outback communities embraced by tall mountains, magical forests, and pure wild country could easily coexist with responsible use of some of the land and permanent protection of wild places. I agonized over why achieving harmony among people and their homeland seems so difficult.

It got to be impossible to talk about that human/land relationship without finding myself outside the circle. So I deferred and went on watching those beautiful gals as they sang and played. And for a brief time, I drank with them and their husbands in the local taverns.

CHAPTER 6
THE FORSAKEN RECREATION AREA

The 1980s were a narcissistic decade: a shapeless blob of time headlined by Ronald Reagan and putrefied by disco and big hair. I was listening to country rock and bluegrass and wearing a T-shirt that explained, "Disco sucks." My distaste for the urban culture of the time had been quenched by taking up residence in Joseph. There were no discos in the small mountain towns of the west.

I wanted to be far from the chaotic corruption of urbanity, but once again, my naivete about rural culture left me unprepared for the level of cognitive dissonance that I found in my new home.

The onset of the new president in January 1981 was an ecological tragedy. With all his "Mr. Nice Guy" ambiance, Reagan was the worst thing that had ever happened to the American environment. The first thing he did was deregulate the oil industry. His administration eventually facilitated unrestrained industrial exploitation of millions of acres of federal land and set out to gut any and all environmental regulations.

Reagan was the first president who had the gall to appoint resource-extraction industry figureheads to oversee federal land management and environmental protection agencies. His first appointment was anti-environmentalist James Watt—a lawyer and lobbyist for the mining industry—to be Secretary of the Interior.

To oversee the US Forest Service, Reagan followed the same strategy, appointing John B. Crowell, Jr., as an Assistant Secretary of Agriculture. Crowell was an attorney for Louisiana-Pacific Corporation, a leading manufacturer of building and lumber products. He proclaimed his intent to triple the already-voracious logging levels in the national forests. Ironically, Secretary Crowell and his family had lived a block away from my family in Lake Oswego, and he had been my Little League baseball coach.

Reagan was incredibly popular in Wallowa County, mainly due to his positions on the exploitation of federal land. I felt the attraction of country people to a Hollywood city-boy actor was incongruous, but it's the ideology that matters.

As I contemplated the horrors that would come with Reagan, my thoughts turned to what might happen to local federal land, particularly the Hells Canyon National Recreation Area (HCNRA). I first discovered the HCNRA on a Forest Service map, which outlined a 652,500 acre area that was designated by Congress. I needed to learn more about the HCNRA—Who had engineered local political support? How had they defied local sentiment? What was the level of protection required? The HCNRA had been designated only four years prior to my arrival. I was impressed by how the state and national interest in protecting Hells Canyon had managed to out-shout the Wallowa County status-quo.

I'd remained in close touch with Tim Lillebo, who often made the long drive to Joseph from his abode in Prairie City to encourage me to start organizing locally. Tim imparted his wisdom and gave me the history lesson I was looking for.

The Hells Canyon story began after public power interests sued private power producers in 1968 over who got to build the dams on the Snake River in Hells Canyon. But there were some who didn't want dams to be built at all and formed the Hells Canyon Preservation Council (HCPC) to try to stop them. Newly elected Oregon Republican Senator Bob Packwood became one of the strongest proponents of protecting the area and eventually enlisted legendary conservation-minded Idaho Democratic Senator Frank Church to bring bipartisan power to neutralize the strongest opponent of protecting Hells Canyon—Idaho Republican Congressman Jim McClure.

Even after Packwood and Church joined the effort, established national conservation organizations like the Izaak Walton League told Hells Canyon advocates they were embracing a "no-win" cause. Opposing dams was just something one did not do in the 1960s, when hydropower was the darling of society.

It was Brock Evans, newly appointed western regional director of the Sierra Club, and co-founder of HCPC, who argued in federal court that there should be *no* dams in Hells Canyon, a heretical position in the age of hydropower worship. But his work eventually led to the stunning Supreme Court decision that the legal question was not who got to build the dams in Hells Canyon, but as Justice William O. Douglas ruled for the majority, "whether it is in the public interest that no dams be built." This temporarily halted planning for the various proposed dams, and lit the fuse of activism to further protect the area.

Regional and national voices for protecting Hells Canyon grew. National personalities like Burl Ives and Arthur Godfrey were among its proponents. The national support out-shouted the local opposition.

In 1975, the Hells Canyon Preservation Council fulfilled its mission with passage of the Hells Canyon National Recreation Area Act. It was an awe-inspiring victory that is still referenced by conservation veterans as "the lost cause that was won." Designating the 652,500-acre HCNRA, thus stopping the damming of the Snake River. It was accomplished against gargantuan political odds, including the staunch opposition in Wallowa County.

The Act was a gem of legislation. It went far beyond prohibiting dams. Most of the land it protected is outside the canyon proper. It required restrictions on logging and livestock grazing while mandating the protection of ecosystems, wilderness, and fish and wildlife habitat.

But the Wallowa County timber and cow forces—and the Forest Service—refused to accept defeat. In the summer of 1976, a group of local ranchers and loggers marched a huge coffin in the usually apolitical Chief Joseph Days rodeo, bearing a banner that read "Hells Canyon National Recreation Area—The Death of Free Enterprise."

At that time, most of the incredible HCNRA ancient forests were still untouched. But without hesitation, the Forest Service gladly honored the wishes of the local timber backers and began planning massive logging projects.

In addressing logging, the Act mandates any timber removal be only by selective cutting, and limits logging to places it had occurred prior to passage of the Act, and made it subject to special regulations that would ensure ecological protection. The Forest Service virtually ignored the Act's restrictions on logging and its protection of ecosystems.

Tim and I had numerous discussions about our respective visions for rescuing the HCNRA from the unexpected logging that was going on, fueled by the Reagan juggernaut. We discussed addressing the same threats to wild but unprotected areas surrounding the HCNRA and the Eagle Cap Wilderness. It was a tough time for someone to try and build local support for protecting local wildlands, but the previous success with establishment of the HCNRA gave me a spark of hope that perhaps something could be done—even as the political tide was flowing in the opposite direction. But I wasn't considering all the deeper intricacies of activism; I wasn't keen on organizing but was eager to find a way to share those visions locally and learn what it would take to advance them.

My organizing efforts began in earnest after Tim introduced me to Lori Aschenbrenner and Ken Witty, who became invaluable allies. Lori was my main cohort in efforts to rescue the HCNRA. She was a politically wise, energetic activist. She and her husband, Steve, owned a convenience store in Enterprise, the 1,900 person business hub of Wallowa County, about six miles northwest of Joseph. Ken was a fisheries biologist employed by the Oregon Department of Fish and Wildlife. He was one of the founders of the Hells Canyon Preservation Council, and he acquainted me with the other players involved in the organization. Dale Storey, Tom Derry, June Davis, and Vic Coggins were among those in Wallowa County who were actively involved.

Ken spoke of other movers and shakers of the Hells Canyon campaign from outside Wallowa County with tremendous respect—Loren Hughes, Bill Brown, and Jack Barry from La Grande; Annette Tussing and Carmelita Holland from Baker County; Russ Mager from Washington State; Pete Hennault, Floyd Harvey, Jerry Jayne, John A.K. Barker, Boyd Norton, and Al McGlinsky from Idaho.

In Ken's mind and many others', the leader of the campaign had been Brock Evans. And it was Brock and Ken who had interested Senator Packwood in spearheading the legislative effort to protect Hells Canyon. Most of the players involved would admit that the main impetus of the legislation was to stop the dams. Many people, particularly from Forest Service leadership, say the issue was all about the dams, and other considerations were secondary. But don't tell that to Brock Evans, Bob Packwood, or Ken Witty.

The actions of the Forest Service infuriated Witty. He took me to the sites of timber sales and road construction in the HCNRA. I witnessed logging operations that nearly liquidated forests of giant ponderosa pines. I saw logs being skidded through salmon streams while salmon were attempting to spawn, and logging roads lacerating former pristine backcountry and wet meadows. I saw excavation of gaping gravel pits to surface logging roads, and cattle on Forest Service allotments fouling streams and denuding hillsides.

I was determined to enforce the law. Lori Aschenbrenner was eager to leap into the fray, while Ken did his best to be involved, with deference to his job with the State of Oregon, sensitive to all the political considerations it entailed. But most of the original HCPC cadre had scattered, thinking their arduous task was done.

In 1982, Tim, Lori, and I decided to form a Wallowa County organization. We called it the Wallowa Resource Council. I quickly learned this brand of activism focused mostly on organizing people. I was definitely not in Tim's league in this aspect of the work, but I persevered with his and Lori's help. About thirty-five people with a progressive mindset and appreciation for the outdoors showed up at our first meeting. I felt it was a tremendous success.

I wanted to defeat the Forest Service, but the prospect of being a public crusader was not at all attractive. Getting on the bad side of the local status quo didn't concern me. I was as adept as anyone at living cheap, and I had no desire to be "popular," or to buck up with the predominant local mindset. I wasn't cowed by the local timber industry, which was represented by three big sawmills in the Wallowa Valley and a half dozen logging companies. Excursions into wild country was where my passion lay, not public exposure.

With my often-reckless enthusiasm, I disregarded the potential for conflict and set forth as one might set off to a one-sided war, diving into the realm of activism. However, I was not even slightly aware of what the first steps were to start the process. It was a leap without a glimpse of what the bottom of the cliff might look like. But given my adamant dedication to protecting the land, that became an afterthought.

HELLS CANYON FROM BARTON HEIGHTS

CHAPTER 7
THE ONSET OF ACTIVISM

Lori and I became the drivers of what we hoped would be a new wilderness uprising in Wallowa County, focusing on mismanagement of the HCNRA. We didn't realize at the time how important Wallowa County would eventually become in the future age of increased emphasis on "local control." We only wanted the folks in Wallowa County who revered local wildlands to have an organized voice.

But there were clear signs of anxiety that could be described as "peeking over the shoulder to make sure no one was looking." The old Wallowa County status-quo intimidation machine was always at work, whether it was publicly visible or not.

In the fall of 1982, Boise Cascade, a major lumber and building-products wholesaler, held an "economic forum" in La Grande, the largest town (population 13,000) in Northeast Oregon, where Secretary Crowell was the keynote speaker. The secretary did agree to a perfunctory meeting with a few local "environmentalists" prior to the event.

I walked up to my former coach as he entered the meeting place, a building on the Eastern Oregon University campus. Crowell recognized me and we chatted briefly. He seemed a bit shocked when he saw me take a seat among the "enviros."

Local wilderness stalwart Laurel Reuben, Tim Lillebo, and I had tickets to the banquet that evening. As the festivities were about to begin, Fred Ebel, the Boise Cascade public-relations guy, strode up to us. He knew who we were, and asked for our tickets. We obliged. He then informed us that only two of us were "invited." One of us had to leave. We'd never heard of any invitations, there were simply tickets for sale, and we each had bought one. I had no intention of budging an inch. As the discussion heated up, a crowd of onlookers began to gather.

Laurel was not one to be pushed around either. Both of us lit into Ebel while Tim played the rational middleman. It was a good example of the "good cop/bad cop" routine Tim and I eventually perfected (I was always the bad cop). I told Ebel, "Okay, I'll leave your dog-and-pony show, but I want my twenty-five bucks back." He refused.

The argument heated up again. Finally, Ebel realized he was in a public confrontation that wasn't going to shed positive light on his cozy forum with Secretary Crowell. He pulled $25 out of his wallet and said, "There you go, now leave." I gave him a caustic look, hesitated, then walked out of the building with thoughts of blood and fire.

From then on, I took it upon myself to lead the Wallowa Resource Council into challenging the Forest Service's HCNRA logging projects, and Tim patiently taught me the intricacies of the Forest Service administrative appeals process.

Lori's inherent political wisdom and knowledge of the local community and its issues was complemented, often awkwardly, by my own bull-in-the-china-shop commitment. The learning curve was bluntly short, but it's important to note that our appeals and harsh criticism of the Forest Service were not advanced without prior attempts at collaboration with them.

My main contribution to timber sale appeals was my physical knowledge of the HCNRA via firsthand observations. In 1981, after one year as a firefighter on a suppression tanker crew, I was promoted to the helitack crew, a prestigious initial-attack squad that descended upon wildfires in a helicopter. We were stationed at Memaloose Helitack Base on the west rim of Hells Canyon. That job and my Snake River float-boating excursions and hikes quickly familiarized me with the country—its magnificence and the Forest Service encroachments upon it.

Unfortunately, many people involved in the Wallowa Resource Council started getting nervous as our appeals became more public. Some were small-business owners, and some worked for the Forest Service. They knew that stirring up controversy would rouse the Wallowa County status-quo guardians.

It turned out that my cavalier attitude about being popular in Wallowa County was a mistake. I learned quickly, but too late, that likability was an activist's most important capital. Unfortunately, I had zero training in media relations, so being in the local newspaper was more of a curse than a benefit. Designing a message that would appeal to the audience we really needed to reach—the locals with an open mind—wasn't foremost. Anger toward the Forest Service besotted my messages.

Eventually, I was branded locally as an angry troublemaker, and though exaggerated, it was partly true.

Our influence over Forest Service activities went beyond appeals against HCNRA timber sales. One of the first appeals Tim and I wrote was to protect the Wallowa Mountains from the proposed Eagle Cap Wilderness Management Plan. The Forest Service proposed, among other caustic actions, to place radio transmitters on peaks within the wilderness area and to allow individuals with mining claims unlimited motor vehicle access on wilderness trails.

We began to prepare a legal challenge to the Eagle Cap plan. But before we filed the appeal, the three of us attended an event in Portland. The chief of the Forest Service, its top official, was speaking at a public meeting on federal land management.

Tim managed to corral Chief R. Max Peterson for a three-minute standing discussion. After we described the Eagle Cap Wilderness proposal, Peterson expressed visible disgust at its directives, about which he had no prior knowledge.

Within a few weeks, Eagle Cap Ranger Bob Casey withdrew the plan without explanation. Apparently, Peterson was concerned over the precedent of locating radio transmitters in the wilderness, lest the army or some other agency follow suit with their own transmitters.

A phone call from Peterson to Casey was all it took to defeat the proposal. This was a valuable lesson in politics. It debunked the assumption that one must mobilize an army of support, go through appeals, litigation, and even legislation to achieve something significant. One short conversation with the right person could do the trick.

After that success, Tim, Lori, and I worked local and regional media in an attempt to inform the objective populace about what the Forest Service was doing to their HCNRA. We also briefed local congressional staff. Sadly, our outrage was not shared. Particularly in congressional offices, most felt the battle to save Hells Canyon had been won, and resurrecting it was not worth the effort.

I was perplexed by the lack of concern over flagrant Forest Service violations of the HCNRA Act, and even more so with the agency's lack of accountability. There was never an apology, no "We'll do better in the future." There was no acceptance of responsibility by the agency.

In media accounts, local Forest Service spokespersons denied our specific accounts of their atrocities. Realizing we were in an unresolvable confrontational relationship with the local agency officials, Tim, Lori, and I set up meetings with Forest Service leaders at the regional office in Portland, but all we ever got after showing photos of atrocities within the HCNRA was a litany of poor excuses.

After a year of trying to influence timber sales by meeting with Forest Service officials, I saw it as a waste of time. There was virtually no acknowledgment of our concerns. The condescension of Forest Service leaders only inflamed my mistrust of, and contempt for, the agency.

Eventually, support for the Wallowa Resource Council began to fade. I incorrectly assumed others were as passionate as Lori and I were about protecting local federal lands. We gave up organizing in Wallowa County. But we didn't give up fighting HCNRA timber sales. This was a good thing for me, because I felt like a failure at trying to organize people.

Despite the fizzling of the Wallowa Resource Council and diminished hopes for Wallowa County support, many people in La Grande were prepared to help address the threats to the HCNRA. Plus, there was a flash of hope for national backing. Tim suggested we reach out to Brock Evans.

I had been looking forward to meeting Evans in person. I wanted to shake hands with the mastermind. Still, bringing him into the fray was a long shot, as he was taking on national issues in Washington, DC, from his new seat as National Audubon Society vice-president for national affairs.

I finally met Brock in 1983 at a Portland meeting of wilderness advocates. His knowledge, conveyed with an engaging cordiality, was humbling. With Brock, there was no political elitism. Activists were all equal confederates to be respected. His humility was matched by his political smarts and contagious passion for wilderness. Brock's attitude was a welcome respite from some of the other DC-based leaders of national conservation organizations, who treated grassroots activists like mosquitoes.

Brock, engineer of the HCNRA Act, was deeply moved by my depictions of HCNRA mismanagement. Soon after our meeting, he got involved. He personally helped me with everything: letters to the Forest Service on behalf of Audubon, outreach to the congressional delegation of Oregon, even fundraising.

Brock was there whenever I called, which was often. "Hey, compadre, how's our favorite area!" was his usual greeting. With his willingness to help, and the stalwarts in La Grande ready to move, I was heartened that our attempts to organize people were not completely fruitless.

Somewhere in those early days, it hit me like a sledgehammer that I was now speaking to the head of the US Forest Service and filing "official" administrative appeals. I was talking with members of Congress and appearing in local newspapers, dubious 'privilege' though that turned out to be.

On occasion, I'd snap out of the weird trance. What I was doing was so completely out of character, it made no sense. But what I had begun kept driving me forward. It was now a war, and unbeknownst to me, I was wading into it without being fully armed.

And so it was with my entry into activism—I was the leader of the resistance against the Forest Service's war on the HCNRA's forests. But I still had no idea where all this was leading. The enemy had been identified, and the game was on.

CHAPTER 8
A RADICAL DIGRESSION

I was first exposed to *Earth First* in 1983 when co-founder Dave Foreman visited the Oregon Wilderness Coalition conference at Malheur National Wildlife Refuge's field station in the desert hinterlands of Southeast Oregon. (Yep, ironically, that's the same place the Bundy ranching clan would occupy in their well-publicized protest in 2016.). This self-proclaimed "radical" movement was a response both to Ronald Reagan's shameless anti-environmentalism, and the growing ineffectiveness of the high-profile wilderness advocacy groups.

Eventually, I learned that Earth First was a collection of original ideas and unstigmatized paradigms without adhesive. It seemed to me that adherents could do whatever they pleased with the proselytization of Foreman, Howie Wolke, and Wildcat Annie. It was a free-flowing movement where no one needed to accept responsibility toward the collective for anything.

The founders of Earth First openly embraced monkey-wrenching—more formally known as *ecotage*—as a principle for defending wilderness. There was a lot more to the founders' principles, but of course, that was the most controversial aspect and thus received the most attention. Pulling up road survey stakes, spiking trees, and pouring sugar into bulldozer fuel tanks were celebrated—either in philosophy or practice—by the expanding cadre of wilderness lovers.

Earth First was a spirited flame that gave voice to folks who were frustrated with the bureaucratic condescension of the establishment conservation groups. I'd wasted time trying to set up meetings with the Sierra Club brass in the Pacific Northwest with little success. If given audience, I'd listen to their pessimistic and timid excuses why a Hells Canyon bill would never fly and why they couldn't help.

I had an enlightening one-to-one conversation with Foreman at Malheur and was impressed. He wasn't a reckless, wild-eyed radical, but a genuinely sharp dude with a lot of conviction and original ideas.

The founders of Earth First were former employees of mainstream wilderness advocacy groups rebelling against their politically pandering bosses. They claimed the Wilderness Society, National Wildlife Federation, Sierra Club, and other mainstream ministries were ignoring new science on the need for protecting vast stretches of wildland. They used their rejection of political and educational moderation to promote strong measures to defend wilderness.

One afternoon in March 1983, I got a phone call from Dave Foreman: "You ever hear about the North Kalmiopsis and the Bald Mountain Road?" he asked. I had, via Oregon Wilderness Coalition. "We're putting together a blockade." A blockade? It sounded exciting.

Two days later, I read about four people who'd stood in front of a bulldozer to block the construction of a road incision into pristine forest. Next thing I knew, the Southwest Oregon rain forest appeared through the windshield of my old pickup truck.

After meeting with Earth Firsters Mike Rozelle, Mary Beth Nearing, and Kevin Everhart, I took a hiatus from appealing HCNRA timber sales. I got adopted as an "action organizer." We took refuge in the hippie domain of Takilma, enjoying the warm hospitality of residents sympathetic to our cause.

I fought off poison oak, an unfamiliar culture, financial ineptitude, and my own demons of depression and anxiety to be part of something new and bold. Although a sidebar in my activist career, Earth First was an effective outlet for my ever-escalating anger. Its lure was almost as much about the cultural background of its founders, who were cowboy bar bouncers like Howie Wolke and keen-edged feminists like Nancy Morton, as it was about being "radical."

I spent Cinco de Mayo 1983 with eight other activists chained to a bulldozer deep in the Siskiyou National Forest. We were the second blockade dedicated to a continuing effort to stop the Forest Service's devious attempt to loot one of the most intact bastions of ancient forest left in western North America.

The agency was constructing a road on the northern border of the Kalmiopsis Wilderness which, with its accompanying clearcuts, would cleave the wilderness area from a 125,000-acre tract of immaculately forested but unprotected wild country to the north.

After pleading guilty to disorderly conduct, my Earth First involvement went from the blockade to recruiting more blockaders by giving presentations at colleges.

More Earth First blockades ensued, all generating substantial regional and national publicity. Most of it was surprisingly sympathetic in an age when protests and civil disobedience weren't exactly cool. This helped the Oregon Wilderness Coalition raise the funding to litigate against the Forest Service's shameless effort to destroy the Kalmiopsis forest. The mainstream groups, particularly the Sierra Club, were discouraging lawsuits as "politically unwise."

Although OWC did most of the legwork on the case, including securing the services of pro-bono attorney Neil Kagan, Earth First was the lead plaintiff, as OWC didn't have proper legal standing to be plaintiff. We won the case, an affair where I got to testify before Federal Judge James Redden in support of an injunction to stop the timber sale. The attorney representing the timber company that had bought the timber sale cross-examined me by presenting a clip from the *Earth First! Journal* that described how to disable a bulldozer. It was a tense moment, but I felt a lot more comfortable after Judge Redden seemed to be unimpressed by the attempted character assassination.

Later that year, I used an alias to develop Earth First wilderness proposals that dwarfed what Oregon Wilderness Coalition was proposing, even though OWC had included all the roadless areas in Oregon in their proposal.

* * *

It was in those "radical fringe" Earth First circles that I first heard the terms *deep ecology* and *biodiversity*. The latter eventually became the scientific principles on which wilderness defenders base their strategies for protecting undisturbed ecosystems. The loss of biodiversity and species extinction have spurred present-day calls for preservation of all remaining wilderness and rehabilitation of vast habitats to avoid ecological collapse.

Due to my Earth First connections, I was pleased to make an international contribution to the bold defense of ecosystems. Sea Shepherd

Conservation Society Captain Paul Watson, co-founder of Greenpeace, needed a remote hideaway to avoid an international arrest warrant. He and his crew had pulled the plug on a couple of whaling ships at port in a Spanish harbor, sinking them. My Joseph cabin fit the bill as an isolated refuge for Captain Watson.

Exposure to the Earth First philosophy of advocating for large tracts of wilderness, rather than just the remnant roadless areas, inspired expansion of my Hells Canyon agenda. Eventually, I strengthened positions on protecting Hells Canyon, like favoring the reintroduction of wolves and grizzly bears, removing Hells Canyon Dam, and obliterating the wilderness-incising, twenty-two-mile-long Hat Point Road.

As for ecotage, my position was tempered by the reality that I was engaged in forcing the Forest Service to obey the law. So, I could either justify my own lawbreaking to counteract Forest Service lawlessness, or take the moral high ground. I toed the line by keeping my establishment persona pure, but I value my brief involvement with Earth First. It was more than an education; it was conscientious inspiration.

AN OPEN STAND OF PONDEROSA PINES

CHAPTER 9
MANAGING AN UNPAID "CAREER"

It's easy to accept exile when you're naturally a recluse. I ultimately avoided socializing in public in Wallowa County as my infamy increased. I was unflinchingly dedicated to activism, but repulsed by being in the limelight.

I rarely participated in community or organized events. No yoga, no book club, only a few soccer matches and volunteering as an instructor for special needs kids at the grade school.

The only regular social event I participated in, and looked forward to the most, was the Thursday night poker game. I first got into the game five years after moving to Wallowa County, at Mel's Tavern in Joseph. The regular players included a few retirees, the chamber of commerce manager, a couple of ranchers, a gyppo log-truck driver, and owners of local businesses, including the drug store, bowling alley, junkyard, and taverns. The game started at 8:00 p.m. and often ended after 3:00 a.m.

Although never spoken out loud, I'm certain that on the minds of some players was an opportunity to "skin the environmentalist." But at the game, politics took a back seat to clay chips valued from $1 to $25. There were several good poker players, and no "mechanics" (otherwise known as cheaters). Then there were other guys who apparently could afford to lose $500 or more most weeks.

The ante was a dollar, the limit was table stakes or $40, depending on the game. It was fun, but unabashedly also lucrative, a welcome supplement to my meager income. In over thirty years of playing, I had only one year when I wound up in the red. My biggest winning night was $870, my worst losing nights were $400. That was good, because with my skinny wages, I couldn't afford to lose too often. I limited my losses by taking only $400 cash to the game. If it was gone, so was I.

I met some fine people during my first couple of years in "The County." The old salts and the young millworkers and loggers were keen working-class people. I considered myself in the same corral. Yet from the perspective of the dominant local mindset, one could not be an advocate for protecting land and also be a participant in blue-collar trades.

My main concern in interactions with closeted sympathizers became making sure my eco-cooties didn't infect anyone else. I did my best to respect their sensitivities.

I wasn't just initiating a campaign. I was also forming an organization and morphing it into a sanctioned nonprofit. This involved researching how to write bylaws, file corporate papers, and secure charitable tax-exempt status. I was also trying to collect members and assemble a board of directors. Such tasks were completely foreign, and to this day, I don't know how I managed to get it done.

It took quite some time for me to slow down enough to analyze where I was going with my mission. I never thought much about parameters in managing the impossible revolution I was trying to start—what amount of time and effort would be required, or where exactly this fast-developing "job" was leading.

The work was self-propelling. I managed to figure out how to do things as they became necessary. Tasks like setting up press conferences and tours and consulting with environmental attorneys were tests for an inexperienced activist. I still spent lots of time in the backcountry, although much of it was not for pleasure, but for examining Forest Service activities.

During those early days, I approached all aspects of my activism with my compulsive desire to *win*. That drive was born of the same urgency I had felt seven years earlier at Nesmith Point in the Columbia Gorge—wilderness is vanishing and I have to save it *now*! My activist workload got to the point I had little time to even consider a full-time job.

My summer job on the Forest Service helitack had come to a rude ending in 1982. Even before I became publicly known as an activist, the Forest Service brass knew my opinions on forest management. I didn't make any concerted attempt to hide my opinions from my workmates, or even the upper-echelon bosses.

During my third season, the Forest Service fired me after accusing me of stealing a chainsaw from the fire crew cache. The Wallowa County district attorney charged me with theft. At the trial, all three of my supervisors from the Forest Service fire management office, Steve Harbert, Art Keener, and Duke Denny, testified on my behalf. The forest supervisor, Jerry Allen, later repudiated them for it. The jury deliberated for less than half an hour before bringing their correct verdict: not guilty.

Still, that was the end of my cherished firefighting job with the Forest Service. I was technically a temporary employee and thus afforded few rights to employment. I desperately needed a job, so I drew on the truck-driving experience I'd gained at the steel mill a decade earlier to begin cross-country truck driving for Willis Shaw Express out of Boise, Idaho.

It worked well, as I could come and go as I pleased. When my funds ran low, I'd hit the highways across America for a few weeks, then rush back home to a full plate of activist tasks. But at the end of a long trucking stint in the winter of 1983, I longed for another outdoor summer job.

As if by magic, in 1984 I met wilderness advocacy icon and outfitter Martin Litton at a public meeting in Lewiston, Idaho. Idaho Power Company bureaucrats were discussing the operation of Hells Canyon Dam. I spoke at the meeting and drew scowls from the Idaho Power stuffed suits when I enthusiastically suggested removal of the dam.

Afterward, Martin approached me. "I've always appreciated a guy who says what he really thinks," he exclaimed, grinning. With his casual yet profound demeanor, Martin explained that he owned a river outfitting company.

"I've guest-guided on a few Hells Canyon trips for James Henry River Journeys," I told him.

Martin laughed. "Well, if you're as adept at rowing a hard boat through whitewater as you are at articulating the ridiculousness of dams, how'd you like to guide dory trips for me in Hells Canyon and the Salmon River?"

I was elated. After I learned more about Martin, one of the godparents of wild river protection and river outfitting, the honor of working for him became one of the defining moments of my career. But, er, a *dory?* Once I finally rowed one of the picturesque, high-prowed wooden dories, inclusion in that exclusive niche of river-guiding culture became a source of tremendous pride and satisfaction.

Given meager financial requirements, I was economically set—spending summers guiding dory trips and winters driving trucks—and had ample time for activism in between multi-day river trips and three- to six-week trucking excursions.

Truck stops were my office for writing many of the timber sale appeals. I'd often sit in a crummy cafe off an interstate highway in the middle of the night reading a Forest Service timber sale environmental analysis to figure out legal arguments against the project. In the early-morning hours at a truck stop in Walcott, Iowa, I penned what would become an infamous appeal of the rapacious Skook Timber Sale.

Long-haul trucking was nice because I was alone 95 percent of the time, but it was otherwise a hideous job—piloting a huge, roaring diesel tractor-trailer back and forth across the USA, contributing to virtually nothing except the hollow perpetuation of the industrial beast. My habitat was the cavernous, growling Peterbilt cab, the hostile cops, the cocky union geeks at the loading docks, and the company that treated its drivers like juvenile delinquents. Then there were the persistent "lot lizards," desperate young women looking for quick cash whom I circumvented like rusty barbed wire. I worked in the most depressing culture I could imagine, entrenched in the dregs of toxic industrial zones and trash-laden highways.

While hauling fifty thousand pounds of frozen fish sticks from Boston to Oxnard, California, the only thing that kept my own wheels turning was thoughts of my dory trips once summer came. While grinding gears, I fantasized wandering aimlessly through untouched mountain meadows and groves of giant trees, and pacified myself knowing that cozy mountain town was waiting.

But the activist tasks were accumulating, and I was forced to dedicate less time to both money-making jobs. Activism was my priority over income, so how I'd survive financially became almost a secondary consideration. I rarely bought anything. Stout hiking boots were my only shoes, and I perfected the art of making two pairs of Levi's last for several years. I never paid more than $150 for cabin rental.

As my dedication to activism increased, I wondered how I could ever again work a job only to make money. It would feel like a self-serving waste of time. I loved river guiding, as it allowed me to share natural history and river-protection efforts with clients. Eventually, I gave up trucking completely. I looked for occasional jobs outside river guiding to make meager ends meet.

By accident, I found a high-paying job with a company called Bart Associates. It had a contract to build a Forest Service campground at Anthony Lake, in the Elkhorn Mountains, south of the Wallowas. I gratefully accepted the $16.40 per hour, an incredibly high salary at the time.

My main job with Bart was logging the right-of-way for the campground roads and campsites, and driving a dump truck. I felt no guilt, as I was not felling ancient ponderosa pines in a vast commercial timber sale. I took comfort in defying the false edict that one can only be either pro-logging or anti-logging. I didn't live in a world of black and white; my activism was about how and where to log, not whether or not to log.

Working only enough to support my activism was another art form I needed to perfect. Maximizing my income was not a personal principle. I regarded the very term *career* with disgust. What was the point? To dedicate yourself to doing basically the same thing all the time?

I began to see a career as something important for those who raise families. But that was no more on my radar than building a career. My romantic attachments were all punctuated by staunch informality; activism had become my "career," and activists my family.

* * *

Into the mid-1980s, Lori and I were achieving significant success appealing timber sales and interesting other conservation groups in Hells Canyon issues. We had also begun to interest hunting and angling groups and the Nez Perce Tribe in stopping the logging in the HCNRA. The more popular our work became, the more work was added to my docket.

I dismissed every suggestion to try and raise enough money to receive a salary for my Wallowa Resource Council work. It seemed a ridiculous notion given the paltry donations WRC had been receiving. We took in maybe $3,000 per year. Where would I raise more? Besides, I despised fundraising. I was never comfortable asking for money: it implies the asker is a beggar. My upbringing sanctified privacy and stigmatized nosing into other people's business—particularly their finances. Discussing finances with anyone was strictly verboten. I never knew what my parents were pulling in.

I had no intention for activism to become a paid job, nor a career. Looking back, I should have focused on determining my own limitations. My only thought of constraints was that I feared being tied down, overcommitted, depended upon, and inextricably locked into responsibility for something that I might not be able to unlock because I deeply believed in it.

Along with the workload, my stress was escalating. I began to pay more attention to my moods, considering the cause of episodes of deep depression. I had assumed they were a part of everyone's internal psyche. Yet I became convinced it was something more serious once anger became a dominating emotion.

I wasn't convinced the depression was something permanent. I wasn't able to parse the dark feelings that came out of nowhere, and those that came from the stress of the job. I hadn't found ways to temper my workload and had no idea how to find the means to address the depression.

By the time I began to accept that depression would impact the activism and vice versa, I'd already set a course of action I could not back down from. The alternating fulfillments and stresses of the work became a paradox of cause and effect that spun me toward what might be called a meaningful oblivion—I was satisfying myself with my work, but it was simultaneously shredding my brain.

After I began to accept that stress was not solely responsible for the depression, it became irrelevant—I was compelled to advance my crusade no matter how much it was eroding my will. Depression became a phantom compeller of dread, just another demon to fight, like the forces of darkness destroying the land.

I eventually figured that if my instinctive love of wilderness was to have a name—the "eco-psyche"—the demon that beset my brain must also be branded. Perhaps I could fight it better if it had an identity. On one particular sleepless night, after awaking in a cold sweat, I named my pain: Dagloth.

CHAPTER 10
A COMPLICATED IDENTITY

During my time advocating for forest wilderness protection, the pro-logging vs. anti-logging labels became even more mutually exclusive, more starkly black and white. Any gray area was left as a sickly hue to feed irrational conflict and confuse purpose. During the heyday of anti-wilderness fanaticism in the Western United States, nearly every reference to "environmentalist" was accompanied by the words "radical" or "extremist."

Locally, my tacky "environmentalist" brand was set in concrete; by default, I was "anti-logging," and by default, the local media were going to support the local timber industry. I was presented in the local press as a radical environmentalist whose heartless appeals against timber sales were threatening local jobs. I wasn't sure how to wriggle out of that stereotype, but I resented being viewed as anti-logging and began to loathe the term "environmentalist."

The reality was that a wealth of timber was available outside the HCNRA, on hundreds of thousands of acres of public, corporate, and private land within the county. If managed sustainably, it was more than enough to feed several sawmills. But that was the rub with sawmills; they weren't built based on the ability of the forest to sustain them, but on corporate models of how much profit could be made over the short term.

I did not consider myself an environmentalist, just a working-class stiff who loved the outdoors, determined to stop the destruction of wild places. I felt fortunate being able to sneak into some outdoor jobs in Wallowa County. My summers working on the Forest Service fire-suppression crew, prior to being unjustly fired and the advent of my activism, were particularly rewarding. I enjoyed the mystique of being a firefighter on the front lines.

I wanted to burst through the contrived image of a spandex-wearing, SUV-driving tree hugger of privileged means. I began to tell local reporters to refer to me as a "wilderness advocate," not an environmentalist, but of course they didn't.

Despite the local media's intractable insistence on painting me as the plotting environmentalist enemy, it became known in Wallowa County that labor, including logging, is my heritage. Lots of folks knew I had worked as a Forest Service firefighter, and some knew that my post-firefighting employment involved running a track hoe for a contractor building a new water main for the City of Joseph.

Others knew I was adept at felling trees, as I once got "caught in the act" when I had a chance encounter with three young men who worked for a local logging company. I was cutting firewood alone near Harl Butte, deep in the woods about forty miles from Joseph. It was late morning, but I'd risen early, and my truck and trailer were half full of split tamarack (aka western larch—the most prized local tree species for firewood). As I was fueling and sharpening my chainsaw, I heard a truck stop on the road above. I knew the occupants were watching, but didn't yet know who they were.

I ignored them, fired up the saw and meticulously felled a good-sized tamarack snag (dead tree) using falling wedges. That's a technical process reserved for the more experienced timber faller. After you've put a "face cut" about one-third of the way into the tree, you start the back cut on the opposite side. As you sink the saw in, you pound wedges into the back cut to compel it to fall in the direction you desire.

It took about ten minutes to topple the twenty-five-inch-diameter snag. I successfully placed the tree where I needed to for easy bucking, splitting, and loading. After I turned off the saw and prepared to limb the tree and mark it into firewood-sized rounds, I could sense the men were still there watching.

I looked toward them through the brush. One walked down the hill from about a hundred feet away. He was straining to see who I was. He may have been disappointed that, by local woodcutter etiquette, I had essentially laid claim to a nice patch of dead tamarack.

As he continued to approach, he yelled, "You gonna take all that nice tammy for yourself?"

"Finders, keepers," I replied, laughing. "If you help me load 'er up, you can have some!"

He hesitated, tilted his head, and stared. I could see a sharp flash of recognition bite him. He spoke suddenly and loudly. "I'm sure as hell surprised to see *you* out here with a chainsaw." He turned and walked back up to his truck without taking me up on my offer.

My closest friends in the wilderness movement had blue-collar backgrounds too—Tim Lillebo, George Atiyeh, and Scott Stouder had worked as loggers. Scott was known as one of the more talented timber fallers on the Oregon coast, a third-generation logger in a family business. He became an incredibly effective advocate for wilderness, proceeding from logging to professional writing and a job with Trout Unlimited helping to protect Idaho forests. Scott proved the politicians wrong, with their insulting implications that loggers aren't capable of doing anything but logging. His migration to forest advocacy was chronicled by Ed Bradley in a 1996 episode of *60 Minutes*.

George Atiyeh, a Vietnam veteran, was about as far from a daisy-sniffing, bleeding-heart "environmentalist" as an advocate for protecting forests could be. He met Forest Service employees who came to mark timber in his beloved Opal Creek in Western Oregon with a cordial demeanor, but also with clear instruction that if they came back with survey stakes and timber sale boundary markers, they faced whatever degree of resistance might be needed to prevent them from invading Opal Creek's forests. (Tragically, George perished in the Lionshead Fire of 2020 that completely scorched the Opal Creek Wilderness he labored so long to protect. He chose not to evacuate. Later, Pacificorp power conglomerate was found negligent for failing to properly maintain the powerlines that created the sparks that ignited the fire.)

My friends were also a living counter to the stereotype held by some wilderness advocates who assume that because most loggers and cowboys don't have college degrees and live in isolated rural areas, they're not too sharp. Frankly, some of the smartest people I've ever met are loggers and ranchers.

My philosophical allegiance was with both the conservation ethic and the working class, but adamantly not with the timber companies or the Forest Service. I respected and admired most of the loggers and millworkers I met. Still, their trade associations and most prominent spokespersons defended the timber industry party line that federal land should be dedicated to supplying timber without regard to impacts on other forest resources.

Eventually, the fact of my blue-collar background increased local enmity. My work history tainted the contrived mask political detractors had painted, muddying the myth of who the supposed oppressors of the working class really were.

The fact that there was a living, breathing "environmentalist" in Wallowa County was a matter of shame to the more hostile local timber workers. In their neatly contrived world, environmentalists simply didn't live there. That the one who did live there had a blue-collar background was offensive and incomprehensible.

Even though I had worked for the Forest Service and had witnessed firsthand that *they* were the ones breaking the law, behind closed doors in meetings with county commissioners, congressional staff, and local economic pundits, the Forest Service brass contributed to the negative branding of environmentalists in general, and me in particular. They named me as the obstructionist filer of lawsuits and impeder of conscientious Forest Service management activities. I know this because I was informed by a sympathetic Forest Service employee who'd sat in on some of the meetings.

I was pleased that, despite the attempts of my detractors to frame me as a wealthy elitist and rob me of my jobs, many local folks were well aware of my work background. But my future as a blue-collar worker in Wallowa County was squelched by my political enemies. About six weeks after I'd secured the job running a track hoe in the operation to build the Joseph water line, I saw the person who had become my primary detractor, Boise Cascade Corporation millworker Paul Morehead, on the job site speaking with the company owner. The next day, I got the pink slip. But in my conversation with the owner, he gave no reason for the firing, saying only, "Sorry, we appreciated your work."

Back then, I simply ignored the backbiting, but I now regret that course of strategy. Without resistance, my reputation crumbled over time. I loathed the categorization of my identity. Why was it not possible to be a blue-collar worker and a wilderness advocate, not just an "environmentalist"? I cherished the times I had sat with Tim and envisioned more protective lines on the map, invisible but effective barriers against intrusions into pristine groves. I'd dream of the day when I could walk into the Imnaha River's ancient forest knowing the Forest Service's timber planners, with their accursed cans of blue paint, would never set foot there again. What I didn't envision was the accumulation of tasks that outran my ability to keep up, and the increase of hostilities to a point I could never have imagined.

BOY SCOUT FALLS ON THE WALLOWA RIVER

CHAPTER 11
SCHEMING A LEGISLATIVE SOLUTION

In the Hells Canyon National Recreation Area, blue-painted "marked to cut" trees proliferated like noxious weeds. Trying to keep the Forest Service timber machine out of HCNRA forests became like trying to keep a pack of hungry jackals off a carcass.

Initially, Lori, Tim, and I stopped several HCNRA timber sales by convincing the Regional Forester's office in Portland, which reviewed most of our administrative appeals, that they were illegal. Eventually, however, HCNRA's head ranger, logging-centric Al Defler—who rode in on his father's coattails—and his timber staff adapted to our arguments. They began writing more concise environmental assessments. Defler also convinced the regional and national offices that if our appeals continued to be upheld, it would dismantle the HCNRA's contribution to the timber output in the region, something they did not look kindly at. Our appeals were henceforth denied, and the logging of the HCNRA progressed apace.

The Forest Service contrived some of the most horrific logging projects in some of the most magical places. The worst was the Skook Sale, located on a magnificent slope above the Imnaha River near Coverdale Campground. This blatantly rapacious timber sale became our poster child against HCNRA logging.

The 3,000-acre Skook Sale invaded a dream world of picturesque slopes adorned with tall bunchgrass and clear, cold-water springs surrounded by glowing aspen groves. Huge ponderosa pines, some over five feet in diameter and approaching two hundred feet in height, stood like noble sentinels amid dark but radiant volcanic rock domes.

The Forest Service didn't even attach some contrived rationale as to why they "needed" to deface this idyllic place. There were no "problems" pulled from the industrial forester's bag of tricks to try and justify logging, like "excessive fuel loading." No "invasive insects." No "overabundance of dying trees," nor fire danger. The only reason for the project was to provide the Boise Cascade Corporation, eventual purchaser of the sale, with priceless giant ponderosa pine trees.

I first learned of the Skook Sale in 1984. When I spoke with HCNRA timber sale planner Jerry Magera, he said, "We're just gonna get rid of some of that ol' spike-top stuff (trees with dead tops)." When I went to the newly laid-out sale area, I found maybe four or five "spike-top" trees among hundreds of trees marked to cut.

I later learned that the largest aspen grove in the Skook Sale area was referred to by longtime locals as the "Cabbage Patch." I have no idea how it got that name, but anti-protection county commissioner Ben Boswell, an amicable guy and one of the few Wallowa County commissioners who would even speak with me, admitted his adoration of the Cabbage Patch in one of our conversations about the Skook Sale. Ben described how as a teen he used to go to the Cabbage Patch on summer afternoons with his girlfriend. It was one of his favorite places. It became one of mine. I often wondered if that helped him to understand why I was challenging federal timber sales.

Yet, when I asked him during one of his visits to my office, "Why don't you oppose the sale?" his response was disheartening.

"I can't," he said, an obvious allusion to the political flack he'd receive if he even questioned a federal logging project.

On my first visit to the Cabbage Patch, the grotesquely fluorescent blue "marked to cut" kiss of death was splashed across the base of giant pines and firs—trees with no "defects." During my logging career, I cut down many trees, but it struck me as incomprehensible that anyone with the slightest ability to perceive natural beauty could disgrace such a magical place.

*　*　*

Tim, Lori, and I realized the Forest Service had an inexhaustible supply of excuses for logging, and we were never going to slow down their HCNRA chainsaw binge. So after nearly three years of appealing timber sales, we considered another option with permanence—legislation.

I hadn't the slightest idea what was involved in a legislative campaign nor how to "play politics." But I had Tim and Lori's knowledge and eventually, the backing of the most prominent and principled wilderness advocacy group in Oregon, the Oregon Natural Resource Council (ONRC).

As I considered the challenge in getting Congress to pass a bill, an agonizing irony nipped at my politically uninclined conscience—we'd be engaging in a complex and expensive effort to maintain the status quo—keeping the remaining vestiges of wild land the way they already were in an area that was supposedly already protected. How many times would we have to do the same job over again?

With the election of Ronald Reagan, the nationally-based movers and shakers of pro-wilderness politics had gone from playing offense to defense. They were concentrating their work in places where they had a strong membership presence, friendly press, and a receptive congressional delegation. There was little interest in lonely northeast Oregon. We got no positive reactions to our suggestion of a Hells Canyon bill.

In trying to engender support from the lobbyists of the Sierra Club and The Wilderness Society, Jim Blomquist and Mike Francis, we heard all about what *couldn't* be done. I preferred to consider what *must* be done. The snub didn't discourage me, nor Tim or Lori, from pushing for legislation.

As our pursuit of a bill became known, Boise Cascade Corporation rose with wrath. With its Joseph sawmill and three more mills in adjoining Union County, Boise controlled the economic and political agenda in Northeast Oregon. There's no finer proof of this than when Boise financed the campaign of one of its employees, Mark Simmons, and got him elected to the 58th District seat in the Oregon House of Representatives.

My first meeting with Simmons just prior to his election was tense, but entertaining. It occurred during the Forest Congress in Washington, DC, an event designed to bring people involved in forest management together to discuss ideas and issues. I'd never met Simmons, so when I saw a man with a name tag indicating he was from Elgin, Oregon, I walked up to him and extended my hand as a fellow resident of northeast Oregon.

The man withdrew his hand after looking at my name tag and said, "It'll be a cold day in hell before I shake your hand." I shot a puzzled look at him. Suddenly, one of the event's organizers, a young woman who heard his comment, walked him over to a secluded section of the conference room. All I could see was her scowling at Simmons as she spoke to him. When I inquired with a guy who'd been speaking to Simmons, I found out he worked at Boise Cascade's Elgin sawmill. Little did I know he'd soon be elected to the state legislature.

Coincidentally, I sat directly behind Simmons on the flight back to Oregon. We couldn't ignore each other's presence and, amazingly, had a cordial conversation.

But Boise Cascade came after me, Lori, and Tim with tooth and nail. Its public-relations people conjured images of sawmills closing, hordes of people out of work, and empty storefronts throughout Wallowa County. Their self-serving proclamations were spoon-fed to their work force and other local businesses. It was utter nonsense. In the worst-case scenario, eliminating logging in the HCNRA would have reduced timber entering the sawmill pipeline by a paltry ten million board feet. And there wasn't even any guarantee that HCNRA timber would go to local mills.

The Wallowa-Whitman National Forest was logging close to 250 million board feet outside the HCNRA, and even more logs were rolling out of Boise's 150,000 acres of private timberland in Wallowa County. There was plenty of timber available to feed Boise's sawmills many times over without cutting a stick of timber from the HCNRA. But economic blackmail is the robber baron's best friend.

Lori, Tim, and I were now public enemy number one. Going to public meetings was risky. We were always vastly outnumbered by hollering detractors. Yet we persevered, and began to flesh out ideas for a bill to re-protect Hells Canyon.

Planning a legislative vision for protecting the HCNRA was empowering. I'd become sick of trying to appeal to stone-faced Forest Service leaders. Our urging that the HCNRA Act presented an opportunity to show they could treat forests with special care flew over their heads like a drunken pigeon. Playing in a new arena allowed us to plan a positive vision for the HCNRA.

But how could we take on the Forest Service, the Reagan administration, Boise Cascade, and volatile Wallowa County in the legislative arena? It would be like a kid with a willow switch challenging mail-clad knights. I didn't even know what weapons we had. But I had just enough blind ambition to take the plunge.

The HCNRA Act was a huge part of Bob Packwood's senatorial legacy. He had to be our champion. Unfortunately, the Reagan revolution strapped our second congressional district with the far-right, anti-wilderness Republican Denny Smith. But the fact that Packwood was a Republican was of course helpful.

We needed to find allies who had his ear to impress upon the senator there was a dire need for a legislative fix to correct the Forest Service's perversion of the law he had championed. Packwood was fond of Ken Witty, so over a couple of beers at Stockman's Tavern in Enterprise, Tim and I asked Ken to risk emerging from his politically sensitive position working for a state agency. We needed his help.

Witty put in a call to Packwood. The senator was impressed, and receptive. Thankfully, Tim had already mobilized the ONRC, and its executive director, James Monteith, joined in. He, Tim, Ken, and I drew up maps and finalized language for a Hells Canyon bill.

It was a knee-jerk move to designate more wilderness in the HCNRA, as this was the most common and effective tool to curtail Forest Service logging programs. It was the "go-to" solution for forest-protection advocates. This made me nervous, because there were valuable ancient forest stands outside of roadless areas that didn't qualify for wilderness designation. So, we solved that by adding a timber-cutting cap of one million board feet per year to the bill. The final draft included the logging cap and 300,000 acres of wilderness.

While Packwood might have been impressed by assumed support from the big DC-based groups with their lobbying capabilities on Capitol Hill, the national groups remained uncommitted, and mostly uninterested. Enter Brock Evans. I met with him in his DC office. Brock eventually gave us all the support we asked for. He was respected and trusted by Bob Packwood.

We began working closely with Emily Barlow, lead on Packwood's natural resource staff. She was on board, but worried about how Wallowa County opposition would play out. We knew the best way to dilute that was to bring out the people Packwood knew and had worked closely with in passing the HCNRA Act—the Hells Canyon Preservation Council.

In the spring of 1985, Tim, Ken, Lori, and I had organized a tenth-anniversary celebration of the HCNRA's establishment. Packwood committed to attend. We assembled at Buckhorn Lookout, a spectacular viewpoint overlooking the north end of the HCNRA. Many of the original HCPC activists attended, as did several Nez Perce tribal leaders. Packwood was impressed; it was a welcome reunion.

Accompanied by Tim, Monteith, Witty, and John A.K. Barker, I stood with Packwood on the edge of the Imnaha Canyon. I placed a paper in the senator's hand—a draft of the legislation.

We pointed out clearcuts and the stumps of giant pine trees. He was clearly disgusted his masterpiece of legislation, an effort that only succeeded because of his relentless perseverance, had gone for naught other than stopping the dams. He agreed to introduce our bill, and did so four months after the event at Buckhorn, just as we had written it. I was elated. We'd taken the first giant step toward Hells Canyon's salvation.

UPPER HELLS CANYON FROM HELLS CANYON CREEK

CHAPTER 12
SPLINTERS OF DESPERATION

The wheels were in motion, but legislation wouldn't come in time to stop the Skook Sale, so Tim and I organized tours of the sale area for whoever was willing to risk experiencing the rationale for our outrage. Our initial tour in the summer of 1985 was the first time I spent in the woods with nationally acclaimed eco-forester Bob Jackson. Bob eventually accompanied us on several VIP tours.

Bob's perspective was spiced with an unmatched knowledge of forestry and understanding of forests. His explanations of why the Forest Service's timber sales were downright bad, even exclusively from an industrial forestry perspective, were enlightening to many, but not the Forest Service.

Head Ranger Al Defler never accompanied us on any tours. But I met with him in his bland, cinder-block Enterprise office to discuss the Skook Timber Sale. I tried to explain that invading such an amazing vestige of nature to replace it with scarred ground and stumps was not consistent with the "preservation of unique ecosystems–conservation of wildlife habitat–protection of natural scenery" mandates of the HCNRA Act.

Protecting such amazing beauty and ecological richness was exactly what Congress intended when it passed the HCNRA Act, which Defler was mandated by law to carry out. But the ranger was unmoved. He seemed to be restraining himself from eye-rolling in response to my proselytizing. I eventually berated myself for ever speaking to him at all.

During our second tour of the Skook Sale, Bob Jackson measured one white fir tree at 62.0 inches diameter and 145 feet tall, the largest I'd ever seen of that species. We found a ponderosa that he scaled at 66.4 inches diameter (Bob was an exacting guy—if anyone asked him about that big pine in Skook, he'd never say 66 inches, or 67, it was always 66.4). Bob triangulated it at 171 feet tall. We also found a beautiful western larch that was 65.2 inches diameter and 168 feet tall. All the trees Bob scaled bore the fatal blue paint.

Bob was disarmingly compelling. In his inimitable slow and ponderous but lilting voice, he would say, "In any logging operation, ah, you want to emphasize weeding out the genetically inferior trees and keep most of your prime seed stock and, ah, *hab-tat*. You need to think about *hab-tat*. This operation, well, uh, (chuckling satirically) is doing the opposite. They're taking most of the gravy and leaving the culls."

That man was a living druid. Though he only stood about five foot one, Bob was a giant of a man. His personality was what I suspect an ancient pine tree's would be like, akin to J.R.R. Tolkien's slow and peaceful yet huge and powerful Ent characters in *Lord of the Rings*.

Bob Jackson exemplified the theory that some of the world's wisest people are tucked away in the far corners of the globe, and are never "discovered." If I could take all the knowledge from one person and bottle it so the entire planet could partake of it, my subject would be Bob Jackson. Perhaps his halting speech (a result of polio in his youth) was a safety device implanted by fate to prevent too much brilliance from overwhelming the recipient of his wisdom.

After the Forest Service regional forester denied the Skook appeal late in 1985, I attempted a last-ditch plea and met with Wallowa-Whitman National Forest Deputy Supervisor Joe Stockbridge (infamous for being bitten on the ass by a bear in Hells Canyon) and Ranger Defler. As purchaser of the Skook Sale, two of Boise Cascade's representatives showed up at the meeting—Paul Morehead and the aforementioned banquet bouncer, Fred Ebel. Joining me were Tim Lillebo and National Wildlife Federation scientist Rick Brown.

At the meeting, we pleaded our case and asked for reconsideration of the decision to award the sale. The entire time, Morehead, sitting across the table from me, issued snide, half-whispered mutterings toward me. He was rubbing my face in the fact that we lost the Skook appeal, and the Forest Service wasn't going to reconsider. At one point, he whispered, "You're a radical, and *you ain't no working man*."

Rick, Tim, and I had been aggravated by Stockbridge's deferral to Morehead's remarks, and admittedly, I snapped. "We set up this meeting, Paul, so be respectful and cut the sarcasm."

"Respect?" Morehead spat.

Stockbridge didn't hesitate to rebuke me. "Come on now, Ric...," he said. It went downhill from there, with Tim and Rick Brown playing the good cops to my bad cop, with Stockbridge repeating the word "respect" in a hopeful tone. At that moment, it came into my head that respect is never inherited nor assigned—it can only be earned.

Rick Brown seemed as pissed off as I was, but he wisely directed his comments at Stockbridge and Defler. The meeting was futility in action. I began to lose my composure, leaning across the table toward Morehead, who began leaning back toward me. Tim and Rick walked me out of the room as Stockbridge hemmed and hawed.

Only once did I ever see Tim lose his cool, and of course, it was after a healthy helping of Forest Service bullshit. We were leading a tour of the HCNRA for some high-profile staff and officers of the National Wildlife Federation. At the head of Horse Creek where the Forest Service had authorized a new set of clearcuts in an ugly timber sale, we stood at the edge of one of the cuts as Tim explained that the HCNRA Act requires logging by selective cutting, the intent clearly to prevent clearcutting.

Tim was interrupted by Forest Service silviculturist Steve Fletcher, who insisted the trees removed had blown down in a storm. Patiently, Tim pointed to the symmetrical thirty-acre stump field and replied, "So, the wind blew down a perfectly rectangular block of trees, jumped up and left another rectangular block standing, then blew down another perfectly symmetrical thirty-acre patch?"

Fletcher responded emphatically that by technical definition, this was not a clearcut, and that the trees had been felled by the wind. He added that the beautiful ancient forest along the Imnaha River we had visited two hours earlier was a result of Forest Service management.

Tim tried to move the conversation forward, as he'd made his point and Fletcher was making an idiot of himself, but the timber man wasn't finished. "You people are always misrepresenting us," he spat. "We're helping the forest, and you're not telling the truth."

His Norwegian skin tone quickly reddening, Tim shot back, "You and I are going to get into it!" as he took a step in Fletcher's direction. Fletcher wisely withdrew.

A few days after the train-wreck meeting, I met again with timber sale manager Jerry Magera, who I always found to be an honest and forthright guy. I asked him, "Can you do us one small dignity—go in and 'unmark' the big pine and that giant larch tree?" It was within his authority as contract officer.

He replied, "I'd get into deep doo-doo with Boise Cascade and besides, they'd probably just take them anyway." I noted that he didn't say he'd be in deep with his boss, Al Defler.

About a month later, the logging company moved into Skook. Roads were built and giant pines were felled. I didn't monitor the logging—I didn't have the stomach.

It wasn't long after the logging started that the local press learned many of the trees at Skook had been supplemented with twelve-inch spiral spikes. The *Wallowa County Chieftain* spin was that loggers and millworkers were being endangered.

The peril of tree spiking to loggers and millworkers is recklessly used to demonize tree defenders. In my time cutting wood, I've harmlessly run my saw into fence staples and nails from signs. I've never heard of anyone being hurt by a spiked tree. Wildlife biologists sometimes spike trees to protect nesting birds.

Whatever opinion one has of such desperate stratagems, the spiking of the Skook Timber Sale was inspired by someone's dedication to a sacred place. Such opinions are value judgments. In judging ecotage, any objective view of lawless behavior must avoid a double standard. If ranchers kill wolves, if loggers steal federal timber, or if poachers kill game animals out of season, their condemnation of ecotage is patently hypocritical. This is true even if one believes a bulldozer engine is more valuable than a wolf or a grove of five-hundred-year-old trees.

I couldn't just cry in my beer after Skook was doomed. My anger at the ignorance and malice of the Forest Service and the taunting of Morehead rang in my head like the screaming of tortured souls every time I considered Skook's epitaph.

I admit to sometimes being overcome by my emotional-control issues. It was at least a year before I calmed myself enough to go back to the Cabbage Patch and review the aftermath. When I did, the giant stumps, ripped up ground, and piles of logging slash littering the ground were devastating. It felt as if someone had taken a jagged razor to a da Vinci portrait.

I spat at the pine stumps and log-skidding ruts. I walked to that big larch tree. It hadn't been saved by the five spikes sunk into its lower flanks. But when the larch hit the ground, it had shattered into a mass of giant splinters. None of it was even hauled to the sawmill.

Photo by Ric Bailey TIM LILLEBO SAYS FAREWELL TO A GIANT PINE TREE WITHIN THE SKOOK TIMBER SALE

CHAPTER 13
THE MAULING OF THE PACKWOOD BILL

James Monteith, a former resident of Wallowa County, put the Oregon Natural Resource Council's strength into the Hells Canyon legislative effort. Their statewide presence and loyal membership could help diffuse the toxic Wallowa County opposition, with its general volatility toward any protection of the land. Hells Canyon was revered among wilderness lovers throughout Oregon.

I was still dangling my hat on the tenuous hook of the Wallowa Resource Council. Tim asked, why not *officially* resurrect the Hells Canyon Preservation Council? With the approval of the HCPC originals, I became the voice of the Hells Canyon Preservation Council. The Wallowa Resource Council dissolved into thin air.

I filed articles of incorporation and got approval for tax-exempt status from the IRS, things the original HCPC never did. Tim and I put together a solid board of directors that included two of HCPC's original founders, Jack Barry and John A.K. Barker, two political bulldogs.

After Packwood introduced the bill in the Senate, the Wallowa County forces exploded. Boise Cascade openly threatened to shut down their Joseph sawmill if Packwood's bill passed.

Boise's job blackmail was the same draconian fear tactic it used to manipulate their employee's wages. It still worked. Wallowa County millworkers lived in almost constant fear of the mill closing. With fear-driven opposition from practically the entire economic infrastructure of Wallowa County, we faced emotional resistance that defied any rational reading of Packwood's bill.

Wallowa County forester Bob Jackson publicly commented that Boise's corporate land, if managed sustainably, could alone produce enough timber to feed at least two of Boise's four Northeast Oregon mills with no federal timber supplement. But the details didn't matter. The millworkers and loggers swallowed the industry line.

Angered by Boise's dogma, Packwood informed us he wanted to hold a public meeting in Wallowa County to set the record straight about his bill's impact on timber supply. Tim and I advised against it. We knew the chances were slim we could get many supportive people to the meeting, whereas Boise Cascade would shut the Joseph and La Grande mills for the day so their entire workforce could attend. On January 9, 1986, a defiant Packwood held a public meeting at Toma's restaurant in Enterprise.

Bob Packwood was a statesman with oratory skills that would match any member of Congress. But at the meeting, he was nearly overwhelmed by sheer numbers and rank hostility. More than three hundred people, mostly angry millworkers, stacked the room. Despite my desperate local organizing, few pro-wilderness people attended. Tim Lillebo and I were virtually alone.

There were several tense moments at the meeting. Packwood's presentation of historic HCNRA logging levels was challenged by Wallowa County Chamber of Commerce Manager Jerry Perren.

There was no reason to be debating historic logging levels, as the HCNRA Act has no requirement for maintaining historic timber production. But the red-herring issue stole the show after the Forest Service later confirmed Perren's figures, higher than what Packwood had received earlier from the agency, were accurate. Packwood was seen browbeating Perren after the meeting, and later had to apologize after the Forest Service presented the new information, which they claimed they found in a box stuffed inside a closet.

As for the Forest Service's blunder in giving Packwood the wrong numbers, Forest Supervisor Jerry Allen was soon after relieved of his position. I figured Packwood had flexed his political muscles in retribution.

The biggest incident at the meeting began while I chatted with Tim and Emily Barlow. The three of us were suddenly surrounded by millworkers. Suddenly, Packwood motioned for us to join him while he spoke with Perren, but we didn't say anything to either of them. I walked outside to place my jacket in my truck. It was *hot* in the restaurant. Just after I exited the building, a man walked up to me, flanked by three other men. He spoke in emphatic terms, his pitch rising. "If I lose my job over this, we're going to nail your ass, and I'm talking tar and feathers and guns and the whole works." As he spoke, I tried to look nonchalant, but it did come as a shock.

I spoke directly to him. "Hey, I respect concerns about your job. But if I were you, I'd be more concerned about logs from local forests going to outside sawmills and the unsustainable management of Boise's forestland." He grimaced and acted like he didn't hear me. The men walked away.

It was my first death threat. It felt surreal, despite the local hostilities that had been occurring for months. Wild thoughts rushed through my head. What if the encounter broke out in fisticuffs, the violence spread into the building, and a US senator was exposed to a one-sided riot? What if someone pulled a gun? But I didn't consciously take the threat seriously.

* * *

The circus atmosphere of that meeting continued when Packwood held a public hearing in La Grande in August 1986. He was joined by Oregon's other senator, the equally powerful Mark Hatfield, who chaired the Senate Energy and Natural Resources Committee.

Somehow, Tim, James Monteith, and I were able to inspire many leaders of the greater conservation community in Oregon to attend. We also got a good showing of people from the La Grande area. I put together some sideshow events, including a barbecue at Loren and Betty Hughes' ranch.

Of course, Boise Cascade mobilized their forces for the hearing. It made for a wild affair, including an arrest when Jack Barry was tackled by three policemen in the aisle of the hearing room as his son Peter testified. Jack later sued the local cops over the incident and settled out of court for an undisclosed amount. The cops never said why they arrested him.

Hells Canyon protection forces presented eloquent arguments in their testimony. An economics expert testified that HCNRA timber was inconsequential to local sawmills. Scientists noted the ecological significance of the HCNRA. Representatives of the timber forces could only come up with the same worn-out arguments—any reduction in timber production from federal land would derail the local economy.

Senator Packwood was discouraged by the local opposition to his bill. Still, Tim, James, and I continued our push to advance the bill in the Senate. I went to Washington, DC, to lobby. Navigating the marble halls of Congress was like a weird dream. I was a fish swimming in oil.

I showed congressional staff scenic photos of Hells Canyon and spoke of the creatures and plants that existed there, but nowhere else. I quickly learned the best weapon I had was not facts and figures, but my passion toward what I believed in.

Tim, James, and I searched for co-sponsors. With the Republican Packwood supporting one of the Democrats' platform issues, there was opportunity for bipartisan support.

Foremost in our considerations was to find a sponsor in the House to introduce a companion bill. The obvious first choice was dedicated wilderness champion Jim Weaver, a Democratic representative from Oregon's fourth district. We got an enthusiastic response from Weaver.

But then a strange thing happened. Weaver announced his intention to challenge Packwood in the upcoming senatorial election. That essentially excluded him from being involved in Packwood's bill.

Coincidentally, I had been elected to the board of "Wild PAC," a fund started by James Monteith to support pro-conservation candidates. Weaver was the obvious choice over Packwood for Wild PAC's endorsement in the Senate race, as he had been a stalwart for Oregon wilderness his entire career. Conversely, Packwood had adopted specific conservation causes and fought mightily for them, but his support was infrequent.

Wild PAC delayed its Senate endorsement to avoid alienating Packwood. Meanwhile, ONRC's Andy Kerr attended a meeting with Weaver on an unrelated issue. As Weaver, a passionate guy with a notorious temper, spoke with a person across the room from Kerr, he pointed a finger at Kerr. When he finished, he turned to Kerr and shouted, "Where's my endorsement!"

A week later, an even stranger thing happened. Hopelessly trailing Packwood in the polls, Weaver dropped out of the Senate race. Packwood, obviously discouraged by the lack of local support, informed us the Hells Canyon bill was "on hold" until we could find local support. I was devastated.

It seemed all the bill did was show Packwood the wilderness movement in Oregon had weakened since his tryst with HCPC in the 1970s. The reality was—and Packwood knew it—the big national groups wouldn't be involved in actively supporting his bill, Brock Evans notwithstanding.

On top of that devastation, immediately after the La Grande hearing, Lori Aschenbrenner, my close local cohort for five years, vanished.

She and Steve sold their house and convenience store and moved out of Wallowa County with no explanation. I sorely missed her political wisdom and energy.

Meanwhile, the anti-wilderness fire continued to burn in Wallowa County. So it is in rural politics—once the mob gets its teeth into an issue and smells blood, it's easy to rile them up.

Overwhelmed by the workload, I desperately needed time for some personal introspection. I was overwhelmed. I figured a couple of months guiding river trips and walking in the mountains would be healing. Not so much.

Contemplating the defeat of Packwood's bill and the hostilities, my days were dark. And in the shrunken enclave of that ramshackle cabin on Hurricane Creek Road, my depression began to grow. It was inconsistent and difficult to predict, but characterized mostly by sleepless nights filled with thoughts of hopelessness and self-loathing, expanding anger and intolerance.

I tried to shrug it off with as much resolve as I could muster. I had no inclination to get help because I didn't know there was anything medically wrong with me. "Suck it up," I'd tell myself. "Be the mountain." Self-debate muddled the theory that the darkness was inflamed by the public controversy wherein I was always the bad guy. I resisted the conscious acceptance that activism was inflaming my depression.

I was driven by my cause, and clung to salvation in the job I had to finish—legislation to re-protect the HCNRA. There was too much to be done to just crawl into depression's ragged hole and lie there.

CHAPTER 14
LITIGATION AND A DISTURBING REVELATION

Early in 1987, Tim came to Joseph and spent a few days with me. We took counsel after the demise of the Packwood bill. Our days fighting Forest Service timber sales were exhausting. After our administrative appeals were no longer successful and the legislation tactic on hold, Tim and I decided to do what I'd long wanted to—find a lawyer and file suit against the Forest Service to enforce the HCNRA Act's directives for protection of the ecosystem.

I wasn't familiar with suing the federal government. In my lingo, lawsuits involved one person suing another, or someone suing a restaurant because their coffee spilled. But the more I learned, the more I felt we might actually put a long-term halt to the Forest Service's unchecked logging agenda.

The 1980s were days when the question of getting attorneys to file an environmental lawsuit was not "which lawyer should we try to interest?" it was "can we find a lawyer?" With the help of University of Oregon Law School Professors Mike Axline and John Bonine, we soon had two attorneys, Gary Kahn and Kerry Rydberg, working on a lawsuit. We filed against the "Mud Duck" Timber Sale, with its proposed clearcuts and logging of ancient pine and spruce stands.

We set out to prove that the Forest Service was blatantly ignoring all four requirements of the HCNRA Act for logging—it can only occur in areas it has previously occurred; it must be *compatible* with the protection of fish and wildlife habitat and unique ecosystems; it must be subject to special rules to ensure compatibility with resource protection; and it must be carried out only by "selective cutting."

We wound up in the Ninth Circuit Court of Appeals. Unfortunately, the court's ruling on the selective cutting stipulation showed us that trying to legislate logging prescriptions is about as futile as trying to regulate abstract art. The law's intent is obvious—log with special care and don't clearcut. But the Forest Service, masters of manipulating language, simply renamed clearcutting. In HCNRA timber sales, they referred to clearcutting as "group selection." Thus, clearcutting became "selective cutting." I wasn't sure which was worse, the agency's sleazy semantic manipulation, or its compulsive desire to engage in the ecologically ruinous practice of clearcutting.

On the positive side, regarding the critical issue of the HCNRA Act mandate that logging and livestock grazing be "compatible" with ecosystem protection, the court ruled that compatibility must be enforced via the special regulations the Forest Service is required to write.

But, to our complete dismay and in incomprehensible defiance of the judicial branch of government, the court's mandate was ignored by the agency. Despite our insistent reminders, the Forest Service ignored us and declined to write the special rules. Shockingly, the Hells Canyon Preservation Council had to go back to court twice more to force the agency to write the rules. We sued a fourth time to challenge the weak rules they finally published.

* * *

While I was navigating the path toward correcting the Forest Service's legal negligence, I got better connected to the growing cadre of environmental attorneys. Eventually, I met Vic Sher, one of the engineers of the famous spotted owl lawsuit. A staff attorney and eventually executive director of the Sierra Club Legal Defense Fund (now called Earthjustice Legal Defense Fund), Sher adopted our cause. He described "a series of lawsuits to clarify and enforce the intent of the HCNRA Act." Suddenly, we had the best of legal representation for environmental causes in our corner. Adam Berger, one of Sher's understudies and a precise litigator in his own right, adopted HCPC's cause and became a powerful ally.

Diligent litigation became the short-term solution of our multifaceted campaign to protect the HCNRA. HCPC filed more than a dozen lawsuits to enforce the HCNRA Act's directives. All but three were successful to one degree or another.

We didn't sue because we liked to, but because we had to. Never once did I take pleasure in authorizing a lawsuit. They require a lot of work and they're expensive, even with pro-bono representation. The

Forest Service, however, did whatever they wanted to, and dared us to file another lawsuit while they complained about those litigious radicals at HCPC.

The badmouthing of litigation sticks in my craw. When you're right on the law, why would you not enforce it? I often told people who criticized our lawsuits if they don't like the laws, they should work to change them, or convince the federal government to obey its own laws.

Those who oppose environmental protection speak of lawsuits like they're a disease, as do the federal agencies that get sued. I'd always assumed it was self-evident that citizens' ability to hold the federal government accountable to the laws of our country is as much an inalienable right as free speech. In fact, it *is* free speech.

Laws are what make civilization, well, civilization. In the absence of laws protecting the environment, we would have to rely on the goodness in the hearts of intractable federal agencies and corporate America. I've seen very little of that. Or, we could resort to guns to defend our home, our health, and our lives. A lot of people would be willing to fight for their country, but we shouldn't have to.

As we discovered with the local Boise Cascade Corporation timber machine, the most vocal critics of those dreaded environmental rules are heirs of the original robber barons. They long for the old days when industry could take whatever it wanted without any interference.

Dictionaries define *robber baron* as "a ruthlessly powerful US capitalist or industrialist of the late nineteenth century considered to have become wealthy by exploiting natural resources, corrupting legislators, or other unethical means." Today, robber barons like Dick Cheney and his cohorts have maintained control of federal land by co-opting both federal land-management agencies and members of Congress.

The barons line up the working class to support their causes with the threat of job losses and wage cuts if their agenda is not carried out. Amid the clearcut oblivion of the once-bountiful public forests, the barons contend the problem besetting the timber worker is "environmental obstructionists" filing "frivolous lawsuits" and "locking up federal timber."

In a sense, the Forest Service actually benefitted from our lawsuits. Its leaders knew the more lawsuits we filed, the more the local workforce hated us. It was my despair over the conflict between HCPC and the working class that inspired me to intensively manage the publicizing of our lawsuits.

HCPC made it clear in speaking to the public and the political establishment that litigation was always a last resort. We sued the agency only after collaboration with the Forest Service failed to produce a solution, and I made sure we had a paper trail to prove it. We produced letters and meeting minutes articulating our disclosure to the Forest Service that it was violating the law. They ignored us, so we sued them and won.

Equally important, we produced alternatives to Forest Service logging proposals, illuminating natural means of dealing with alleged problems. We proposed dealing with supposed insect "epidemics" with use of pheromone baiting as opposed to unscientific and ineffective efforts to control indigenous bugs by (surprise, surprise) logging. Providing alternative solutions presented our litigation as the constructive work of concerned citizens rather than obstructionists who oppose everything.

It didn't work.

Defenders of environmental law are ever more widely scorned in today's confused world. There is tremendous value in having enforcers of the law. It's important they use law rather than monkey wrenches or gunfights with the henchmen of the robber barons.

One of the biggest mistakes the forest advocacy movement ever made was allowing the media to frame the public forest logging issue as "loggers vs. environmentalists." Defenders of forests allowed themselves to be framed as adversaries of working people.

I've been criticized for "bashing" the Forest Service. I won't apologize. Because it wasn't loggers and millworkers who deliberately violated federal law, ignored science, lied to the public, and presided over the dismantling of forest ecosystems. It was the Forest Service—in service to the robber barons.

As an employee of the Forest Service, I worked with many fine people. While doing battle with the agency, I regretted criticizing the Forest Service collectively when there were dedicated folks working in the biological sciences, courageous firefighters, and competent recreation managers. But the agency culture and brain trust are a very different story.

I used to say asking the Forest Service to protect ecosystems is like asking Madonna to sing gospel. Its answer to every question and its solution to every problem is logging. Its defiance of law and subversion of science is compulsive. The agency commercially logs during firefighting activities to escape environmental review, and it initiates prescribed burns in select areas so it can initiate "salvage" logging of the trees it burned. It initiates logging projects for "public safety," that remove trees along hundreds of miles of forest roads where many of the roads are not even open to the public.

In filing lawsuits, we forest advocates were defending our country's ecosystems and natural resources by enforcing laws and holding a federal agency accountable. We were defending the working class by compelling sustainable resource management. We were the good guys, but were out-shouted by the spin doctors of the timber industry and neutralized by the Forest Service, which hid its real agenda behind the brilliant façade of Smokey the Bear.

THE SEVEN DEVILS MOUNTAINS FROM NEAR SADDLE CREEK

CHAPTER 15

BIRTH OF THE HELLS CANYON–CHIEF JOSEPH CAMPAIGN

I was still painfully mindful of Senator Packwood's requirement of "local support." I knew he wasn't referring to La Grande, where support could be marshaled. He meant Wallowa County, within which the vast majority of the HCNRA lay.

His position indirectly validated Wallowa County government's claim of lordship over federal land within county lines. If given authority, Wallowa County would log and overgraze the HCNRA with no plan for sustainability nor consideration of ecological impacts.

Of course, that was pretty much what the Forest Service was doing anyway: the American taxpayers funded administration of the HCNRA, but they didn't matter to Wallowa County government—the county wanted their money, not their opinions. But luckily, the prospect of a Wallowa County takeover of federal land was a local pipe dream.

Perceiving the near-impossibility of the "get local support" task, I huddled with Tim and the HCPC Board over strategy. Paul Fritz, former National Park Service Superintendent of Craters of the Moon National Monument in Idaho, was on the board and contributed mightily to the discussions. During our talks, I wondered at the knee-jerk compulsion of the wilderness movement to fall back on wilderness designation as the answer to every problem. Perhaps it was time to broaden our thinking with respect to a legislative solution—one that might neutralize local antagonists.

I had once offhandedly broached the idea of switching management of the HCNRA to the National Park Service to Tim. "If the problem isn't the law, but the agency that's failing to comply with it," I explained, "why don't we change the agency?"

Establishing a national park would give us an opportunity to approach Packwood with a new idea, one that might garner some local support due to tourism-based economic opportunities. The Forest Service's failure to promote the HCNRA for visitation was often criticized by Wallowa County business leaders.

I entertained the National Park Service idea with hesitation, as I was a "park skeptic." I didn't want hordes of tourists pouring into the Wallowa Valley and overrunning Joseph. I was loathe to welcome an agency which, I naively supposed, might be paving roads and constructing developments.

I conducted my own intensive research, and eventually toured some of the newer national parks like Capitol Reef, North Cascades, and Great Basin. I soon realized the Park Service's pro-development reputation is a myth.

The developments in Grand Canyon, Yosemite, and Yellowstone National Parks were not authorized by the Park Service. Prior to the establishment of the agency in 1916, the parks were managed by the railroad companies and the US Army. The railroads were marketing rail travel from the Eastern United States to the scenic wonders of the West. With the army's cooperation, they built the rail lines, roads, hotels, and other developments.

I contrasted Grand Canyon roads under the Park Service with Hells Canyon roads under the Forest Service. There are no roads in Grand Canyon National Park that descend from the rim into the canyon over its entire 226-mile reach, and only one two-mile-long road runs along the south rim. Conversely, in the HCNRA, four roads run from the rim all the way to the Snake River, and roads traverse almost the full length of the rims on both sides.

The Park Service has closed many roads after a park's designation. It tried to rid Yellowstone of snowmobiles, and eliminate motorized boating in Grand Canyon, but was thwarted by the local congressional delegations.

It didn't take long before Tim, Paul Fritz, and I wrote a bill that would designate 1.5 million acres of protected area encompassing the HCNRA, Eagle Cap Wilderness, and roadless areas adjacent to them. Within the overall boundary, some areas were designated as "park," while some were "preserve." The national preserve sections would allow continued hunting. We had never deemed hunting to be an ecological problem, and had potential allies among the hunting constituency.

Why stop at the HCNRA, we mused, when we really wanted to protect the entire Hells Canyon–Wallowa Ecosystem? Besides, the Forest Service was also marring the Eagle Cap Wilderness and adjoining roadless land in the Wallowa Mountains. They had proposed constructing radio transmitters on peaks within the wilderness. They were authorizing the introduction of hordes of domestic sheep. They planned to log—and eventually did—roadless areas and the Lostine River Corridor, a narrow finger of undesignated, recreationally popular land surrounded by the Eagle Cap Wilderness.

After releasing our proposal to select individuals in the northeast Oregon conservation fold, we were disturbed by skepticism over the Park Service idea. Among Wallowa Valley progressives I spoke with, the common perception was that with a national park, we'd be enabling a phalanx of giant recreational vehicles to course through every road like reckless bacteria through besieged veins. We'd be confronted with condominiums on Hells Canyon's rim and glitzy park entrances with lines of vehicles waiting to pay exorbitant fees to enter.

I privately laughed at the depiction—even from people I considered intelligent—that national parks were like "Jellystone," with bumbling rangers protecting hordes of RVs from Yogi Bear. Actually, the Park Service has proven adept at managing the zip-in, zip-out "been there, seen that" crowd by concentrating motorized visitors into already developed places. I fantasized about being in front of every resident of Wallowa County and saying, "I don't want more tourists either, but the raw truth is, *you can fence yourself in, but you cannot fence the world out.*" (gratitude to J.R.R. Tolkien.)

HCPC enabled a fine tool to combat the Park Service tourist myth, a study and prospectus called *Not Another Yellowstone*. Written by students from the Environmental Studies Program at the University of Montana, their paper was supported by months of research and field trips. The document provided a wealth of evidence that the imperiled Hells Canyon–Wallowa Ecosystem, as well as the constituency of people who love it, would benefit from Park Service control. But it didn't seem to persuade the doubters.

With respect to the "tourist explosion" contention, we found that North Cascades National Park, designated in 1968, ranks fifth among national parks with the lowest visitation. The only locations with fewer visitors are four remote parks in Alaska. This fact alone would seem to assuage fears of Hells Canyon and the Wallowas becoming tourist traps under Park Service management.

HCPC had a vision for what the national preserve would look like, and how local community character and culture would be affected. The vision wasn't one of more people, it was of protecting rural character and managing tourists rather than increasing them.

In conjunction with local chamber of commerce materials, Park Service descriptions of the park and preserve could disclose that space for RVs would be limited, and there would be few snowmobile, motorcycle, or Jet Ski accommodations.

Descriptions could encourage Nordic skiing, winter and summer backpacking and biking, whitewater boating, and dispersed camping. There could be local zoning rules to prevent resorts and RV parks in local towns, using existing state land-use laws.

The enabling legislation we drafted prohibited road construction and development of modern facilities inside the preserve. It called for hands-on ecological and recreation-infrastructure restoration, which would put local people to work.

HCPC advocated for a restoration plan that would include invigorating riparian areas by planting willows and cottonwoods, conducting prescribed burns to reduce wildfire risk, and re-planting clearcuts. Contracts would be issued to local companies to eradicate weeds, turn old logging roads into single-track trails, and reconstruct campgrounds and trailheads.

Every overture we made to the Forest Service to collaboratively pursue such a vision fell on deaf ears. The Forest Service was doing nothing to manage the growing visitation to the HCNRA, except to build more accommodations for the additional people showing up. Managing tourism was not even being attempted in Wallowa County, and the juvenile whining over more prospective tourists when they were coming anyway became nauseating.

My frustrations mounted. I found it difficult to respect those who purportedly supported protecting wilderness, ecosystems, and rural character, but who resisted considering options to reverse their deterioration. That any conservation-minded person would accept the continuing ruination of the Hells Canyon–Wallowa Ecosystem because they might encounter a few more tourists was dumbfounding. I'd done the research on the Park Service, and relentlessly crossed swords with the Forest Service, and the skeptics hadn't.

If there was a "do-over," I'd begin the Park Service campaign with a strategic dispersal of information to re-educate the general public *and* the wilderness movement on the true nature of the Park Service. No, there's no such thing as a perfect federal agency, and the Park Service is no exception. But from the standpoint of biodiversity awareness and wilderness salvation, the Park Service stands for everything wilderness advocates support, and the Forest Service stands for everything we despise.

In national parks and other designations managed by the Park Service, visitation is managed to protect natural values. The agency protects land and manages people, while the Forest Service is a corporate contracting agency that "manages" land for commercial exploitation.

* * *

As weird as it may seem, proof of the disparities between agency philosophies lies in an issue I was deeply familiar with as a river guide running both the Snake River in Hells Canyon and the Colorado in Grand Canyon—the depletion of sand bars along each river's banks.

In Hells Canyon, the Brownlee, Oxbow, and Hells Canyon Dams trap the sand and gravel deposits that move down from the mountains. In Grand Canyon, Glen Canyon Dam also traps in-stream sediments.

The problem is exponentially worse in Hells Canyon than it is in Grand Canyon. Nearly all the beaches have vanished. But the Forest Service is doing virtually nothing about it. So, what about the Park Service in Grand Canyon?

Many Grand Canyon river guides have benefitted from the procession of Park Service–sponsored science trips, rowing geologists, fish biologists, and hydrologists downriver to find solutions to the beach-erosion problem. Yet in Hells Canyon, despite the HCNRA ecosystem protection mandate, no guide would know what a science trip is.

Moreover, at the behest of the Park Service and river advocates, federal legislation was passed to strictly regulate the flows from Glen Canyon Dam to protect and restore Grand Canyon's sandbars from erosion caused by sudden releases from the dam.

The Park Service also pulls political strings to trigger accelerated water releases from Glen Canyon Dam to stir up the sand at the bottom of the river, where it is deposited along the shores.

But the "park" designation wasn't winning us any allies in Wallowa County, so we dropped it in favor of only a national preserve designation. Going with a straight "preserve" designation, where hunting is allowed, might also assuage the hunting constituency.

Still, Wallowa County remained the fifty-thousand-pound bulldozer in the ointment. I learned that most local progressives were more concerned with protecting the rural character of the communities than the surrounding ecosystem. Not that I didn't share their opinion of protecting community character—I did. But I professed that protection of the land and the rural community character needn't be an either/or proposition.

Time and again, I spoke with Wallowa County individuals who would say they opposed a national park. But when I told them what we wanted was a national preserve, not a park, the ears of listeners seemed clogged with dogma. There was no distinction between a park and a preserve, or the Park Service. It was always "the national park thing."

As we struggled to gain Wallowa County support, Tim did what he did best—impress people and attract allies. His opportunistic outreach had discovered a group of people in the small community of Halfway, Oregon, on the opposite side of the Wallowa Mountains from Joseph. This philosophically diverse collection of folks was interested in protecting roadless areas on the south side of the Eagle Cap Wilderness.

In the tiny community of four hundred people, Tim secured the active involvement of people like Mike Hammar and Mike Higgins, Raz Rasmussen, Tony Sowers, and Marion Crow. The latter was a strong conservative with an open mind and an understanding that the Forest Service's logging in the mountains above Halfway was not helping local agriculture. And oh, yeah, there were no sawmills in Halfway.

Tim successfully nurtured Halfway support for the national preserve. He was assisted by Kate Crockett, who was hired by ONRC to support and further Tim's efforts. With Kate's consistent presence, Halfway soon became a bastion of *local* support, but still, it wasn't in Wallowa County.

Mike Higgins and Tony Sowers were impressed enough with the national-preserve proposal that they worked with me and Tim to organize presentations in the towns around Hells Canyon. In particular, the meeting in Lewiston, Idaho, was fruitful both in terms of gathering some interested folks and sympathetic press. It didn't take long for the

Lewiston Morning Tribune to endorse the national-preserve proposal with a fine editorial, titled "TELL THE PARK SERVICE TO GO TO HELLS CANYON."

But the crowning event was the meeting in La Grande, where most of the local conservation community attended—more than one hundred people showed up. The event turned out to be a raucous gathering of people who were fed up with the Forest Service and open to new ideas. No one in the congregation expressed fear of more tourists, or the ridiculous superstition that the Park Service would begin constructing hotels on the rim of Hells Canyon.

When long-time hunter and conservation advocate Bill Brown expressed opposition based on the hunting restrictions he envisioned, he was countered by wilderness advocate Charlie Jones. "We expect people to make sacrifices when we designate wilderness, so we should be expected to take risks ourselves."

With Halfway and La Grande on board, and prospects in Lewiston, Idaho, and Baker, Oregon, could we create enough of a groundswell to neutralize Wallowa County?

With regional support growing, Tim and I turned our attention to one of the most critical players—we desperately needed the blessing of the Nez Perce Tribe.

The Nez Perce remain not only a sovereign nation, but also an assembly of fiercely independent people. The tribe is not prone to simply applying a rubber stamp onto someone else's initiative. Fortunately, Tim had good relationships with several tribe members, whom he had already alerted to the illegality of the logging in the HCNRA.

With follow-up visits to those members, including Levi Holt, Allen Pinkham, and Tribal Council Chair Pete Hayes, we managed to schedule a presentation to the Nez Perce Tribal Executive Council (NPTEC).

To our everlasting joy, we secured the tribe's permission to use the name of one of their most revered ancestors, Chief Joseph, in the name of the proposed national preserve. Thus was born the name Hells Canyon–Chief Joseph National Preserve. NPTEC also wrote a letter that endorsed the national preserve, with contingencies to ensure protection of tribal treaty rights and involvement in Park Service decisions.

Tim and I returned to Wallowa County with a lot of fist bumps and some vigorous toasts to success with Ken Witty.

Meanwhile, the support of Brock Evans legitimized the preserve campaign among organizations in Washington, DC. He helped me set up a meeting with Dave Simon, issues coordinator for the National Parks Conservation Association (NPCA). Simon was enthusiastically supportive of our campaign, and quickly got the Association to endorse our proposal.

With support growing, HCPC, NPCA, and ONRC held a joint press conference early in 1988. We got incredible regional and national coverage. Suddenly, writers and reporters were interested not only in the national-preserve campaign, but also in Forest Service mismanagement, and surprisingly, the hostility toward me in the local community.

As I moved forward with all kinds of plans for the national preserve, there was this nagging vulture on my shoulder. The reality was that the Forest Service was not going to stop abusing the HCNRA while we went about our business of firing them and replacing them with the Park Service.

With our publicity increasing, the Forest Service responded with media tours that claimed logging in the HCNRA was designed to "open up views" and produce other benefits like protecting campers from falling trees. I was amused with these dog-and-pony shows. They didn't really appeal to any demographic, whether loggers or recreationists.

But still, the Forest Service merrily logged away.

HELLS CANYON NATIONAL RECREATION AREA LARCH TREES IN NOVEMBER

CHAPTER 16

TWO CANYONS AND A LINCHPIN

As the national-preserve campaign advanced in notoriety, I illuminated a national audience on the ecosystem's singular physical and ecological attributes. I dropped semantic anecdotes like Hells Canyon being the deepest canyon in North America, and talked about how diverse, rugged, and visually striking the place is.

I emphasized reasons why the Hells Canyon-Wallowa Ecosystem is worthy of the strongest protection beyond its scenery: its natural assets, from the Imnaha River's incredible salmon to rare species of birds and flowers, to huge elk herds and endemic butterflies.

While proselytizing, I privately considered how well-protected Grand Canyon is, and how Hells Canyon is not. I'd developed an intimate relationship with both canyons after spending hundreds of days buoyantly traversing their river basements as a river guide. Both places are spectacular but, to some degree, for different reasons.

The Grand Canyon, as we all know, has been idealized into stony immortality. Hells Canyon is much less celebrated. That's because when America set out to safeguard its special lands, the ones that got protected were not only the most rugged and pretty to look at, but also the most publicized. Not that Hells Canyon isn't rugged and pretty, it certainly is. But it never got the press of places like Grand Canyon, Yosemite, and Yellowstone. That was actually a good thing, up to a point.

Grand Canyon's ten distinctive rock layers, patiently incised with erosive precision, are piled atop one another in a veritable stone lasagna. But its majesty goes far beyond its geological uniqueness and sheer depth. After one gets beyond the picture-book views from the top, at the bottom the Colorado River ride is 237 miles of untamed water. The river presents a radical "pool and drop" alternation of rapids, laden with liquid turmoil, and tranquil reaches—all framed by stunning walls of sheer redrock.

I pity the people who go to its top edge amid tour buses and rented SUVs, look down, and think they've seen the Grand Canyon. They haven't sampled the flash-flood-sculpted slot canyons, adjacent tributaries that suddenly appear like voluptuous terrestrial icons in an earthly beauty pageant. These are components of a delectable geologic magic arranged in the glorious, yet treacherous aisle of the Colorado River.

Until Grand Canyon voyeurs have cast down their burden upon a stretch of sand along the riverbank, contemplating two billion years of the Earth's torment, and until they've listened to wordless tales from the ageless stone amid the concert of the river's voice, they haven't even shaken the canyon's proverbial hand. Until they've rocketed over the crests of eighteen-foot waves to be cast into the boiling hydraulics of angry beige water, they haven't paid the price required for the honor of the visitation. To truly experience the Grand Canyon, they must amble into a slot canyon to see turquoise pools that capture waterfalls sparkling like uncut diamonds framed by misanthropic ferns.

I've been exhilarated watching the fat old sun cast its brief radiance into chasms twenty feet wide and over a thousand feet high with no break in vertical relief. I once sat on the beach with fellow guides at Blacktail Canyon and howled at the comedy of twelve snowy egrets that ran Blacktail Rapid, then repeatedly flew back up to the entry pool to float it again and again. Above Granite Spring, we witnessed a flock of seventy white pelicans on the far horizon flying in a vertical formation, turning their bodies in perfect unison, all their bellies shimmering in the sunset.

* * *

In Hells Canyon, the magic of nature's graces is alive and well. Parsing them from the distinctiveness of Grand Canyon is like contrasting joy and happiness. From the physical perspective, Grand Canyon is more than double the length of its Northwest counterpart, but Hells Canyon's measurements are nonetheless impressive: even with the two sides differing significantly in height, the distance from the Snake River on the lower (west) side is greater than Grand Canyon on either side.

Hells Canyon isn't as vertical as Grand Canyon, yet the visual perspective from the Snake River looking upslope is strangely deceptive—a prominent summit like Dry Diggins on the east side appears to be a relatively manageable hike from the river's edge at the mouth of Sheep Creek. Yet it would actually take a full day to reach Dry Diggins for a strong hiker, with an elevation gain of 6,500 vertical feet. And Dry Diggins isn't even the top of the east rim, which is an impressive set of jagged peaks known as the Seven Devils. There's still more than 1,700 feet of climbing from Dry Diggins. It's just the highest point you can see from the river. There is no point along the river where you can see the highest point on the east rim.

Hells Canyon and the unique ensemble of tributary canyons that surround it began forming around seventeen million years ago, after flows of Columbia River basalt oozed from subterranean wells to cover most of the land in West Central Idaho and Northeast Oregon. That's when the Snake River began forming Hells Canyon. It is a rambunctious but massive infant within geology's vast timetable. Compared to Grand Canyon's two billion years of geologic legacy, Hells Canyon is the new kid on the North American block.

Underlying the basalt extrusions are limestone and sedimentary rock. The oldest rock in Hells Canyon is 260 million years old. It was part of a volcanic island that collided with the North American continent around 130 million years ago.

Hells Canyon's composition experienced another bold reformation a mere twelve thousand years ago, at the end of the last major ice age. Lake Bonneville, which was about twelve times the size of its remnant, the Great Salt Lake, and one thousand feet deeper, drained after the ice that plugged the lake's northern outlet melted. An incredible volume of water and rock suddenly poured through Hells Canyon over a matter of mere weeks.

Rattled with thunder and seared by lightning, wildfires sculpt Hells Canyon's vegetation as profoundly as wind and water sculpt its stone. Oceans of the peculiar clumps of bluebunch wheatgrass and Idaho fescue bind its precarious slopes.

Ecologically, the diversity of elevations, landforms, slope aspects, and subsequently, vegetation in Hells Canyon provide incredibly diverse habitats for scores of wildlife species. Its southern end is at the 45th parallel, the geographic center between the equator and North Pole, and the temperate midpoint.

Hells Canyon's forests are headlined by giant ponderosa pines. Their vanilla scent is as enticing as a delicious elixir. They stand solitary, or in small groups joined only by grasses and brush.

Great herds of secretive elk carry out a key function in Hells Canyon's life cycle, browsing the rich native vegetation. In Wallowa County, which encompasses the majority of the Hells Canyon–Wallowa Ecosystem, elk outnumber humans five to one. The hulking ungulates graze the grassy openings and find thermal and hiding cover in the timber.

And today, thanks to visionaries who compelled the reintroduction of wolves, resurrecting them from history's pitiful slaughter, the elk and wolves have resumed their fascinating survival dance.

Eagles and peregrine falcons trace the heights. Endangered salmon and ten-foot-long sturgeon haunt the depths. From the rarest of rare—the endemic rhododendron-like McFarlane's four-o'clock—to the blue camas that fed the Nez Perce Tribe for centuries, the density and diversity of life in Hells Canyon is fascinating.

Similar to Grand Canyon, wanderers exploring Hells Canyon's floor find they are in a sparse desert that often heats up to 115 degrees in summer. Ascend a couple thousand feet, and desert changes to boreal forest. On the east side of the canyon, ascend another few thousand feet and you are in the high alpine terrain of the Seven Devils Mountains. To the southwest, the bruising hulk of the Wallowa Mountains, with their rampaging streams and wet meadows filled with wildflowers, lend their granite souls to the conjoined mix of topography.

While Grand Canyon feels like a sacred temple, Hells Canyon feels more like a mortal chalice of life within a veritable stadium of habitats.

The Hells Canyon–Wallowa Ecosystem is an isolated wildland complex embracing a million and a half acres of roadless backcountry. Yet even with all its habitat and landform diversity and unique features, the ecosystem hasn't received the statutory protection required to ensure it remains inviolate.

If America were to prioritize the protection of ecosystems, Hells Canyon merits at least as much consideration as Grand Canyon or any other national treasure.

* * *

The respective political histories of Hells Canyon and Grand Canyon are telling. While the latter has enjoyed numerous federal administrative and legislative acts that range over more than a century, Hells

Canyon has only once been decorated with legislative protection: the 1975 HCNRA Act.

With advancements in conservation biology, I felt there must be some way to incorporate the Hells Canyon–Wallowa Ecosystem into the ecological connectivity discussion. As it turned out, I almost accidentally discovered that the Ecosystem's ecological bounty is critically important to places far beyond its perimeter.

I was sitting with Tim Lillebo on the moraine of Wallowa Lake after a long hike up Chief Joseph Mountain on the outer edge of the Wallowas. We were looking at one of Tim's wrinkled old maps from his inexhaustible collection, one that showed the interior Pacific Northwest. As is my wont, I saw the map as a whole, without tuning in on details. But Tim, a detail guy whose skill with a map was unparalleled, was trying to get me to focus on something.

Suddenly, it clicked. When I asked Tim if he saw what I saw from a wide lens, he hesitated. I eagerly explained that the Hells Canyon–Wallowa Ecosystem appears to be the central wildland complex—the hub and heart of the ecological wheel of the Pacific Northwest, connecting all its ecosystems. His excited agreement was beyond affirming.

The connectivity principle holds that isolated wild expanses where ecosystem function is mostly intact must be connected by undisturbed pathways that allow for genetic interchange to flow between them. After becoming familiar with the concept and recognizing the ecosystem's geographic importance in regional biological interchange, I incorporated the principle into HCPC's programs.

Presenting Hells Canyon–Wallowa as the "linchpin" ecosystem of the Northwestern United States became the cornerstone of HCPC's national-preserve campaign. Our promotion brought the ecosystem to the forefront of discussion toward protecting critical islands of biodiversity and establishing connecting corridors.

The Hells Canyon–Wallowa Ecosystem provides a central pathway amid the greater Salmon Ecosystem of central Idaho and western Wyoming; the Selkirk Ecosystem of western Montana, southeastern British Columbia, and western Alberta; the Blue Mountains of northeast Oregon; and the Owyhee and Great Basin Ecosystems of southeast Oregon, southwest Idaho, northwest Utah, and northern Nevada.

* * *

But convenient geography wasn't enough. In my media forays, I searched for a way to convey the spiritual aura of the Hells Canyon–Wallowa territory without venturing into philosophical gibberish. For me it's not about religion. It boils down to the phenomena of having feelings about a place rather than applying conscious value judgments.

For me, Hells Canyon feels like a place of organic kinship and deep sentiment. I feel at home. When I am in Grand Canyon, I feel like a visitor. In Hells Canyon, there is a presence that engages, as if the land were alive and speaking in the parlance of existence. It's always fascinating when myth encounters a grain of plausibility.

To describe the feeling of kinship, I hearken back to hints from members of the native tribes. It was during political work that I befriended Umatilla Confederated Tribes member Louie Dick Jr., whose grandmother was Nez Perce, and Levi Holt of the Nez Perce Tribe.

Even after we developed friendships, both were hesitant to reveal any secrets to *Sooyapo* (the common term of Pacific Northwest tribes for Europeans). But through Louie and Levi, I caught just enough glimpses of mysticism to validate my feelings. There's magic in the Hells Canyon territory, and the human/land connection is powerful. Louie and Levi both spoke of spiritual presences, but with little elaboration. I didn't pry.

However, a wildlife biologist from Vermont, Jamie Sayan, once told me of an experience he had while with a Nez Perce elder at Dug Bar in Hells Canyon in the 1970s. Jamie heard strange sounds during an ominous lull in the conversation—distant voices mixed with the swirling sounds of the river. The stunned biologist asked the elder in a shaking voice what was going on. The elder suddenly laughed, amused and maybe impressed that *Sooyapo* could hear them.

"That's the ghost walkers," the elder replied slowly, his demeanor changing from amusement to a calm intensity. "At this very place they swore an oath to the eldest of elders, their forefathers and grandmothers, that when the white man's spell is broken, the people will return home. Still they wait—impatiently." (In his novel *Winterkill*, Oregon author Craig Lesley makes a similar allusion.)

Writer/photographer Vera Jagendorf was alone on a slope above Dug Bar when she heard something similar—echoing voices and drums. The sounds came as she picked up a strange stone off the Nee-Me-Poo Trail, the route the Nez Perce used in their exile from the Wallowa territory in 1877.

After hearing their stories, I spent many a night near Dug Bar listening. Although I could feel the magic, I never did hear any voices.

There's more validation for Hells Canyon's supernatural aura, should one choose to give credence to vague histories and explore the limits of coincidence. Three people very familiar with Hells Canyon, all involved in river guiding in some capacity, have died near the tiny settlement of Oxbow at the southern entry to Hells Canyon: Outfitter Jim Zanelli, his wife, and two others perished when Zanelli crashed his pontoon plane in the Snake River in 1982. In 1994, jet-boat outfitter Gary Armacost severed his femoral artery and bled to death while working with a power saw. Gus Garrigus died while shuttling a vehicle back to the boat launch site at Hells Canyon Creek in 1997 when he tried a shortcut down the old power-line road from Lonesome Saddle, and took a header off a cliff.

All three tragic deaths occurred in the same general proximity, within about a mile of each other. According to reliable sources in the river outfitting community, Zanelli, Garrigus, and Armacost were all suspected of unauthorized collection of Hells Canyon's Native American artifacts.

Then there was Joel Ryan, a guide who accompanied several of us on a river trip with Forest Service archaeologist Bruce Womack. Womack was lobbying guides to "adopt" archaeological sites to monitor for disturbances. When we stopped at Granite Creek to look at some ancient middens, Joel abruptly lay down in one of them, defying Womack's instructions.

Less than an hour later, Joel flipped his eighteen-foot dory in Granite Rapid, his first flip ever. I saw him several weeks later, and he mentioned nervously that there had been an unusual profusion of crows circling his home.

Readers can take these stories with however many grains of salt they wish. But whatever it is that makes the Hells Canyon Ecosystem feel so poignantly singular and magical, it nailed me. I didn't choose Hells Canyon, it chose me, as it chose many others before.

MOUNTAIN GOATS AT DRY DIGGINS

CHAPTER 17

THE UNANTICIPATED RISE OF HCPC

Ever decided to move some furniture around your one-room apartment one evening, and you wake up the next morning to find you're constructing a two-thousand-square-foot house and carrying couches up the stairs on your back?

With HCPC organizational tasks, lawsuits, and the national-preserve campaign, my desk was overflowing. I never took stock of the tasks I was taking on, nor where I was going. My activist world was moving at such a tremendous pace, *it* was driving *me* rather than vice versa.

Visiting the history of HCPC's progression conjures fond memories, but all of them bring back the associated stresses.

When HCPC began to vigorously expand around 1990, Tim could see I was stressed out and struggling financially. One autumn day, we went on a hike along the rim of Hells Canyon from PO Saddle to the breathtaking viewpoint called Black Mountain. Upon the escarpment, I told him about something I'd never shared with anyone—my bouts with depression. He responded with empathy and wisdom. "This place needs you, but you have to protect yourself first."

Tim was anxious to help, but unimposing. "Have you ever thought about getting off the trucking circuit and getting paid for your HCPC work?" He followed up by speaking with folks in the wilderness movement who were raising money from family foundations. Finally, the light of getting out of trucking and not paying for expenses out of pocket dawned, and I was soon submitting grant proposals to foundations in the Pacific Northwest that were supporting regional wilderness initiatives. The publicity we were receiving gave us a solid boost.

Individual donations from $25 to $100 had been the limit of HCPC's funding. When the check showed up from our first successful grant proposal of $12,000 from the Max and Anna Levinson Foundation, I was stunned. I'd never seen a check for that amount of money.

None of the Levinson grant was dedicated to paying me a salary. It went toward publishing a brochure and producing a video program to promote the national-preserve campaign. For the video, I approached friends Karen and Ralf Meyer, who had just started a video production nonprofit called Green Fire Productions.

Complete with original footage, the video was exquisite. Together with the colorful brochure, it further legitimized the national-preserve effort. Eventually, I showed the video in congressional offices and at gatherings of wilderness advocates. I also dangled it in front of select Forest Service employees. I had no problem letting the Forest Service brass know through covert channels that taking Hells Canyon and the Wallowas away from them was a serious venture. I secretly delighted in the shock wave that went through the Forest Service offices, as explained by an agency insider.

A $20,000 Bullitt Foundation grant followed the Levinson check. The thought that my activism might become a bona fide paying *job* entered my mind, but it still didn't sit well with me. On one hand, I fantasized about no longer needing to pick up side jobs, and maybe even hiring an employee to relieve some of my workload; on the other, I couldn't get over my long-held aversion to asking people for money. Aside from that, I believed that getting paid might dilute the outward appearance of conviction.

Eventually, I became comfortable soliciting foundations for grants, because that's what they expected me to do. But when it came to individuals, well, suffice it to say I recall asking a person for money face-to-face maybe a half dozen times in my entire career.

I wasn't aware that a board of directors is supposed to assist with fundraising. I never asked them for money, or for them to ask others. They donated as they saw fit with no prodding. My priority for a board was people dedicated to organizational objectives and willing to invest some time and ideas.

My self-taught skills with grant writing and foundation outreach grew. HCPC received funding beyond the notable wilderness funders in the Pacific Northwest, including the W.K. Kellogg Foundation in Michigan, which had never funded public land protection. A connection made with a client on a river trip connected me to Kellogg.

In 1990 the board approved a $19,500 annual salary. Unfortunately, that didn't decrease the workload, but it did allow me to quit truck driving, freeing up more time. It was a great relief retiring from the growling diesel.

Regardless, working a forty-hour week was a far-off fantasy. I often worked seventy-hour weeks. But I continued to spend a couple of months spread out over the summer guiding river trips in Hells Canyon and Grand Canyon. It was a welcome reprieve and an income supplement.

As more grants came in, I hired HCPC's first staff, Marnie Criley. While at the University of Montana, Marnie had done her master's thesis on the impacts of jet-boats in Hells Canyon. She joined me in the Joseph office we opened in 1991. Marnie took a chunk of work off my desk. She quickly became adept at monitoring and confronting Forest Service activities.

Our membership began to experience consistent growth. It expanded with clients from my river trips. We sent our brochure to people who had signed local trailhead registers. We had to fight the Forest Service for the hikers' addresses, but eventually we proved people on a public register for entry onto public land were not their sole property.

Our members were precious. We honored them by not trading or selling their names to other organizations. Our membership was family, not a random collection of names to be bartered. I knew many of them personally. I kept our members informed via the newsletter we called the *Hells Canyon Falcon*. It became arguably one of the best newsletters for a regional nonprofit.

The desire to continue expanding income increased with my anxiety over making sure Marnie and I had a long-term pool of dollars, while considering hiring additional staff. Soon, I came to a startling revelation: the challenge of raising money in a rural location. This was never fully understood by fundraising consultants and the foundations that insisted we leverage their money with income from other sources. In Northeast Oregon, the vast majority of local money was against us. Most of our foundation funders and donors lived in faraway locations, making it tough to maintain person-to-person contact.

Still, by 1993 HCPC's income had expanded enough, mostly through foundation grants, to hire more staff. We had successes to show, mainly our effective lawsuits and the legislative campaign. We had a vision to share, and a committed staff and board to pursue the vision to fruition. Still, the prospect was troubling, as the monkey on my back was the constant worry over making sure I had enough money to pay our people over the long term.

It was terribly difficult to accept the reality that HCPC had become an "official" organization with budgets to meet. All my anxiety aside, the growth of HCPC in the 1990s was an exhilarating time. I welcomed a number of excellent activists into the fold. I always looked first for people with energy who believed in the wilderness cause. I used our rural location, accommodating to outdoor lifestyles, as a selling point.

With an increasing budget and expanding staff, HCPC had the horses to promote the national-preserve proposal while thwarting Forest Service plans. By the mid-1990s, we had an incomparable staff complement, with Brett Brownscombe as conservation director; Kathleen Ackley as development director; Jennifer Schemm as legal counsel; Lisa Dix as forest watch coordinator; Juanette Cremin as outreach director; Darilyn Parry-Brown as office manager; and Min Lee as our Hells Canyon–Chief Joseph National Park and Preserve campaign coordinator, stationed in our newly opened Portland office. Dogged activist Mary O'Brien, a PhD in botany working on contract, expertly assumed a wide range of projects.

I had no idea how to manage staff at a nonprofit. I had been a foreman on work crews, but this was something completely different. Since I never had plans to *build* HCPC, when it did grow, I found myself hesitant to delegate my responsibilities to others. Trust came with the quality of people I was honored to have join us.

I was adamant in counseling staff not to make the same mistakes I had made. I admit to sometimes being overbearing, but I simultaneously made it a priority to allow each person to play to their strengths. The toughest part of staff management was reigning in my passion and sense of urgency. The intensity of my drive to prevent every single Forest Service indiscretion could be overwhelming, as was my penchant for mistrust of the Forest Service. The new staff's instinctive propensity was to build relationships with those they came in contact with. That was great, but I reacted honestly and firmly to the question of "working more closely" with the agency. It didn't take a lot of exposure to the Forest Service for them to understand. But I eventually welcomed staff developing new relationships with agency personnel, mainly for the purpose of gaining easier access to information.

I counseled every person who worked for HCPC that not only did we need to replace the Forest Service, but the National Park Service would be an advocate for the Hells Canyon–Wallowa ecosystem. Park Service myths and the desire of staff to work with rather than against the Forest Service made for some tough learning.

Another challenge was acquainting staff with the nature of rural politics and the hostility I'd experienced in the local communities. It took a lot of patience from me, and from them. Our dubious reputation locally was tough for some to grasp. Going out in public without realizing many people would rather yell at you than speak with you was a startling experience. Thankfully, it was rare that HCPC staff experienced the kinds of hostilities I had become accustomed to. Most of the hostilities were personal. The organization wasn't the demon, *I* was.

I slowly adapted to having an office with competent, dedicated fellow activists. It was as if I woke up one morning, walked into an office, and found a collection of bright, top-notch people, and a stable of volunteers and interns, flexing their muscles toward a common vision. With no clear intent, I had moved HCPC from a one-person show to a bona-fide, multitalented, and, eventually, nationally-recognized organization. We were an excellent team. I look back at what we had with humility and deep gratitude.

THE WALLOWAS' MATTERHORN FROM HURRICANE CREEK

CHAPTER 18

THE DELIGHT OF UNFORESEEN CHANGES

In 1992, less than two years after I'd begun getting paid as an HCPC employee and a year before I hired our second staffer, the Hells Canyon–Chief Joseph National Preserve campaign burst from the blocks like a spirited sprinter. Once a one-horse show in a territory far away from the illumination of the greater wilderness movement, HCPC was now a player: a force for protecting and restoring an important ecosystem.

Media consultant John Hough of the Rockey Company, a contractor with the Bullitt Foundation, took a particular interest in HCPC. I leveraged Hough's media expertise by organizing several river trips through Hells Canyon. He brought in noteworthy journalists to attend.

I shared the whitewater and majesty of Hells Canyon with Charles McCoy of the *Wall Street Journal*, Jeff Rennicke with *National Geographic Traveler*, Bob Howells from *Westways Magazine*, John Balzar with the *Los Angeles Times*, and Mike Wyatt from *Backpacker* magazine. Joel Connelly from the *Seattle Post-Intelligencer* and Kathie Durbin with the *Oregonian* wrote a number of quality pieces on the Hells Canyon controversy.

Independent writers Richard Lovett, Kathy Witkowski, and Bill Dietrich contributed stories that brought the Hells Canyon issue to a diverse cross section of readers. We hosted a team from ABC News, which did a fine piece that aired on *World News Tonight*.

HCPC's national exposure had escalated to new heights. Our notoriety brought us into the broader corral of federal land management policy, where we worked closely with other organizations on everything from proposed National Park Service designations, regional wilderness bills, and reducing the Forest Service's logging budget.

Also in 1992, the Montana-based Alliance for the Wild Rockies (AWR) was putting together a biodiversity-based wilderness bill for the Northern Rocky Mountains called the Northern Rockies Ecosystem Protection Act (NREPA). They wanted to know if I was interested in designing the Hells Canyon–Wallowa portion of the bill. I gladly agreed.

Through my involvement in AWR, I met Carole King, an AWR board member. I eventually found this renowned musician to be as eloquent an activist as she was a singer-songwriter, and as down-to-earth a person as I'd met. Carole wielded her celebrity with tact and effectiveness. I soon joined her on the AWR board.

NREPA was exactly the kind of vision that had been bouncing around my brain for quite a while. The bill would protect *all* roadless areas in Montana, Idaho, Wyoming, northeast Oregon, and eastern Washington. It also established rehabilitation zones within degraded national forest land and designated connection corridors to facilitate genetic interchange between the major ecosystems.

I loved it—get the whole job done for the Northern Rocky Mountains in one national interest bill. Constantly threatened wildlands and climate change mitigation could not wait for piecemeal legislation that protected only politically safe places. Thanks largely to Carole King's influence, NREPA was introduced in the House of Representatives, and later the Senate, with bipartisan support.

I promoted NREPA, but I continued to push the Hells Canyon–Chief Joseph bill independently. Our national-preserve proposal predated NREPA. We had intricate strategies already in place to gain public and political support, particularly relationships with allies in Oregon and Idaho.

Tossing all of HCPC's marbles into NREPA and abandoning the independent effort would have changed the political dynamic and could have jeopardized the support we'd already gained. This caused some tension in the relationship with AWR.

AWR wanted complete dedication to its bandwagon. But the reality was, I couldn't just toss out the work we'd already done. Still, I took every opportunity to wave the NREPA flag. The fact that we had a Hells Canyon–Chief Joseph bill active in Congress via NREPA was a tremendous boost, particularly in the eyes of the Forest Service.

The anxiety of the Forest Service chief's office escalated with the advancement of our campaign, and the real threat of the Park Service taking over their turf. The soft underbelly of the agency's DC brain trust was its sensitivity to negative publicity. In visits to the chief's office, I always brought press clips that showed the nationalization of our effort, especially the stories where Forest Service negligence was prominent.

* * *

The 1992 election of Bill Clinton brought light to the darkness of twelve years of Ronald Reagan and George H. W. Bush. President Clinton's sympathy allowed us to pursue almost immediate changes to the Forest Service's management of the HCNRA.

Clinton's Department of Agriculture Undersecretary, Jim Lyons, became the first to make the position of Chief of the Forest Service an administration appointment rather than an internal decision. His new chief was La Grande resident Jack Ward Thomas, a wildlife biologist. I knew Jack well.

In the spring of 1993, I scheduled an extended visit to Washington, DC. One key appointment was with Democratic House Committee staffer Jim Bradley, former Forest Service manager of the Eagle Cap Wilderness. He knew the Hells Canyon–Wallowa territory and its issues quite well.

Practically before I could sit down, Bradley asked me, "Ric, who needs to go?" As I began to understand what he was saying, I didn't hold back. I gave him the names of several logging and livestock culprits in the Wallowa-Whitman National Forest, including HCNRA Head Ranger Al Defler, who had been largely responsible for tossing the HCNRA Act into the trash bin. I described how Defler's staff was composed mostly of timber sale planners and silviculturists who wandered around the HCNRA looking for big trees to cut, and how Defler had turned them loose and let them do whatever they wanted, then signed decisions approving timber sales as nonchalantly as scribbling on a bar napkin at the local Elks club.

I wasn't sure if Bradley could just make a few calls and get the changes made, but in no time at all, he flexed his political muscle. Defler was transferred.

Defler's replacement was recreational professional Ed Cole, fresh out of the Forest Service's DC training mill for district rangers and forest supervisors. Cole proved to be a tremendous improvement, departing from the party line of massive timber sales and unmonitored livestock allotments. But he also brought with him a new set of problems, and an entirely new political conundrum for HCPC.

From the outset, our relationship with Cole was tempered by the fact that we were already on record as trying to remove the HCNRA from the grip of the Forest Service. And from Cole's perspective, he was essentially charged with rescuing the Forest Service from the national preserve proposal.

Despite Cole's de-emphasis of logging, HCPC had to look at the big picture. And that meant we could not assume one change in Forest Service personnel, with limited shelf life, was going to permanently solve the problem.

Still, we couldn't appear ungrateful for Jim Bradley's direct and profound assistance. So we put our best foot forward with Ranger Cole. He deserves high praise for many of his actions. However, as HCPC board member Paul Fritz often told me, the Forest Service would fight the Park Service proposal by attempting to "out-park" the Park Service by emulating its false reputation for modern development. He was right. Cole went on a rampage to build modern recreation facilities.

Some of our media coverage began to highlight the friction between me and Cole. Bill Dietrich wrote an excellent story for *Pacific Northwest* magazine that contrasted us at a personal level. I actually carried on a cordial personal relationship with Cole, but we also had many heated arguments.

I told Ranger Cole our root problem with the Forest Service was that it was not fashioning its management from the HCNRA Act, which does not call for more logging, livestock, or recreation development, but repeatedly speaks to protecting and restoring the ecosystem.

In all of my discussions with Cole, I detailed HCPC's vision for restoring the HCNRA's natural attributes by closing logging roads, planting riparian areas, and eradicating weeds. As for recreation, what the HCNRA needed was bricks and mortar for existing trails and semi-primitive campgrounds, not new developments. "Why build new, high-maintenance facilities when you cannot even maintain the existing primitive facilities?" I once asked Cole.

Eventually, Cole went directly to Oregon's congressional delegation for recreation-development money; he had no interest in asking Congress for ecosystem-rehabilitation funding, or even funds for trail and campground maintenance. The continued deterioration of the trail and campground infrastructure was a concern for many HCPC members.

On one occasion, Cole's assistant ranger, Ron Bonar, authorized a massive "hazard tree" removal from all the already-disheveled campgrounds in the HCNRA. Ken Witty, in his capacity as an Oregon Department of Fish and Wildlife biologist, asked Bonar point blank: "Can't you people leave anything alone?" The question spoke volumes.

Soon after, HCPC hosted a news crew from a Portland TV station on a tour of the HCNRA. They interviewed a hunter who sat glumly in Lick Creek Campground, where his family had located its hunting camp all his life. He asked, "Who the hell would clearcut a campground?"

His development propensities aside, Cole did follow through on two critical ends of the management ledger—he ramped down the HCNRA logging program and achieved a tremendous win for the ecosystem by eliminating commercial domestic sheep grazing from the HCNRA. Cole deserves high praise for those actions, as does Jim Bradley for getting him appointed. But as we've since seen, many of his changes lasted only as long as his tenure, which was six years.

* * *

As the evolving conflict with the Forest Service proceeded, I wondered if I was engaged in a war with no light at the end of the tunnel. Was I doomed to fighting a bureaucracy that will go on its merry way defacing the ecosystem in creative ways while I jump up and down on the sidelines shouting and litigating with no end in sight, and pushing a legislative agenda up an insurmountable hill?

I managed to take heart by reminding myself HCPC was riding the crest of a large standing wave. We were no longer just chasing the Forest Service around. We were forcing them to defend themselves against us. We were a player, both defending and playing offense with proactive solutions. Our successful advocacy—from sponsoring the nationally acclaimed national-preserve proposal to our ecosystem restoration plans—continued to earn us credibility among the greater wilderness movement, key players in Congress, and the press.

Still, there were many times I awoke in the middle of the night wondering how I'd created such a movement, and fighting anxiety over how I'd keep it moving. The hours were long and the stress was mounting. I had never wanted to be the leader of an organization. Often, I longed to be back in one of those shabby Wallowa Valley cabins, sipping beer with the locals and communing with wild places. But I was unquenchably dedicated to bringing salvation to the grand ecosystem I had joined with.

CHAPTER 19
"YEAH, SURE. WE CAN *DO* RECREATION!"

One night in 1993, I awoke from a haunted sleep—the kind where you're not completely unconscious, only considering whether to stay awake fighting depression, or go back to dozing at such a shallow level you aren't getting any rest. I stayed awake—my head was on fire with racing thoughts. In depression's throes, I validated despair by revisiting every indiscretion I'd ever perpetrated. I screamed out loud for allowing myself to become a pariah in the community. Every verbal gaffe, every undeserved shun, and every relationship I'd managed to destroy pounced upon me like a bloodthirsty predator. I went to the medicine cabinet, ripped the door off and threw it on the floor, took three Benadryl, and dove headfirst under the bed.

I didn't define it at the time, but that was probably a panic attack. It was the Dagloth at play. I had no idea how to deal with it, or prevent its presence.

I'd charged into forward with a righteous mission to achieve while wrestling with the ever-more-persistent demon on my back. It was almost as if the chemical conflict in my brain was a metaphor for the conflict that defined my activism. If I could win the war to save Hells Canyon, could I defeat depression, or vice versa?

Actually, I had much to celebrate, though I didn't always see it that way at the time. Each achievement, like hiring bright new staff, generating more positive press, or winning another lawsuit brought only brief bliss as I whipped myself toward an invisible finish line.

As I advanced after the panic episode, I realized virtually every stressful, angry period I experienced threatened to unleash the demon. I was ruled by my volcanic moods, and only managed to distract myself by focusing on conservation-based projects. It was invigorating to occasionally depart from fundraising and organizational management to work on real issues.

After that dreadful evening, I got to work on a now-common task—fighting one of the Forest Service's new "recreation developments," another project that would dilute the HCNRA's wildness and frontier character.

I had figured if we could put a stop to the logging, we'd have won the battle to save the HCNRA. But the emergence of a new threat under a new ranger who didn't want to log everything was perplexing, and terribly frustrating.

The first of Cole's developments was a "visitors center," constructed just below Hells Canyon Dam where the free-flowing Snake Wild and Scenic River begins. It's an architectural imitation of modern art that fits with the towering cliffs of Hells Canyon about as well as a Dairy Queen would meld with Manhattan's Park Avenue.

The building, surrounded by its vast asphalt parking area, was located at a virtual dead end, sandwiched between vertical cliffs rising thousands of feet above the river. Tour buses and wandering cars now bustle around the steep, narrow cove in twisted traffic jams, joining jet-boaters and floaters trying to get their trucks to the launch ramp. Originally, the Hells Canyon Creek site was only a boat launch.

There are no trails, nor a picnic area. There's no room for either. There was no point to making Hells Canyon Creek a destination. The project was the first testimonial to the Forest Service's lack of acumen in recreation development and planning.

A year later, Cole built the "Hells Canyon Overlook," which actually doesn't afford a view of Hells Canyon. Its gold-plated interpretive signs worded for eight-year-olds, slick blacktopped roads, and bright white-striped parking lots, accommodate visitors looking into McGraw Canyon. We were hesitant to challenge it because we didn't wish to appear to be against recreation accommodations.

But by the time the next development hit the planning phase, we'd had enough of Cole's vision for "recreation." When he suddenly pulled the "Overlook II" development out of his hat, much to his dismay we filed suit in federal court. Our lawsuit was successful. The case was distinctly different from our lawsuits challenging violation of the HCNRA Act's ecosystem protection directives. It asserted a violation of the National Environmental Policy Act's (NEPA) requirement that the cumulative impacts of connected actions be analyzed. The federal court found a violation of NEPA in the proposal to construct a motorized recreation spread that would have extended the Hells Canyon Overlook development north another twelve miles.

The Overlook II development would have paved a mostly primitive road to PO Saddle, a rustic trailhead for hikers and horse packers. A modern campground would have been built near PO Saddle, and the road would have been pocked with an array of RV turnouts with paved parking areas, restrooms, and more sappy interpretive signs designed for the "been there, done that" crowd.

We were angry about Overlook II for several reasons. The first was that Cole had convinced Oregon Senator Mark Hatfield to appropriate funds for it without ever telling us there was a project in the works. Thus, Hatfield didn't know we opposed it. After we won the lawsuit, I got a phone call from a high-level Hatfield staffer saying, "What the hell is wrong with you people? Don't you want recreation?"

I tried to explain: what we wanted was maintenance of existing dispersed-recreation facilities. The rim of Hells Canyon shouldn't look like the south rim of Grand Canyon. Our vision didn't resonate with Hatfield, but with the lawsuit win, we'd sent a clear message that the development of the HCNRA would not go unchallenged.

After that conflict, I set up a meeting with Cole and Assistant Ranger Ron Bonar, his right-hand guy. I asked them, "What's your long-term recreation vision for the HCNRA?" No response. "Do you have a plan to organize recreation use, or are you simply building developments willy-nilly, with no idea how visitation will be changed, how recreationists seeking primitive accommodations will be displaced, or what the final portrait will look like?"

Bonar unwisely responded before his boss. He referred to the new developments as an effort to show they could "do recreation." (He actually used those words). I was struck with the thought that these guys had no overall plan. It was as if recreation development was some exciting, chic new fad the Forest Service was getting hip to.

The development push was actually nothing more than appeasement for the Wallowa County development crowd, headed by the chamber of commerce. It had an incongruous vision of both unlimited cows and logging conjoined with more tourism.

I couldn't stomach the prospect of a disorganized mishmash of modern campgrounds and motorized accommodations, with no consideration to retain some of the HCNRA's places where one could experience a quiet, uncrowded refuge.

The Forest Service's rationale for the new developments was, "We anticipate recreation use will increase, and the new users will need accommodations." The construction of modern developments was thus a self-perpetuating phenomenon: if more use occurred, more developments would be built, apparently with no end in sight.

In further meetings with Cole, I suggested a change to better protection and accommodation of dispersed camping and hiking. Would they consider maintenance of Hells Canyon's once-incomparable trails, where one can find some of the most incredible winter backpacking anywhere in the country?

The answer? "We don't have the budget."

How about marking and grooming some cross-country ski trails? "That's not in the management plan." Might they repair some of the existing, disheveled campgrounds? "We don't have control of our budget."

But Cole did have control over seeking funding to do the things he wanted to do.

During the development foray, existing rustic campgrounds like Evergreen and Hidden on the Imnaha River deteriorated to the point Cole closed them due to "lack of maintenance funding." Buckhorn Campground was falling apart. Even an experienced hiker would be challenged to follow the once-popular but deteriorating mid-slope Bench Trail that traverses Hells Canyon's western expanse.

However, the cash for new developments just kept flowing in. Thus, we were eventually confronted with a project on the Idaho side at the floor of the canyon at Pittsburg Landing. I'm still not sure where the funding for this development came from, whether appropriated by Congress at the behest of the Idaho delegation, or from Forest Service general funds. It seemed to come out of nowhere.

This project was overseen by the Wallowa-Whitman National Forest supervisor's office rather than Cole at the district level. After our successful Overlook II lawsuit, Forest Supervisor Bob Richmond stepped in and figured out a way to circumvent our challenges—spring the project silently, and issue contracts before anyone could mount a legal challenge.

The Forest Service was doing exactly what some feared the Park Service would do if it was in charge. The irony never escaped me. But I was never able to use the Forest Service's development craze to leverage opposition from the local people who were against development.

The development at Pittsburg was constructed on a huge alluvial fan, an expanse of relatively gentle gradients and flat benches that rise to timbered slopes, picturesque cliffs, and basalt outcrops. The "Landing" is a boat ramp on the Snake River. The only other feature was an old house built by ranchers nearly a century ago.

Pittsburg presented the rustic charisma of a bygone era. The ramshackle ranch house, a few dirt tracks, and the rusted old plows and broken wagon wheels were the dominating features. Twisted strands of barbed wire, wrapped like ivy around rotting fence posts, seemed to reverently cling to that brief pioneer history.

But the diamonds of Pittsburg rest in a secluded meadow, where there's a curious boulder field surrounded by contorted hackberry trees. Strange, indiscernible symbols are etched on the boulders. An archaeologist told me the inscriptions are probably well over two thousand years old. A geologist told me the Volkswagen-sized boulders were brought there from somewhere else. How, he couldn't say.

On river trips, I used to walk people up to the Petroglyphs from the river. Like me, many of them could feel the mystic, indescribable magic of the place. Pittsburg feels sensitive in an incomprehensible way. I've moved soil and stone with machines during my work history, but carving into that alluvial fan with excavators would be like lacerating skin. I could never lay the scourge of steel to this place.

I paid Pittsburg a final visit in 1994 after the machines had moved in. There were cranes, D8 bulldozers, stacks of concrete and metal pipes, and excavators. They cast shadows of despair. Their handiwork created an ugly mosaic of road incisions, culvert ditches, and gravel quarries. With the invasion of the machines, the Nez Perce and pioneer ranching cultures wavered, flickered, and expired.

After the development's completion, new roads reached to every attraction, including the old ranch house and the new jet-boat fuel station, large rectangular metal tanks that loom like latrines above the riverbank.

Worst of all, a new paved road leads visitors—aided by a sign that points them to "petroglyphs"—directly to the rocks with the wondrous, thought-provoking ancient markings. The sacred site is stained with a paved parking lot and trail. Predictably, less than a year after the development was completed, the boulders inscribed with the petroglyphs were vandalized.

The final indignity of the Pittsburg development is its new, modern recreational-vehicle facility. At its location on a treeless grassy bench just above the river, this monstrosity looks like an alien encampment descended upon the peace of primitive ground. Next to each campsite is a corrugated metal "shade structure" that resembles the roof of a squared-off Quonset hut.

The wisdom and respect in allowing the remnants of a culture to lie unchanged in their natural setting as a living testament was virtually unknown to Forest Service leaders. They converted the very context of the Nez Perce habitation into a gaudy tourist trap. They changed objects of cultural identity into drive-up museum pieces.

They could not grasp the reality that what was sacred about Pittsburg Landing wasn't just the graven stones or the topography, it was the magic of the *place*.

After the defacing of the petroglyphs, I sternly questioned Ed Cole's boss, Wallowa-Whitman National Forest Supervisor Bob Richmond, about the Pittsburg development. He told me he was required to "provide public access" to the petroglyphs. I replied that the HCNRA Act specifically mandates protection of archaeological sites as a clear priority over access to them. I added that if the objective was to get as many people as possible to see them, he may as well dig up the rocks and ship them to the Smithsonian. He gave me a strange look and walked out of the meeting.

At Pittsburg, the Nez Perce remnants no longer blend with the natural setting and meld with the bountiful land that begat and held them. All chances of experiencing the thrill of finding the unadvertised petroglyphs—wondrous things whose designers carved their messages about the same time the world saw the rise of the Roman Empire—were dashed.

Today I see the petroglyphs as figuratively framed in plastic—encased in glossy display windows. Detached, like flowers plucked from the soil, soon to languish and die in the vase, or pressed in two-dimensional memory inside a book that laments the past.

It wasn't just the logging and the development that haunted my nights and fueled my expanding nightmares. It was the combination of abuse and neglect, the ignorance and the corruption.

CHAPTER 20

THE JET-BOAT WAR

Speaking of recreation, it is with great loathing I recount another example of indefensible Forest Service negligence: its failure to comply with the HCNRA Act's requirement to regulate jet-boat use on the Snake River in Hells Canyon.

The consequences? I was leading a six-day float trip down the Snake River during one particularly hot August day. On the second day of the trip, we pulled into Salt Creek camp at 4:00 p.m. It was 108 degrees. Seven kids, ranging in age from eight to twelve, excitedly buckled their life jackets. Led by seasoned river guide David Sears, they began to swim across the placid, seventy-foot-wide section of river toward the trail on the opposite side.

The children welcomed relief from the blistering heat. Shouts of excitement resonated as they frolicked in the cool water. David and the kids intended to swim across the river, then walk up the trail to Suicide Point for an elevated view of Hells Canyon. They were halfway across when the guides on shore sprang to attention at a familiar, yet dreaded sound—a dull vibration that began to interrupt the peaceful swooshing of the river and the kids' laughter.

Within seconds, the disturbing rumble became a full-throated roar. Around the second bend of the conspicuous "S" curve in the river, just upstream from Salt Creek camp, three twenty-five-foot-long jet-boats appeared, and accelerated.

The boats bore the inscription "North River" on the stern, but other markings on the boats were in a distorted font. Without slowing, they rocketed between the swimmers at an estimated forty miles per hour. Shrill screams from the children could be heard amid the mechanical din.

Miraculously, there were no hits, only near-misses, as the jet-boat pilots used the youngsters as slalom buoys and raced downriver without slowing, or showing the slightest hint of concern. The father of two of the children was sitting at the edge of the river. He rose, fists raised. "Bastards!" The guides restrained him from boarding one of our dories and going after the jet-boats with nothing but oars to give chase.

After the trip, the father and I wrote to the Forest Service to report the incident. We received a disappointing response: "There's nothing we can do without positive identification of the boats and drivers . . ."

Such was the case with all incidents reported by floaters complaining about the unsafe use of jet-boats. In my over one hundred river trips in Hells Canyon, I reported many near-misses, jet-boat wakes pounding moored wooden dories against rocks, jet-boats repeatedly re-running rapids, not giving waiting floaters a chance to get through, and thundering noise from endless parades of jet-boats wrenching tranquility from an entire river trip. I've found no record of a jet-boat operator facing any consequences for reckless driving or violating any rules.

That's probably because there were no rules.

But there was one complaint the Forest Service took very seriously. Jet-boat outfitter Mike Luther accused me of trying to ram his forty-foot, five-hundred-horsepower metal-hulled jet-boat with my oar-driven wooden dory. The day before Northwest Dories manager Curt Chang and I were scheduled to meet with Luther and the Forest Service to discuss the incident, Luther bailed out of the meeting. Maybe he felt his complaint seemed too outlandish and whiny to defend.

The jet-boat issue became a personal campaign, influenced by my experiences as a guide. I didn't burden other HCPC staff with work on that issue. I sank a lot of time and energy into doing battle with the Forest Service, and the jet-boaters themselves.

Admittedly, jet-boats on the Snake River don't cause much ecological damage. Their wakes erode sand bars, and it's likely their pressure waves displace eggs from salmon redds embedded in the gravel of the river bottom. Controlling these loud, speeding thrill machines is mostly a matter of protecting wilderness values and recreation quality in Hells Canyon, although protecting quality recreation experiences is important to millions of people who want peace and quiet.

The jet-boat war was unique: unlike the other adversarial jousts I had over Hells Canyon issues, our adversary wasn't just the Forest Service. The constituency opposing us wasn't the diverse and amoebic "timber industry." It was the jet-boat lobbying organization, a well-financed entity headed by former senatorial staffer Sandra Mitchell.

I had many colorful debates with the politically astute Ms. Mitchell. Her array of reasons why it was okay for jet-boaters to have free run of the river with no rules of the road were pitifully dazzling and nauseatingly inept.

And that's the really agonizing part: even two decades after the HCNRA Act required rules to control the use and number of jet-boats on the Snake River in Hells Canyon, there were still none. Describing the history of Forest Service river management in Hells Canyon is easy—there wasn't any. As the Forest Service did with all the other directives in the HCNRA Act they didn't like, the agency simply ignored the act's requirement that it "control the use and number of motorized rivercraft."

There were no speed or decibel limits, no use restrictions like slowing down for float boats or swimmers, and no requirements for reducing wakes when encountering moored float parties. There was also no limit on the number of jet-boats that could roar up and down the river in the otherwise wild and tranquil reaches of Hells Canyon.

But here's the nonsensical part: for the entire period when innumerable jet-boats illegally cut up the waters of the Snake River, *nonmotorized* boaters were strictly regulated. To secure a permit for a noncommercial launch, a person had to enter an annual lottery for a chance to score a permit—each floater could only qualify for one launch permit per year. Yet any jet-boater could run the entire river every day of the year if they so desired.

In 1979, a group of river guides had concocted a plan to place outboard engines on their boats and run the river without a permit. Why couldn't they launch at will since they had a motor? The Forest Service caught wind of the plan and sent word to outfitting companies that the guides would be cited if they tried it. Since the guides' licenses would be in jeopardy, they relented.

In her ignoble attempts to defeat any effort to regulate jet-boats, Mitchell espoused what she and her followers called *shared use*. The cushy term was meant to illustrate that there was no problem in having concurrent jet-boat and float-boat use in the narrow, turbulent confines of the Snake River.

Among her collaborators, Mitchell embraced a group of maybe thirty people who floated the river in rafts in addition to jet-boating the river. The group, an anti-regulation outfit called "River Access for Tomorrow," was Mitchell's less-than-shining proof that floaters were happy sharing the river with jet-boats.

Meanwhile, I managed to line up a coalition of all twenty-four of Hells Canyon's float outfitting companies, the three largest float-boating advocacy organizations in the United States, and the two largest river-protection nonprofits in the country to support rules governing jet-boats.

Revealingly, joining Mitchell in her public appearances was Art Seamans. Prior to his activism on behalf of unlimited jet-boat use, he served as the Forest Service's Snake Wild and Scenic River manager. That's right, the guy who was supposed to be managing river use in Hells Canyon was a dedicated jet-boat sympathizer, and it showed.

But Mitchell's most revered cohort was her chief financier, Joe Scott. The grandson of famed supermarket patriarch Joe Albertson, Scott's wealth supported his personal love of thrill-motoring through the great outdoors of Idaho. He jet-boated through Hells Canyon, snowmobiled across the otherwise pristine Boulder–White Cloud Mountains, and unquestionably blue-smoked his way into other places that the rest of us otherwise call wilderness. Scott's deep pocketbook was wide open in his efforts to torpedo any rules that limited his motorized access. And of course, his economic and financial influence placed him firmly atop the agenda of the Idaho congressional delegation.

However, Mitchell's cadre of financial and political support didn't help her win public support. The only people her arguments appealed to were jet-boaters. And while she spoke loudly of "responsible shared use," I was dreaming up colorful ways to make her sound silly.

Mitchell claimed that since jet-boats had, to one degree or another, run through Hells Canyon for around fifty years, their use was sacrosanct. This claim had no basis in either law or common sense. The motorhead mantra and false standard of "traditional use" claims that the unchecked proliferation of the latest craze in motorized toys cements its continuation, whereafter it cannot be challenged or reduced.

I responded that the longest standing river use in Hells Canyon was dugout canoes and fishing by the Nez Perce, uses incompatible with jet-boats. But my favorite sound bite was developed with the assistance of Bullitt Foundation Director Emory Bundy, who had joined us on a river trip during which Mitchell jet-boated in for a chitchat around the campfire with a collection of journalists.

While Sandra parlayed the mantra of "responsible shared use," I heard Emory—from a position outside the circle of pens and notepads—say something about "smokers." I didn't catch the whole statement, but a phrase jumped into my head—Mitchell's rosy depiction of "shared use" was tantamount to smokers being fine with sharing a room with non-smokers. The non-smokers make all the sacrifices in the "relationship." That became the impactful, one-sentence hallmark of my counter to "shared use."

Along with a lot of other nonmotorized boaters, I'd been badgering the Forest Service over their patently unfair use allocation for many years. Around the same time, our national-preserve campaign had taken wing and, two years after the incident at Salt Creek, I finally backed agency leaders into a corner over their defiance of the law requiring jet-boat rules in Hells Canyon. Between the threat of a sweeping lawsuit and the national publicity illuminating their egregious malfeasance, HCNRA Ranger Ed Cole finally agreed to write a new management plan for the Snake National Wild and Scenic River.

The Forest Service engaged the process for developing a new river plan by hiring consensus guru Ed Krumpe of the University of Idaho to facilitate twenty-four people representing "user groups" into a panel to assist the Forest Service in developing a new plan. Krumpe did a fine job in a tough situation, but it became a convoluted exercise in Forest Service hand-wringing and manipulation. Endless discussions and debates ensued over things like campfire rules and requirements for toilets on commercial jet-boats.

It was my first and only experience in consensus groups. I was the representative for conservation interests. After two years of attempting to steer the process toward honoring the law as the guiding principle for discussion, I became completely disillusioned. It wound up being nothing more than a circular debate between jet-boaters and floaters, with no rational parameters for jet-boat use limits and rules of the road.

The biggest questions the plan needed to answer were how many jet-boats would be allowed on the river and what rules of the road would they need to comply with. This is where we ran into the problem with Forest Service control of the process.

Instead of basing jet-boat use levels on those that existed in 1975, when the HCNRA Act required regulation of jet-boat use and numbers—and also the protection of Hells Canyon's wilderness values—the

Forest Service baseline was the use that existed at the time the plan was being written. In other words, when they finally implemented jet-boat rules, they essentially rewarded themselves for illegally failing to regulate jet-boats by locking in the use that had increased unchecked for over 20 years. It was considered a *minimum* in the new plan.

In the final river plan, sixty jet-boats per day are allowed to launch. Any jet-boater can apply for as many launch permits as they'd like each year. Jet-boaters can camp anywhere and for as long as they wish. They can run upriver, downriver, up and down rapids, or back and forth across the river.

There are virtually no rules of the road. Incomprehensibly, jet-boaters are encouraged to "self-police." There are no speed limits, no wake-free zones, and no requirement of slowing for floaters. Jet-boat domination of Hells Canyon is the reason it is by far the easiest river trip for which to win the lottery to obtain the one launch permit the applicant is allowed. Floaters want a wilderness experience, not a "vacation" on a river with motor traffic resembling the New Jersey Turnpike.

There is, however, one crumb of comfort in the plan. For eighteen days per year on a twenty-one-mile segment of the river, jet-boat use is prohibited. Of course, the jet-boaters went mad over the tiny exclusion. It was a petty protest, since even during those eighteen days per year they still had full access to the other sixty miles of the river corridor.

In the end, the river plan only reinforced the reality that the Snake River in Hells Canyon is managed on behalf of Sandra Mitchell's financiers. Spoiled as they were, the jet-boaters refused to accept the non-motorized period. They filed suit in 1998 in an attempt to remove it from the plan. HCPC also filed suit challenging the number of jet-boats allowed and the absence of "rules of the road." We claimed jet-boat use should be limited to the maximum number of boats that were using the river when the HCNRA Act was passed. But the judges in the Ninth Circuit Court of Appeals apparently saw the issue as a conflict between user groups, and deferred to the Forest Service plan.

Joe Scott's control over the Idaho congressional delegation was apparent, as was the delegation's control over the Forest Service, a phenomenon that began soon after the HCNRA Act was passed. In 1981, Idaho Senator Jim McClure had told Ronald Reagan's assistant secretary of agriculture, John Crowell, to suspend any restrictions on jet-boat use in the original HCNRA plan. Oregon Senators Packwood and Hatfield—

fellow Republicans—battled with McClure over his manipulation of the plan. But McClure was chair of the Senate Natural Resources Committee and had the last word. According to a Packwood staffer, during a meeting to discuss the plan, McClure defied the Oregon senators to the point Hatfield walked out of the meeting in a huff, while Packwood "stayed in the room and yelled at McClure."

Senators using their power to support the interests of their big funders is, of course, nothing new to American politics. But the Idaho delegation's dogged insistence on ensuring Scott's uninhibited jet-boating in Hells Canyon exposes how flagrant and vain such political/financial servitude can be. As the great political cartoonist Tom Toles once noted, "The great American principle—one man, two senators."

After the courts ruled against legal challenges to the plan, the Idaho delegation faithfully stepped up with legislation that would gut the river plan's minimal restrictions on jet-boat use. Idaho Republicans Senator Larry Craig and Representative Helen Chenoweth introduced the bill.

I lined up outfitting-company owners and representatives of noncommercial float-boating associations to testify at the hearings in Washington, DC. My allies and I held a press conference at which we presented a compelling record of the Forest Service's disregard for the HCNRA Act's requirement of jet-boat use restrictions.

Hearings on the legislation produced some humorous moments. At the House hearing, Chenoweth presided, sitting beneath a mural on the wall behind her that proclaimed, "She flies with her own wings." An irony if there ever was one. At one point, she asked Idaho float outfitter Peter Grubb what kind of car he drove. "Um, a Subaru," the outfitter disclosed. "Well, then how would you like it if Subarus, but not other cars, were banned from the road?" Grubb looked mystified by the bizarre analogy, but issued the perfect response: "I suppose if Subaru were creating impacts that other cars weren't, I'd accept some restrictions."

The jet-boat bill died a miserable death, and the time spent opposing it was well worth it.

* * *

But the story doesn't end there. After the river plan and its environmental impact statement were finalized in 1994, Wallowa-Whitman National Forest Supervisor Bob Richmond refused to sign it. Why?

Richmond was intimidated by Idaho Senator Craig, though I cannot say what he was threatened with. Ed Krumpe spoke out publicly, criticizing Richmond for stalling the plan. Richmond retaliated by threatening that the Forest Service would shun the University of Idaho, but he didn't have a leg to stand on. He had no excuses for his failure to implement the plan and couldn't tell the truth about why.

In 1999, as Richmond continued to sit on the plan, I attended an event in La Grande to honor Forest Service Chief Jack Ward Thomas. There stood John Lowe, deputy chief of the Forest Service, and by most accounts the number two guy in the agency.

Coincidentally Lowe, who I knew as a straightforward guy while he was forest supervisor on the Umatilla National Forest in Northeast Oregon, had recently spoken to my father about buying a house in the Portland area. I used that connection to initiate my approach.

I asked if he could assist me with a pertinent political issue. He was receptive, but seemed to blanch after I dropped Senator Craig's name. I pressed him, politely but directly. "John," I said, "why do we have to sue you guys just to implement a management plan that's already signed off? Is the Forest Service managing the Snake River, or is Senator Craig?"

Lowe didn't acknowledge any truth to Craig's role in delaying the plan, but I could sense he was aware of the situation. I was asking him to defy Craig and, despite his hesitation, I also sensed that he wouldn't have a big problem doing that. Larry Craig was not generally seen as a highly respected Senator.

Less than two months later as I was planning another lawsuit, Bob Richmond signed the river plan. After seven years of hair-pulling over the river plan issue, I look back at that ten-minute conversation with Lowe as the one event that brought to fruition the only thing we gained out of the entire process.

* * *

There was one other simple thing I did to protect Hells Canyon's wilderness values that didn't involve spending seven years and tens of thousands of dollars. It involved my dory, three friends, and a chainsaw.

I got the idea after hearing of an announcement from the Army Corps of Engineers. The corps was calling for bids to remove its navigation markers from Hells Canyon. These were eight- to ten-foot-tall, three-foot-wide, bright-green "mile posts," like what you see on freeways. They were cemented into the ground at all the rapids on the Snake River.

The impending removal of these eyesores was a delightful revelation, and I wanted in on the fulfillment of removing them. So I called the corps and spoke with the presiding colonel whose name, unfortunately, I cannot recall. I asked how to submit a bid. He said the call for bids had been withdrawn on account of the jet-boaters, who told the corps they would maintain the markers. "They are adamant that the markers stay," the kind and helpful colonel explained. Thus began an interesting conversation.

"So, Colonel, the corps cannot afford to maintain the markers, and thus you are turning maintenance over to the jet-boaters?"

"That's correct, sir."

"So, would I be correct in assuming that from a legal perspective, the corps has abandoned the markers, and the jet-boaters are volunteering to maintain them on their own time?"

"Yes, sir, that would be a fair statement."

"Would it then also be correct to assume that the markers are no longer US government property, and if someone considered them to be objectionable, one could legally remove them?"

The colonel hesitated a bit before replying, but said, "I suppose, well, that could be one way to look at it."

I had the strong feeling the corps would prefer to see the markers removed. The colonel's statements were enough for me, Tim and Karen Lillebo, and ally Gilly Lyons. We ran a one-boat float trip in May, 1998, as a cleanup project. The river was roaring at sixty-five thousand cubic feet per second. I loaded my chainsaw into the dory and off we went.

My best estimate is that we sawed off over seventy navigation markers. We bucked them into pieces to discourage reinstallation and let them lay for the jet-boaters to glue back together if they were so inclined.

* * *

I no longer run river trips in Hells Canyon. Between the jet-boats, the disappearance of the beaches, the unchecked proliferation of weeds, and the defacement at Pittsburg Landing, I can't stomach it. Seeing this supposedly protected place literally falling apart in every way imaginable is beyond depressing.

I cannot count the eighteen-day-per-year nonmotorized period in the upper part of the canyon as a significant win, regardless of all the energy that went into it. Still, my allies and I went up against a very powerful lobbying group and came away with something to show.

Sometimes I fantasize about an earthquake that would take out Brownlee, Oxbow, and Hells Canyon Dams above the free-flowing section of the river. This event could create new rapids that jet-boats might not be able to navigate, flush away the development at Pittsburg Landing, and give us back the beaches. A USGS study reports that a 4.6 earthquake would do the trick.

Yes, it is with a stout Shillelagh that I thump the US Forest Service. For credibility's sake, my only wish is that the agency figureheads would either try and dispute my claims, or apologize to the country.

OVER 8,000 FEET OF VERTICAL RELIEF FROM GRANITE RAPID TO THE HE-DEVIL

CHAPTER 21

CRYING WOLF

In dealing with so many battles, my tendency was to fix one problem, then move on to the next without proper debriefing or archiving. I never took time to celebrate or publicize the wins.

Beginning in 1998, HCPC played a strong role in one of the greatest ecological restoration initiatives of the past hundred years—facilitating the reoccupation of the western United States by wolves. Reflecting on this achievement helps to stave off the demons of depression that unravel my objectivity.

The significance of wolf restoration is that the deed will likely stand forever. Wolves are back in the Northwestern United States to stay. The only thing that could reverse it is an organized effort by state governments to slaughter the packs that have developed.

From a philosophical perspective, seeing society right a wrong that had always seemed permanent was intensely satisfying. The reintroduction of wolves was the fulfillment of a dream heretofore deemed impossible, or like a legend that donned flesh and walked in the light of day. The return of wolves has shown there is no such thing as an impossible dream for those who want to see ecosystems restored.

Aside from all the depictions of wolves, both positive and negative and wrapped in romanticism, wolves are a keystone species at the top of the food chain. Their removal created serious ecological consequences that eventually were accepted as "normal." After Defenders of Wildlife compelled the reintroduction of wolves into Yellowstone National Park and the Frank Church–River of No Return Wilderness of Central Idaho in 1996, positive changes began almost immediately.

While wolves were absent from Western US mountain and forest ecosystems, ungulates like elk and deer got lazy and dwelt along streams, denuding vegetation. This led to warming and sedimentation, which led to the decline of fish. With the wolves back, the deer and elk are once more on the run: the strongest are surviving and the fish are recovering.

HCPC anticipated that wolves from the Idaho reintroductions would migrate into Oregon. In 1999, the wolves obliged. A lone female was confirmed running a pack of deer south of Hells Canyon. In 2000, facing down the vehement opposition of the ranching community, HCPC led the way in protecting the wolves that migrated west from trigger-happy wolf-haters and nearsighted legislators.

After the first wolf was reported to have entered Oregon via Hells Canyon, I directed most of the HCPC conservation staff to drop everything nonessential and leap to the wolves' defense. We developed a strategy to protect the returning denizens.

As with every other important issue and opportunity that came into our sphere of influence, HCPC didn't wait until we could raise money to act. We made time and dug up the dollars to get the job done. We set projects that were not time-sensitive on the shelf, and sought emergency funds from major donors and loyal foundations.

* * *

I enjoy philosophical discussions about the pros and cons of wolves. Kicking the idiot position that killing off all the wolves in the West was somehow a good idea can be fulfilling. I enjoy gunning down the proposition that when the last wolf was killed in Oregon in 1937, that was the end of wolves and the end of the argument.

I had several opportunities to debate those curious souls on the other side of the issue. The arguments in favor of exterminating wolves, and against restoring them to Western ecosystems, are among the most ridiculous I've heard on any issue.

I was once lassoed in Joseph outside the grocery store by a fellow who recognized me, and began to describe God's plan for wolves. It was entertaining. "Wolves were a placeholder for humanity. They were designed to be eliminated when we were strong and wise enough to rule the food chain." I asked him if he was open to other interpretations of "God's plan." After he muttered something about "human destiny," I thanked him for his insight.

Outspoken Northeast Oregon rancher Sharon Beck graced the pages of the *Oregonian* newspaper with a startling quote: "Wolves are vicious. That's why we got rid of them in the first place, if they were ever even here."

I engaged in a lot of dances with wolf rhetoric, and they were all fun. I fantasized about conducting a play in downtown Joseph, a parody of "Little Red Riding Hood" where Little Red finds a gun-toting redneck in Grandma's bed and says, "My, what false teeth you have!"

Actually, HCPC did support considerations for ranchers who might lose some stock from wolf predation. For a period of five years after wolves were reintroduced, ranchers would be compensated for livestock lost to wolves. This would give them a window of time to adapt, and prove they are smarter than the wolves. But in the end, if a rancher is going to operate an open-range livestock business, wolf predation is part of the natural cost of doing business. Eliminating all the wolves is unconscionable, as is having taxpayers perpetually compensating them for those little inconveniences of nature.

In Minnesota and Wisconsin, ranchers have been operating alongside wolves for over a century. There, domestic dogs kill one hundred times more cows than wolves do. Those ranchers adapted, and it's an insult to Western ranchers to suggest they cannot.

In discussing the wolf issue, I suggested the more enlightened Western ranchers threw away an excellent opportunity to give themselves the moral high ground in accepting the inevitable—that wolves were back to stay. They could have shown the world they have advanced both technologically and philosophically from the old days when they just killed everything that threatened their business. But unfortunately, they let the radical arm of the ranching community hog the microphone.

* * *

HCPC's advocacy to protect wolves ran beyond our home ecosystem in the northeast part of the state and took in all of Oregon. Our strategy involved three aspects: a wolf-naming contest, litigation to prevent the elimination of endangered species protection, and catching a wolf poacher.

The wolf-naming contest was a positive action designed to elicit sympathy with what was, I admit, a sappy dog-and-pony show. We didn't want the first wolf to be seen in Oregon in nearly seventy years to continue being referred to as "B-45." It sounded like a World War II bomber. She deserved a real name, something to give her a personality folks could embrace.

HCPC sent the naming contest guidelines to every public school in Oregon, with an invitation to participate. Nominations were sent to the Nez Perce Tribe, which convened its own panel of tribe elders to pick the winner. We received around 1,800 submissions and widespread regional media coverage.

Nez Perce member, friend, and ally Levi Holt announced the winner: "Freedom." The bureaucratic moniker "B-45" was shelved, and Oregon's first wolf walked to the name offered by an excited school kid—Cedar Hursh, a seventh grader at Lorna Byrne Middle School in Cave Junction, Oregon.

For the second component of our wolf strategy—litigation—we secured a commitment from several environmental lawyers to litigate should the state or federal government seek to kill wolves entering Oregon, or to ignore or reduce federal and state Endangered Species Act protections.

To its great credit, in the initial phases of wolf dispersal into Oregon, the State chose not to pursue lethal control. It convened a panel of wildlife biologists, wolf advocates, ranchers, and others to develop an Oregon wolf recovery plan under Oregon's Endangered Species law. HCPC's Brett Brownscombe was appointed by the governor of Oregon to sit on the wolf recovery panel.

The third component was more challenging—catch a wolf poacher. We figured the best wolf-poaching deterrent would be a conviction for violation of the Endangered Species Act. A hefty fine and a couple of months in jail levied against a poacher would serve as a deterrent to the many who arrogantly embraced the cowardly and juvenile mantra "Shoot, shovel, and shut up."

We nearly succeeded. Two years after Freedom's arrival, three more wolves were confirmed to have entered Northeast Oregon. One of those wolves was shot and killed by an unknown assailant near the town of Ukiah. A couple of months later, HCPC staffer Lisa Dix was at a public meeting in Pendleton. She overheard a man say he knew the guy who shot the wolf.

Lisa couldn't get the witness' name, but we still tried to locate him. We even hired a private investigator, but never found him. Afterward, it appeared that the killing on sight of any wolf was not going to become common practice. The chance there'd be an organized effort to kill all the wolves seemed unlikely.

Our work to protect wolves bolstered our regional reputation among the ecologically enlightened. It also elevated our national-preserve campaign by physically showing that indeed, the Hells Canyon–Wallowa Ecosystem is a critical biological linchpin. Wolves not only found an excellent home in the mostly undisturbed ecosystem, they also used it as a travel corridor to migrate west into the Blue Mountains, the Cascades, and the Siskiyou Mountains of southern Oregon.

* * *

A year after wolves were reintroduced at Indian Creek in the Frank Church–River of No Return Wilderness in central Idaho, I was guiding a river trip on the Middle Fork Salmon River in the heart of the wilderness. Our float party was camped at Marble Creek.

It was a joyous evening with six guides and our twenty-two clients amid giant ponderosa pines, craggy peaks, and the crystal waters of the Middle Fork. Within minutes after the evening festivities subsided and the guides hit their sleeping bags, a faraway howl pierced the silence of sacred backcountry. I was the last to bed, and grinned broadly to myself. The wolves might have been watching us as we partied.

The next morning, a client from New York City, who'd brought his adolescent kids on the wilderness adventure, approached me for a cup of coffee. "We heard something last night," he said with a mix of eagerness and trepidation. He looked at me sidelong. "Was that a wolf?" I nodded and smiled. His glowing response touched me in a deep way; a proclamation I'll never forget—"If I had known my children would hear a wolf in the wild, I would've paid ten times what I paid for this trip."

COW ELK NEAR THE LOSTINE RIVER

CHAPTER 22
A RECIPE FOR SALMON, BEEF, AND MUTTON

In our youth, my pal Jim and I used to walk down to Sucker Creek, the outflow from Lake Oswego. We caught three-foot-long salmon, sometimes with our bare hands, diving into pools and chasing them through small rapids. When the whole family ate them, I felt fulfillment and connection to the wild world, and developed a reverence for these amazing fish.

I used a pole to fish for salmon with my grandparents in the Toutle and Coweeman Rivers in Southwest Washington. I recall listening to my Grandfather Les Bailey telling me the story of the salmon. He was more talkative than grandma Bert, and needed to impress us kids with his stories because Grandma could usually out-fish him. To paraphrase grandpa:

> *The dams should have killed off all the fish. They even log right down to the creek bed, throwing mud into the stream. But the salmon are strong.*
>
> *They come up from the sea, bringing all the secrets of the deep in their flesh. They circulate through all the rivers and creeks. They return to the same creeks where they were hatched.*
>
> *The salmon are eaten by the bears and the eagles, and the soil and tree roots consume them. All the substances of the forest are partly made up of the salmon's flesh. And the fingerlings go back down to the sea, taking with them all the secrets of the forest.*
>
> *Salmon are one way in which the oceans, the forests and mountains are connected. They don't just feed us, they are the cog in the wheel of this beautiful land we call home.*

The wild stocks of salmon that now survive are the last scant remnant of the runs that fed Native American Societies for centuries. The hatcheries that produce genetically inferior fish were only developed because of the sharp decline of the wild stocks.

The Imnaha River provides some of the best salmon spawning habitat east of the Cascade Mountains. To spawn, Imnaha adult salmon must now navigate through seven high dams that plug the Columbia and Snake Rivers. Their offspring must make it past those same dams and the slack reservoirs they created, where there used to be a living, flowing river.

I've swam with the four foot long beauties in the Blue Hole, a magnificent pool in the upper Imnaha River. HCPC advocated fiercely for Imnaha salmon primarily by combating habitat degradation brought about by logging and cattle overgrazing.

There are actually three definitive legal mandates to protect Imnaha River salmon. The first is the HCNRA Act. The second is the National Wild and Scenic Rivers Act, which requires federal agencies to protect the outstandingly remarkable natural values of the river, including native fisheries. The third is the Endangered Species Act, wherein Imnaha salmon are listed as endangered.

Yet even with those unambiguous legal mandates, the Forest Service has done virtually nothing to protect and restore Imnaha salmon, and has repeatedly enabled actions that have perpetuated, and increased the risks contributing to the pending extinction of the Imnaha's wild stocks.

* * *

I can say without caveat that HCPC's accomplishments toward protecting federal land from livestock impacts are among the most profound of any organization working on the livestock issue.

When I started my activist career, I paid little attention to livestock grazing, other than being disgusted by seeing droves of cattle and cow shit almost everywhere I went in the HCNRA. I needed to be educated on the full range of livestock impacts, and that the livestock-denuded condition of the grasslands I was seeing were not "normal."

Most of the cattle that inundate federal land are not owned by family ranchers, but by large corporations, for example, J.R. Simplot. They not only supply the vast majority of McDonald's French fries, but most of the beef for their burgers as well.

These companies enjoy profuse federal subsidies, paying less than one tenth for the use of federal land than they'd pay for grazing their stock on an equivalent parcel of private land. Add in subsidies to grow winter feed and free water rights, and livestock grazing becomes a profound tax-sucking, as well as public land degrading, enterprise.

All breeds and sub-breeds of the cattle used to produce beef, like herefords or charolais, are native mostly to the swamplands of southeast Asia and India. Ecologically speaking, the last place they should be—in the concentrations common to federal livestock allotments—is in the arid and semi-arid desert and shrub-steppe lands of the western United States.

Via direct consumption, the growing of winter feed, and the depletion of moisture-holding soil and vegetation, one cow occupying a federal allotment consumes approximately 30 gallons of water per day. Multiply this by two thousand head, and the water needed to sustain fish and wildlife is severely depleted.

Due to cattle grazing, salmon suffer.

Salmon and cattle are both food for us humans. But cattle deplete water while salmon do not consume water at all. Cattle adversely impact native wildlife and plant species by trampling streamside soils and vegetation, while spreading weeds. This depletes food for native ungulates like elk, deer, antelope and bighorn sheep. Salmon produce no impacts.

Salmon are also food for wildlife, while anything that tries to eat a cow is generally killed by the rancher. And while it's my personal opinion that salmon tastes a lot better, it also happens to be healthier than beef, unless you enjoy high cholesterol and colon cancer.

After such an indictment of cattle grazing, I'm compelled to submit a necessary caveat: that most family ranchers are unaware of, or involuntarily blind to these impacts. Ranchers are generally honest, hard-working people. But I dream that someday they'll end their use of federal allotments and organically raise smaller numbers of animals exclusively on private land under reasonable rules.

* * *

Public land is also impacted by another breed of livestock: domestic sheep. These provide a wide array of distinct problems. The most significant are the literal massacre of overgrazed vegetation, and the spread of diseases to native bighorn sheep. Thankfully, however, open range sheep grazing is a dying industry, as sheep are more efficiently managed in concentrated feed lots.

After herds of bighorn sheep in the HCNRA and the Wallowa Mountains began dying from a disease carried by, and passed to bighorns by privately-owned domestic sheep occupying federal land, we got involved.

HCPC took a very different approach to livestock than we did with logging. Unlike timber sales, with livestock we weren't dealing with a barrage of Forest Service proposals that regularly appeared. Livestock were on federal land under long-term operating permits. There were rarely specific decisions we could influence or challenge.

With cattle grazing, our first objective was to prevent vacated allotments from being re-filled. We worked to ensure that no new permits were issued, and where permittees were violating the conditions of their permits, those permits were revoked. With domestic sheep, we made a solid case for their complete elimination from the Hells Canyon-Wallowa Ecosystem.

Strategically, litigation would be a non-starter, as there were no decisions to oppose. Our success with eliminating livestock impacts depended on impressing the right people that closing livestock allotments is a good idea. But the Forest Service considers its livestock allotments sacrosanct, and serves the ranching industry the same way it does the timber industry. So who would help us influence the Forest Service? Ranchers? Maybe a snowball's chance in hell. But we did figure out one argument that might make sense.

As the beef market declined and the viability of small, local ranching operations diminished, livestock grazing did not entail local ranchers seeking new permits. They had their existing allotments and either did not seek to expand, or vacated their federal turf.

Vacated allotment permits are most often sought by corporate ranching conglomerates. What did local ranchers stand to gain by non-local corporate operations moving in?

We had no inclination to try and run the more conscientious local ranchers off their long-held allotments. Although their operations certainly impact the land, it was in our best interest to focus on out-of-county permittees, where the damage was worse.

Thus, we followed the path of collaboration in addressing the livestock issue. Ally Scott Stouder, at the time an officer with the Oregon Hunters Association, HCPC staffer Mary O'Brien and I initiated fruitful discussions with highly respected and conscientious local rancher Jack McClaran and his son Scott. The McClaran family had been running cattle on their private holdings and HCNRA allotments for a century or more.

At one meeting, Scott, Mary and I explained why keeping vacant allotments closed might be in local ranchers' best interest. Why, we asked, should the family rancher suffer the consequences of stricter policy inspired largely by the destructive practices of corporate ranching operations? Why not close vacant allotments when local ranchers don't need them?

Supplementing our collaborations, Mary O'Brien did an excellent job of illustrating livestock damage to a broad range of people by conducting tours of livestock allotments. The botanist organized what we called "border crossings," that showed the profound difference between an allotment where livestock was present, and one that hadn't been used by livestock for many years.

The most impressive border crossing was in the early summer of 1998 was attended by about thirty people, including federal range specialists, student interns, HCPC staff and three local ranchers.

We walked between the thirty-five-thousand acre Pittsburg cattle allotment and the eight thousand acre Big Canyon Sheep Allotment. Pittsburg had been stocked with cattle almost continually for decades, whereas big canyon had been livestock-free for twenty years.

The examination was stunning. On the Pittsburg Allotment, bare, eroded ground filled our field of vision across thousands of acres. The primary watercourses, Klopton and Kurry Creeks, were bone dry, which under normal circumstances would be unusual for that time of year.

Splats of cow excrement defaced the stream bed. Entire ridges were rife with yellow star thistle, an invasive weed with thorns that can rip a nasty laceration into an unprotected hand. The predominant and most likely more destructive weed, cheatgrass, had spread like mange, in some places inundating entire slopes from top to bottom. The slopes were horizontally terraced from cattle movements, their ruts gouged into the topsoil. It was as if the life had been wrung out of the entire landscape.

Then we crossed the barbed wire fence and entered the Big Canyon Allotment. The land was filled with life. Butterflies danced from flower to flower, and insects buzzed and darted. Large clumps of bright green bunchgrass two feet in height rose from unscathed ground. Deer frolicked on a far slope. It was testimony to what grasslands in the HCNRA and elsewhere could, and should look like.

The power of that visual contrast had a profound impact on everyone present. It sent the message that what we see on livestock-grazed land is not "normal." In making the illustration, we didn't use it as self-righteous proof of our position. We let the land speak for itself.

HCPC did, however, achieve a tremendous success in eliminating and restricting domestic sheep grazing via litigation, and with cooperation from Oregon Department of Fish and Wildlife Biologist Vic Coggins and HCNRA Ranger Ed Cole.

Bighorn sheep were eliminated from what is now the HCNRA in the 1930s. Overhunting, and transmission of diseases from newly-introduced domestic sheep brought about their doom.

In the mid 1970s, Oregon Department of Fish and Wildlife Biologist Vic Coggins, one of the HCNRA's early proponents, began implementing a bighorn sheep reintroduction program. But a few years after the new herds were established, they began to decline. In 1986, the carcass of spot, the largest bighorn ram ever recorded in Oregon, was found in the Wallowa Mountains. This spurred an investigation by Coggins to prove the cause of the dieoffs.

Coggins gathered enough evidence to show that bighorns were dying after they came in contact with domestic sheep. The bighorns had contracted pasteurella haemolitica, a virus carried by domestic sheep that is deadly to bighorns. This convinced Ed Cole to take dramatic action. He brought two sheep scientists together, sheep expert Bill Foreyt from Washington State University, and a domestic sheep specialist recommended by the Wallowa County Stockman's Association, a vehemently pro-domestic sheep group.

Both scientists eventually agreed that when bighorns come in contact with domestic sheep, the bighorns are doomed. Thus, Cole proposed to close all sheep allotments in the HCNRA, due to the Act's prioritization of the protection of fish and wildlife habitat. Both Coggins and Cole exhibited conviction and determination, and deserve high praise.

Actually, pro-livestock at any cost Wallowa-Whitman National Forest Supervisor Bob Richmond pirated the decision from Cole. But in cooperation with National Wildlife Federation attorney Pete Frost, HCPC filed suit to support the decision. With science and law clearly not on his side, Richmond relented.

Although we could not verify that the McClarans were directly influential in the allotment closure edict, it wouldn't have surprised me if they had spoken with Forest Service officials in support of the concept.

But our most powerful ally was the Nez Perce Tribe. Treaty rights give the Tribe preference in the use of lands ceded to them for livestock grazing. They used this leverage to help compel restrictions on HCNRA allotments.

HCPC used both collaboration and litigation to make huge changes in livestock policy in the HCNRA and beyond. For me, the experience addressed the broader question of using multiple strategies to achieve conservation goals.

Another important part of HCPC's advocacy for natural grasslands involved cattle grazing on the private land that was included as part of the HCNRA. This effort stemmed from the successful lawsuit in 1988, when the federal court found that the Forest Service had failed to write regulations to control their activities in the HCNRA. These rules included a requirement to control livestock grazing, and to regulate the use of private land.

The majority of private land in the HCNRA is along the Imnaha River with its critical salmon habitat. Nearly all of these parcels are used for cattle grazing.

Most of the fifty-mile stretch at the bottom of the Imnaha Canyon from the Palette Ranch downstream to Cow Creek is a stinking, demented feedlot. Droves of cattle congregate in the river, destroying streamside vegetation and water quality. They relieve themselves directly into the river. With few exceptions, there is no fencing to keep the bovines out of the river, no alternative watering sources, nothing to protect the water and the fish.

HCPC doggedly hounded the Forest Service, as previously noted, to get the cows out of the river.

* * *

Prior to our success in closing livestock allotments, I met with Del Langbauer, benefactor of the Harder Foundation. Del supported HCPC financially for many years. I assured him at one meeting that HCPC would establish a substantial livestock-free area in the HCNRA. His response was something along the lines of, "I'll believe it when I see it."

We followed through with flying colors. Yet after my retirement, I learned that one of the worst things one could do to bolster their chances of receiving funding from the Harder Foundation was to invoke my name. I'm sure the reasons for this had more to do with personality issues than with conservation policy or organizational integrity. But it emphasizes that often, conservation successes are not what inspires support.

I count HCPC's successful efforts to close HCNRA livestock allotments and defeat domestic sheep grazing among our most stellar accomplishments. But the regulation of cattle feedlots along the Imnaha River to this day remains a critical outstanding issue that needs to be addressed. Present HCPC leadership has not followed through on our success in court to bring that potential victory to fruition.

I often wonder why such accomplishments are rarely given the attention they deserve within the public land protection community. Unfortunately, without the archiving of these successes, as in this book, they would likely be forgotten.

INDIAN PAINTBRUSH AND THE SNAKE RIVER FROM HAT POINT

CHAPTER 23

MINING, SKI AREAS, TRUCK DRIVERS, AND CONCERTS

HCPC stuck to our principles: we were neither capitulators nor knee-jerk compromisers. I believed, and still believe, the Earth is dying. The time for capitulation and compromise must end. That doesn't mean anyone needs to be irrational or hysterically bold, just politely unyielding.

It wasn't until I began writing this memoir that I fully realized how much we had accomplished, apart from our major campaigns. We saved some beautiful country and slew a lot of orcs, and it was all done with very little money. HCPC's annual budget never exceeded $320,000, and my highest salary was $37,500.

HCPC addressed virtually every threat to northeast Oregon public lands: logging, livestock, motorized recreation, modern development, mining, and dams. We did it with very little project-specific funding. I rarely (perhaps unwisely) went looking for money to address a specific issue. We persevered mostly with general support grants and major donor loyalty.

I have the greatest reverence for those individuals and family foundations that believed in us. I am confident we made their investment in our work pay off—Here are some of the highlights of our work that didn't involve major campaigns:

One hobgoblin we slew in 1997 was a Forest Service mining conspiracy. I've always despised mining; it seems the rawest intrusion upon the land, stripping valuable minerals and leaving mountains of undesirable stone and soil to languish with poisonous refining chemicals.

This effort began when HCPC attorney Jennifer Schemm became acquainted with Patricia Hinton, a landowner in the North Fork Burnt River area. In their conversations, Hinton revealed the illegal issuance of mining operating plans in the Wallowa-Whitman National

Forest by mining coordinator Jan Alexander. The latter was a thinly disguised mining industry servant who issued mining permits to her pals, mostly miners with backhoes and suction dredges. The impacts of these intrusions on native trout habitat and water quality had been virtually ignored.

HCPC stopped the illegal mining program by filing a successful lawsuit, laying bare the root of corruption and stopping all mining, at least until a programmatic environmental impact statement is prepared. After our victory, Alexander went to work for the Eastern Oregon Mining Association.

Again due to the efforts of Jennifer Schemm, in 1998, HCPC thwarted a proposed ski resort on Mount Howard in the Wallowas, on the edge of the Eagle Cap Wilderness. The development would have converted the present low-profile tourist scene at the head of Wallowa Lake—a few restaurants, rental cabins, and pack-horse corrals—into a destination ski resort.

We knew the majority of the Wallowa County populace did not support the ski resort, including some of our most virulent detractors in logging and ranching who were opposed to increased tourism and development. But rather than turn our opposition into a circus of controversy, we casually submitted legally-based comments to the Forest Service, highlighting two endemic plants listed under the Endangered Species Act that exist on Mount Howard. These sent the clear message to the agency that the project would not likely survive a legal challenge.

The ski area plan was quietly withdrawn and has never been resurrected. Jennifer Schemm's research was instrumental in this win. I cannot say enough about the value of her legal acumen.

I still mull over the irony that a couple of endangered plants were accepted by the Wallowa County status quo as a means of preventing a ski resort. If the presence of endangered plants had been presented as the reason for withdrawal of a timber sale, the local reactionary faction would have issued frothing protests.

One of my favorite HCPC wins was when we prevented a massive logging project within the Beaver Creek Roadless Area, which serves as the municipal water supply for the City of La Grande. In 2000, the Forest Service proposed to "save" the watershed by logging it. The logic behind their proposed timber sale was allegedly to prevent a supposedly imminent wildfire that might degrade water quality.

The Forest Service presented no support for its claim that such a fire would occur, that it would be of an intensity that would damage water quality, nor that logging the watershed would prevent such a fire. We showed that logging would definitely degrade the watershed. The Forest Service's "mights" and "maybes" just didn't add up to validate creating very real impacts to avoid alleged potential impacts.

On the path to stopping the project, we managed to convince the La Grande City Council, among other constituencies not generally sympathetic to our work, that logging would degrade the watershed, not protect it. We successfully summarized our position with the tag line: "The water is more valuable than the timber."

We sponsored VIP flights over the beautiful, forested watershed and conducted a public forum at Eastern Oregon University, where the Forest Service was forced to (unsuccessfully) defend its proposal against forest scientists and fire-behavior specialists in front of a large audience.

The Service had counted on public support in La Grande, but didn't get much. They withdrew the project, and since then, the Beaver Creek Roadless Area has not experienced a wildfire and still produces pure water and native trout as it has for centuries.

* * *

Amid all the battles on the Northeast Oregon front defending the homeland, I often found myself in strange places doing things that had little direct connection to the local ecosystem, nor to HCPC. It was always refreshing when I was able to break away from my standard routines and help implement ideas for land protection that worked outside the box, and involved tasks that went beyond desk work. One of the most fun was in 1990, a month before I got my first salary check from HCPC. Who would have thought my experience as a long-haul truck driver could benefit forest advocacy?

During one particularly boring moment at a conference, cohort Mitch Friedman approached me: Could we haul a giant log across the USA to draw attention to the plight of ancient forests? Absolutely!

A stellar fundraiser, Mitch attracted the bucks to get the project on the road. A few months later, the "Ancient Forest Rescue Expedition" was touring the country with a 752-year-old, eight-foot-diameter Douglas fir log perched on a drop-deck trailer. Mitch located the log via a timber broker who found it in a shipping yard—ready to be sent to Japan.

Our four-person crew organized media events and presentations as we traveled. It was exhilarating to see people of all cultures across the nation amazed by the giant log and attracted to our presentations, which showed slides and videos of giant trees still standing.

We held one rally in Philadelphia across the street from the Liberty Bell. As I stood atop the truck doing my best to issue a rousing speech to the expanding crowd, I watched tourists walk toward the Liberty Bell, then turn in our direction once they caught a glimpse of our giant log.

* * *

I was busy orienting new HCPC staff in 1993 when President Bill Clinton and Veep Al Gore announced they were coming to Portland to fulfill the president's campaign promise to bring the timber and forest advocacy communities together in what was called a "Spotted Owl Summit."

I considered forest advocates' public presence at the red-carpet event. I knew the logging constituency would be there in force, doing what they usually did to get attention—driving a couple hundred horn-blasting log trucks through downtown Portland. We needed a big, identifiable pro-forest-protection presence.

I mulled over ideas: how about a rally with some noteworthy rock stars? At first, it seemed tacky. But I pitched the idea to some fellow executive directors, and they all loved it. So we went to forest-protection funders to raise the money. The funders jumped on board with no hesitation.

We hired Avocado Productions to coordinate what we called the "Ancient Forest Celebration and Rally." I immediately went to work on music acts by contacting Carole King, who quickly committed. George Atiyeh put in a call to his friend Kenny Loggins, who also signed on. Avocado Productions came on board with Bonnie Raitt, Ann and Nancy Wilson (Heart), David Crosby, and Neil Young. I managed to book some talented local musicians.

An estimated seventy thousand people showed up at Portland's Waterfront Park, dancing and cheering in the midst of a horrendous downpour. "Nice weather for the trees," Neil Young commented during his set, and went to play "Comes a Time."

A reliable source told us the Clinton and Gore families had stationed themselves in the top floor of an office building that overlooked Waterfront Park to enjoy the show.

Although I was thrilled with the success of the rally, I became more deeply acquainted with one of the biggest challenges in organizing an event of this magnitude: egos and micromanagement. Once the rally organizers—a collection of executive directors from Oregon and Washington forest advocacy groups—opened an office to manage the event, a lot of folks associated with forest protection showed up. Some actually took on tasks while others hung around on the chance they'd get an all-access pass to the event and maybe meet a rock star.

My worst taste of egoism came after my initial press conference went awry. Only two reporters showed up. I felt deflated, although we really didn't need it; the musicians we had lined up had the press buzzing anyway.

The next morning, as I walked up the steps to the event office, I heard a familiar voice coming from around a corner past the top of the landing. It was loyal wilderness funder Bill Lazar. He was speaking to a few people I couldn't see. "We removed Ric from media because he botched the press conference."

I was intrigued by Lazar's loose usage of "we," as he was not an organizer, he just kicked in a couple thousand bucks. Despite Lazar's claim that I'd been fired, I continued my media and booking work for the event, with the approval of the rest of the ad-hoc steering committee.

What Lazar failed to mention was that at 5:34 a.m. on March 25, 1993, the morning of our press conference, Portland had experienced the most powerful earthquake in the city's history. The US Geological Survey held its earthquake press conference at the exact same time as ours, 10:00 a.m., on the opposite side of town.

* * *

In 1999, I put together a forum that brought together an impressive collection of leaders of the wilderness movement nationwide. The idea took root on a Grand Canyon river trip with wilderness icon Martin Litton. Carole King joined us on the trip.

During a conversation at the raven-haunted refuge of Saddle Creek Camp, Carole and I resolved to address the lack of cohesion among the local, regional, and national organizations in the wilderness/public lands movement across the nation.

Our aim was to bring together leaders of the movement at Carole's Idaho ranch for a four-day meeting to discuss how we could work together toward a national wilderness campaign. We called it the White Cloud Council, after the location of Carole's ranch.

The forum began with promise. We attracted many influential and visionary activists, including American Lands Alliance co-founder Randi Spivak, Wilderness Society Executive Director Bill Meadows, Conservation Northwest's Mitch Friedman, public lands advocate Judi Noritake, former Congressman Jim Jontz, and wilderness patriarch Brock Evans.

The group conceived a campaign called "Parks to Peaks," an effort to inspire people across the country to join together in protecting America's land, beginning with their own backyards. It envisioned a progressive chain of interconnected protected areas emanating from city parks, advancing to local green spaces, in turn connecting to state and county parks, and from there to federal land, culminating with large wilderness areas and biosphere reserves.

White Cloud faded out, a victim of "lack of funder interest." However, one of its unintended benefits included illumination of the wilderness movement's most glaring shortcoming—that it is composed of many diverse and powerful organizations that can rarely marshal their collective strength toward a proactive effort to protect America's ecological heritage. Each continues to chase (or be lured by) funding to support various individual initiatives, with little or no consideration for how their campaigns tie into a greater vision.

* * *

Revisiting my success with, and outside HCPC, is exhilarating. I should have taken the time to savor the fulfillment when it happened. But there was always another orc waiting in the wings.

PONDEROSA DECORATED WITH SUMAC

CHAPTER 24

KILL BILLS

Traveling the country with the giant log was a lot more fulfilling than my regular travel docket. Early in my career I became a regular visitor to Capitol Hill, mostly to promote the national-preserve effort at congressional offices.

Unfortunately, I also had to work in DC to defeat legislation that would have erased a couple of HCPC's noteworthy accomplishments. In addition to the jet-boat privilege bill, another bill would have moved the boundary of the Hells Canyon Wilderness Area along the west rim of the canyon to allow ORV travel on the Lookout Mountain "road," which is nothing more than an old dirt track.

These bills epitomize the principle of government working for the rich. The level to which members of Congress will stoop to support their big donors is stunning. Introducing federal legislation that would degrade Hells Canyon's wilderness character and impinge upon important fish and wildlife habitat was introduced on behalf of two people—a jet-boater and a jeep enthusiast—to satisfy their motorized recreational desires at everyone else's expense.

I know of no other place where congressional leaders have introduced legislation to decrease protection to federally protected areas not once, but twice.

The wilderness-shrinkage bill was introduced on behalf of Dr. Robert Burns of Baker City, Oregon, who enjoyed driving his jeep along the canyon rim. Like jet-boater Joe Scott, who personally inspired the jet-boat privilege bill, Dr. Burns was a generous contributor to Republican candidates and causes.

I took on the task of killing these two bills myself, allowing HCPC staff to continue working on their own projects. The work was time-consuming, but I felt it necessary to defend HCPC's successes. I was also determined to provide a voice for people other than the wealthy and to defend the integrity of America's wilderness preservation system. The precedent of shrinking wilderness areas is terrifying—wilderness is supposed to be a permanent legacy.

The anti-wilderness bill followed on the heels of HCPC's discovery that a rutted track along the west rim of Hells Canyon was, in several places, inside the wilderness boundary where motor vehicles are prohibited. We never knew anyone was driving out to that section of the Hells Canyon rim.

After we proved our point to the Forest Service, they had no choice but to close the "road." Soon after, Oregon Senator Gordon Smith and Second District Representative Bob Smith, both Republicans, introduced legislation that would have moved the boundary of the wilderness east of the "road," thus allowing Dr. Burns—and others—to again invade the rim with their four-wheel-drive vehicles.

An interesting anecdote concerning the Senate version of the bill is that I had set up a meeting with newly-elected Senator Smith at his Pendleton office in December 1996. Joining me were the writer, geologist, and activist Ellen Bishop, and Oregon Hunters Association leader Scott Stouder. We felt we could find some common ground with the new Republican senator, as he was somewhat of a moderate, and was representing a very liberal state.

We obtained a personal promise from Senator Smith that he would not support legislation to move the wilderness boundary.

After Smith introduced the bill, Scott and I were outraged, and we let the senator know. But it wasn't us who got him to eventually back off the bill. As it turned out, the senator's bill ticked off some local folks far more important to him—local ranchers.

A posse of Imnaha Canyon ranchers who owned property downslope from the road didn't want it open. After getting wind of this, I contacted a couple of people who had cordial relationships with two of the ranchers to alert them to the bill. I knew my attempt to speak with them would have been futile.

A phone call from even one rancher to Senator Smith could kill the bill. And presumably, it did. The ranchers' position showed there's a lot to be said for eschewing stereotypes on land management issues and that "public support" in Wallowa County isn't always black and white.

Senator Smith declined to hold a hearing on his bill. However, Representative Smith did. I went to DC to testify before the House

Natural Resources Committee, chaired by legendary Democrat Bruce Vento of Minnesota.

The Oregon Department of Fish and Wildlife submitted testimony that since the road had been closed, use of the summer range on the west rim by elk had increased dramatically. But contradicting the biologists was the written testimony of Dr. Burns, part of which was read at the hearing by Congressman Bob Smith.

"I've been up there as many times as anybody in my jeep, and I've never seen any elk," Dr. Burns had written. With great vigor and heart-rending passion, Congressman Smith extolled the value and articulate quality of Dr. Burns's testimony.

That was the lesson of the day—you can provide documented evidence from scientists and a state agency that wildlife is impacted, but it can always be countermanded by the observations of one guy in his jeep. I wondered if Dr. Burns might consider his noisy jeep as the reason he never saw any elk.

Thankfully, the wilderness-shrinkage and jet-boat-privilege bills went nowhere. The seven-mile stretch of the Hells Canyon rim beyond PO Saddle remains closed to motor vehicles, and the nonmotorized period on the Snake Wild and Scenic River endures.

I didn't manage to get much in the way of support for killing either bill from the DC-based organizations, given their "it'll never pass" logic. Maybe they were right, but my pleas that the wilderness movement should never fail to attack any attempt to declassify designated wilderness went almost for naught.

But fortunately, one ally, the most effective and eloquent I could have hoped for, came to the rescue—Brock Evans.

Brock testified with me at the House hearing, and his support proved profound. During the hearing, Congressman Bob Smith waited patiently for me to give my testimony, then attacked. He held up documents, waving pieces of paper around while smoking one of his trademark Marlboro cigarettes. I recall hoping his cigarette would ignite one of the mystery documents.

Eventually, Rep. Smith revealed that one of those flailing papers was an article which contained a quote from me. I don't recall its author. After Smith's aide marched the document over to the witness table and plopped it down in front of me like a "presumed guilty" doctrine of doom, Smith pounced. "Mr. Bailey, you claim that the Boise

Cascade Corporation is a herd of prideless robber barons. Do you hold to that opinion?"

I could sense Brock, who was sitting next to me, twitching. My first thought was that he was going to tell me I was screwed. Not so. He leaned over and in clear, plain English, whispered, "Yes! Yes, of course you do!"

I responded accordingly, calmly and matter-of-factly, that despite my appreciation for its workers, I did consider the Boise Cascade Corporation to be prideless robber barons. Smith's attempt to put me on the defensive was squelched, thanks to Brock's bold and timely witness-table counsel. And best of all, Democratic Congressman Vento grinned widely at my reply. Smith's attempt to discredit me was diffused. He had nowhere to go with his sniper shot.

I don't regret the meeting with Senator Gordon Smith, despite his backing off the promise without even contacting us first. I believe that despite his bill, he has personal integrity and some feeling for wilderness. After he lost his 2002 bid for reelection, I maintained contact with him.

THE HIGH WALLOWA MOUNTAINS

CHAPTER 25

A SHOCKING PORTENT: A POSITIVE HCNRA MANAGEMENT PLAN

As the 1990s marched toward the new millennium, my impatience, anger, and hyper-vigilance increased. My workload and emotional attachment to my cause were feeding the depression with relentless stress.

Even as the darkness advanced in frequency and intensity, I still resisted seeking help because I didn't feel there was anything wrong that could be repaired. I accepted my often-abrasive behavior as just a part of who I was.

I figured the only way I could temper my emotions was to reduce stress by retiring from activism. I began to see departure as a mirage of cool, clear fountains. But the wrenching desire to bring permanence to my work remained overwhelming.

While seriously contemplating retirement, I strove to find milestones that would provide a legacy to justify departure. I realized with shock that I'd rarely looked back at what I'd accomplished, and had kept no records.

HCPC's ultimate goal was to designate the Hells Canyon–Chief Joseph National Preserve. But whenever rationality invaded my breakneck desire to buck the odds, it became apparent this was far too lofty a goal to attain with my sanity declining.

Campaigns and tasks drifted away and resurfaced, whether in addressing Forest Service plans and actions, lawsuits, development of the national-preserve strategy, or influencing legislation. I could have hailed the defeat of several timber sales, smothering bad legislation, and the changes in Forest Service personnel as major successes.

I came to realize I was never satisfied, even when HCPC did achieve something big. I had become obsessed with my cause.

Looking back objectively, there is one victory that stands tall: The Forest Service's re-writing of the HCNRA Comprehensive Management Plan (CMP). The quality of the HCNRA CMP was unforeseen and exceptionally visionary in its content as a definitive policy directive. It was compelled by HCPC's dogged, proactive approach to influencing the plan, our litigation, the nationally publicized national-preserve campaign, and influence over changes in local Forest Service personnel. Many organizations might justify their entire existence with such a win.

We had fought the Forest Service for more than twenty years over its defiance of the HCNRA Act. That we could reverse the agency's course was never a serious consideration. But in the late 1990s HCPC's work had the Forest Service playing defense. The Hells Canyon issue wasn't strictly dominated by Wallowa County politics, nor the Wallowa-Whitman National Forest alone. The Chief's office in Washington, DC had gotten involved.

During our efforts to convince the Forest Service to write a new CMP, I spent some time in the Washington, D.C. office of the agency, setting up meetings with the various officers. Amazingly, I found an ally: Jim Furnish. I can't say whether he took action on HCPC's behalf but often, this kind of influence needs to be kept under the rug.

The campaign took wing when Mary O'Brien began working full-time on the project in 1998. A PhD in botany, Dr. O'Brien brought a strong science-based aspect to our work, along with a lot of dedicated energy. She took charge of the CMP effort, which allowed me to enjoy somewhat of a respite. I remained involved, particularly with the establishment of HCPC's vision for what a new plan would look like.

I was surprised when Wallowa-Whitman National Forest Supervisor Bob Richmond, our nemesis, agreed to initiate the process to write a new plan. That may have been Jim Furnish's influence, but it may be that Richmond felt, as long as he was in control of the content of the new plan, its mandates would comply with his livestock and timber agenda.

HCPC mobilized solid support among our membership and several regional conservation groups. For whatever reason, organized opposition to a protective plan in Wallowa County never fully materialized.

As fate willed, Richmond left the WWNF just after the process for developing the new CMP began. His replacement wound up being one of the agency's rising stars, who actually had a science background—Karyn Wood. The friendly Clinton administration may have played a part in the positive change of personnel but again, dabbling in the "why's" was best left unexplored.

The development of a federal land management plan involves the collection of scientific and sociological information, and creation of a wide range of "alternatives," each with distinct policy direction. All information is compiled in a phone-book-sized document which analyzes all the alternatives against each other. Finally, the document is released to the public for comment, whereafter the deciding officer, Karyn Wood in this case, picks one of the alternatives as the new plan.

Mary O'Brien and I felt our involvement in the plan had to be proactive rather than trying to modify Forest Service-created alternatives. Thus, HCPC wrote its own management plan, and pressured the Forest Service to include it in the Environmental Impact Statement (EIS) it was writing to enable the new plan.

O'Brien began by organizing the Hells Canyon CMP Tracking Group, an excellent collective of thirteen seasoned activists, each of whom contributed to our vision for the plan in their particular area of expertise.

The Tracking Group called its plan "The Native Ecosystem Alternative." It included directives for closure of livestock allotments and management of livestock toward restoration of native grasslands; closure of scores of roads, mostly old logging roads; a policy of looking at forests as ecosystems rather than sawmill fodder; consideration of the HCNRA's role in facilitating ecological connectivity; and securing habitat for endangered species. It proposed strict direction for any activity that might occur.

The National Environmental Policy Act, the law that requires the preparation of an EIS, dictates that all "reasonable" alternatives be analyzed in the document. Thus, we had the law on our side. There was nothing unreasonable about our plan in light of HCNRA Act directives.

But initially, Bob Richmond refused to include the Native Ecosystem Alternative in the EIS. His planning team trotted out a number of poor excuses as to why HCPC's Alternative shouldn't be included in the EIS because it was not "reasonable." But Dr. O'Brien took the Tracking Group's case to the Forest Service regional office in Portland.

Surprisingly, the regional office conceded. I suspected it did so because it was afraid of legal action that would result in case law requiring the agency to include all independently developed alternatives in its

EISs. Allowing it without a legally-binding directive from the courts would not create a legal precedent.

Regardless, inclusion of the Native Ecosystem Alternative compelled the consideration of its directives and required its comparison to the Forest Service's alternatives. It also gave our members and allies something concrete to support.

Each EIS is driven by "needs," which on the positive side can include specific ecological restoration priorities, or even providing recreation opportunities. On the negative side, needs can include timber production, meeting draconian economic goals, or even disguising a timber and livestock production agenda with needs like reducing fire risk.

The Native Ecosystem Alternative successfully steered the needs away from timber and livestock production. It pointed to the protection directives of the HCNRA Act as the foundation for the new plan, and emphasized the linchpin principle, that the HCNRA is one of the important pieces of the regional biodiversity puzzle as an ecological connector. Thus, facilitating protection and rejuvenation of HCNRA habitats should be the guiding aspect in developing the needs that would be addressed in the new plan.

Supervisor Wood did not select the Native Ecosystem Alternative as the preferred alternative. But the plan she did select includes many of its principles and directives. It draws upon the latest in biodiversity science. It requires that all management activities respect the ecological attributes of the HCNRA that facilitate regional connectivity.

Perhaps the most significant aspect of the plan is the directive to close nine livestock allotments, resulting in more than 340,000 acres of livestock-free land in the HCNRA. The landmark decision to eliminate domestic sheep from the HCNRA cemented Ed Cole's decision into semi-permanence, at the very least over the life of the HCNRA plan.

The elimination of domestic sheep grazing within the HCNRA later inspired closure of all domestic sheep allotments in the Wallowa-Whitman National Forest. And with the support of Western Watersheds Project attorney Laurie Rule, 70 percent of the sheep allotments on the Payette National Forest in Idaho were also closed.

I was ecstatic over the dreadful bleating of fate.

The HCNRA Comprehensive Management Plan also closed several vacant cattle allotments. I believe this 340,000 acre livestock-free area is the largest expanse of national forest land where livestock grazing is prohibited by legal or administrative mandate.

The plan also mandates the closure of more than two hundred miles of roads and prohibits off-road travel.

Another thrilling aspect of the CMP is that it doesn't set timber output projections—otherwise known as logging quotas—or designate areas where logging is allowed or emphasized. Logging is only permitted when it can be justified toward ecological restoration. The prospect of no timber sales and dismantling of the heinous HCNRA timber sale program is something we could never have dreamed in the 1980s.

Although the CMP victory was huge, there looms a shortcoming. By common practice, these plans only last for around fifteen to twenty years, whereafter they can be rewritten in any way a new forest supervisor might desire. Here again, I lament the absence of permanence in our efforts.

Still, this victory should be enough for lasting satisfaction. But such wins only last as long as constant vigilance is maintained through dogged activism.

* * *

If HCPC was going to pursue permanence by designating the national preserve, my involvement was critical. If I left, the momentum and perhaps even the organizational policies would change under new HCPC leadership. Still, my effectiveness was being compromised by my mental condition. I could feel my staff, board, and others I worked with were impacted by my stress levels. As for retirement, I was unable to make a decision.

It had been too long since I'd spent more than one night in the mountains. Not long after the CMP was signed, I trussed my big pack and headed into the Wallowas for a five-day trek.

At the Bear Creek Trailhead, I heaved a sigh intending to exhale all the stress: the onset of respite from work, the trappings of the imprisoning desk, and the rancid politics. This was my first real "vacation" that didn't involve my job as a river guide.

During my ascent, I was distracted by our fight in 1980 to stop the Allen Canyon timber sale just to the east of my present position. I cast it from my brain like a carcass thrown overboard. The ponderosa pine scent replaced it. The light cloud cover was as welcoming as sunlight.

Graced with precious aloneness, the dour shadow slowly began to fade. Not another soul all day, except for the cinnamon bear and her two cubs, snuffling for grub on a timbered ridge above me.

The gradual change in elevation brought exhilaration as the forest turned from ponderosa and lodgepole to sparse subalpine fir encased in lush mountain meadows, garnished with a proud congregation of multicolored wildflowers. The granite ridges and peaks showed off their nobility with gargoyle shapes complemented by vertical stone reaches smooth as textured velvet.

The gently sloping verdant expanse reached toward a series of stately peaks. Suddenly, a peculiar sound came into focus. Its source was a rill emanating from a high snowfield that found its way into the meadow, lazily wandering until it encountered a two-foot drop into a tiny pool. Its trickling mantra seemed the music of the universe.

Camp was a locket of gaunt firs gathered upon a knoll. No tent tonight. The clouds broke and the last gasp of the sun was glorious. She seemed to direct her radiance in prisms to my brief but precious habitation.

Then came the stars. The constellations to the south and west, a promise of invisible but living worlds. Could there be other planets as diverse and divine as ours? No matter. Earth is all we need. We shouldn't go to other worlds until we can respect our own.

Our world is miraculously alive and heartbreakingly beautiful.

HURWAL DIVIDE IN THE WALLOWAS

CHAPTER 26
A FEW MONTHS IN "THE LIFE"

Inevitably, I landed back at the desk and into the fray. I made the mistake of picking up the local *Wallowa County Chieftain* newspaper. Our local publicity had become even more caustic after our national exposure, as the *Chieftain* editor, Rick Swart, seemed offended by our sympathetic national publicity.

After reading more abrasive reports from the *Chieftain*, I revisited all the hostilities I'd experienced in an almost sentimental way. Recounting them brought a mildly satisfying feeling, given the successes HCPC had achieved despite Swart's reckless spraying of his inexhaustible tub of ink. In particular, there was a prolonged period of harassment that occurred in 1994, after we'd been featured in a number of regional and national publications.

One beautiful spring morning, I began the day with a bike ride to Salt Creek Summit, twenty miles of winding through larch and pine forests. While exiting my driveway, something hanging from a strand of barbed wire on my fence caught my eye.

Hanging there was what my mom used to call a "Kewpie" doll, a plastic figure with a pudgy, cherubic face. This one was naked and had a rusted piece of barbed wire around its neck. Nails punctured its abdomen and posterior, and wood splinters pierced its eyes. There were red and black felt pen slashes across its body. On the doll's belly, *Bailey* had been scrawled in rough lettering.

It was artwork that someone obviously spent some time on. I assumed my recent presence in the *Chieftain* had inspired the artist to drop by under cover of night and leave the surprise.

Despite my puzzlement, I didn't investigate or take the doll to the police for fingerprinting. Contacting the police would seem petty. I left the doll in my pasture and disposed of it after returning from my ride. I considered keeping it, but wasn't sure what noble purpose that would serve.

A few weeks later, I came home from the weekly poker game at 3:30 a.m. to discover a voicemail on my phone. The stark message from a growling voice: "You're going to suffer for what you've done. One day, when you're in your front room, I'm going to be on the hill behind you and put a bullet in your head. Or better yet, I'll do it with an axe on your front lawn."

I attributed the call to someone over-imbibing on a Thursday night. Not that the guy didn't want to do what he was describing, but why announce it? That was before caller ID, and I didn't know how to trace the call. After that one, occasional threatening phone calls came more often.

On October 3, 1994, after returning home from an idyllic eighteen-day river trip through the Grand Canyon, I was greeted by some exciting news. My pal Rhonda hailed me at the grocery store. She seemed surprised I acted normal. She said, "Didn't you know? Yesterday they hung you in effigy." Two life-sized human figures, one with my name attached, and another with fellow wilderness advocate Andy Kerr, had been tarred, feathered, and hung by about 150 people in the Joseph mini mall, where the HCPC office was located. She said the mall's manager, a tough former policewoman, had angrily run the mob off her property. So the mob moved across the street.

I'd have enjoyed the opportunity to offer actual flesh to the lynchers. But I hadn't heard of the hanging event before my departure to Grand Canyon.

The lynching had been conducted in unison with a conference sponsored by the *Chieftain*, which featured a collection of what Rick Swart's stories headlined as the "big guns" of the wise-use movement. (Kerr calls it the "Wise Ass" movement. I commend him for not referring to them by the misleading name they chose for themselves.)

I later spoke with a former logger who attended part of the conference. He declared he had no idea what the conference's purpose was "other than to demonize and threaten environmentalists."

As I pondered a response, Kerr called me. He said the effigies were hanging from a tree on the property of Wallowa County commissioner candidate Dale Potter. Two nights after the symbolic lynching, the two of us liberated our effigies.

As we carried out our caper, Potter and friends were partying inside his house, laughing and drinking as Kerr and I cut the suspension ropes and made off with the effigies. Incidentally, being involved in the symbolic hanging didn't help Potter's campaign, as he got his butt firmly kicked by the established anti-environment incumbent.

We carried our effigies to a remote location in the Wallowa-Whitman National Forest and burned them. We consulted an attorney cohort prior to the next phase of our plan; he assured us the legal consequences of our act would be minor due to the low dollar value of the effigies and the probability we could be exonerated for trespassing, since the branch supporting them was over the public road right of way. So, we telephoned several media contacts and admitted to stealing and burning our own effigies.

The plan was to get arrested, plead not guilty, and have a nice show trial. Surprisingly, we didn't get any bites from the press, which was probably just as well. We both had plenty of circus acts on our plates already. But Kerr mentioned that if we didn't increase our budgets by at least 10 percent due to the publicity from the hanging event, we didn't deserve to be executive directors.

In response to the mock-execution, HCPC successfully applied for an emergency grant from the Bullitt Foundation. We used the money to mail a flier to every address in Wallowa County. On the cover was a photo of an angler holding a fresh-caught, two-foot-long steelhead with the headline *Why do you live in Wallowa County?* It was an excellent opportunity to clarify the motivation for our work.

A few days after the flyer was mailed, I walked to the Joseph post office to see if our mailing had hit the PO boxes. Before reaching my destination, I was verbally accosted. There in his ruddy pickup truck sat Paul Morehead, my most virulent detractor. He had pulled in front of what is now the Embers Pub, in the middle of Joseph.

Morehead opened his truck window and barked, "Bailey!" In his hand were some papers, which he waved like Joseph McCarthy confronting an accused Communist.

The thing I remember most about Morehead was that I only recall seeing him smile once, and when he had, it was only with his lips. The rest of his face remained in a half-scowl. He sat in his pickup and scowled fully.

He said, "If you think all this bullshit you send out and the publicity you get is going to help your sordid cause, you'd better think again. Wallowa County is ours, and we're going to make a living off it." In his hand was our mailing.

I listened patiently, and then responded politely, "Actually, I support your boycotts, effigy-hangings, and death threats, because those are the hooks we're using to attract national press." It was a frozen moment in which the smart-ass in me (as my dad used to put it) just couldn't pass up the opportunity of a perfect setup.

The ex-Marine was furious. I thought he was going to jump out of his rig and we were finally going to have at it, right there on Main Street. I braced myself for a fight officiated by the ghosts of John Muir and John Wayne, and witnessed by the beneficiaries of rural economic myths who inhabited the storefronts. Instead, Morehead sped away with a look on his face that would have curdled fresh milk.

Morehead was actually a smart fellow. But his prejudices and intolerance for divergent points of view made him a dubious spokesperson for his logging cause. In a January 1995 NPR interview, he attempted to characterize the gravity of the conflict in Wallowa County.

NPR narrator: "Morehead speaks of a future in which an environmentalist-run government will seek to depopulate Wallowa County, evicting people from their homes. He sees no irony in his own quest to drive Kerr and Bailey out of town, saying he just wants to make life so uncomfortable for them that they'll leave of their own accord. And if they don't, he says he doesn't know what'll happen."

Morehead: "I've heard people say, 'Well, if I knew I had a terminal illness, I'd go out and I'd take care of these guys.' And I said, 'You mean to tell me that you would go out and you would commit murder, sacrifice your soul?' And they'd stop, and they'd say, 'Well, maybe not.'"

* * *

On behalf of his employer, the Boise Cascade Corporation, Morehead launched many offensives my way during the 1990s. One was a sweeping boycott. According to my fellow poker player Cactus Jack, owner of the Cowboy Bar, Morehead and friends visited businesses in Joseph and Enterprise and told them the local timber workers would boycott any business that would allow me in the door.

Cactus firmly told the instigator he would not allow anyone to determine whom he would and wouldn't allow into his establishment.

I didn't want to damage any local businesses via my patronage. To avoid putting some of them in an uncomfortable position, I used my frequent seventy-mile trips to La Grande for necessary purchases. As it turns out, the boycott became little more than a mild inconvenience.

I had one interesting encounter with John Roberts, a friend of Morehead and a former Boise Cascade millworker. Roberts had opened a "greasy spoon" restaurant in Joseph. I didn't have any inclination to patronize his establishment, but on one occasion, I stopped in. My motivation was admittedly less than pure: I knew Roberts would honor the boycott.

My original idea was to secure the attendance of a journalist to covertly record the encounter. But that didn't work out, as the only objective journalists were far from Joseph, and none accepted the invitation.

On the day I chose for the confrontation, I walked alone into the R&R Drive-In at lunch hour and picked up a menu at the counter. Within a few seconds, John Roberts dropped his spatula at the grill and walked slowly toward me. "Ric," he began. "I don't want you in here." The diners all apparently heard him—there was dead silence.

Though I never knew him before the encounter, by most accounts John Roberts was a well-respected guy. I had no beef with him or his burger joint, and his only problem with me came from second- and third-hand information. He'd never contacted me to inquire about my agenda.

"You don't want me in here?" I suddenly responded in a puzzled tone. "Why not?" He seemed miffed that I'd actually want to discuss the eviction. He was obviously nervous about having to explain himself in front of a couple dozen customers.

He responded quickly, "You have been an enemy of the local economy, and I have a right to refuse service." He pointed toward the door.

"How have I been an enemy of the local economy?" I asked, speaking earnestly.

Roberts seemed unsure of what to say at this point, but wisely finalized his speech without leaving me much wiggle room to continue the embarrassing discussion in front of his patrons. "You have acted to destroy the timber industry. I just don't want you here."

"As usual, you confuse the timber industry with the Wallowa County economy," I replied. "Regardless, this is my home, and I'm not going anywhere, burgers or no burgers." I strode out the door.

I'd be lying if I didn't admit to gaining some satisfaction out of having a little fun at the expense of those who vilified me. I walked home. Twenty minutes later, I rode my bike past the restaurant and saw Roberts talking with Morehead in the restaurant parking lot. A half dozen people stood around them. The conversation seemed intense.

I wondered whether Roberts had used one of the state's loans for displaced timber workers, a program I had supported, to open his restaurant. Looking into that possibility might have revealed some interesting double-standards. But I never seriously considered such a move, mainly because I had no ill intent toward the guy. Besides, engaging in vindictive retaliation would be petty.

More than anything, I wanted to tell Roberts what my agenda really was, and that I was also blue-collar. In one of his letters to the editor of the *Chieftain*, his pal Morehead claimed I was "filled with hatred for people who make their living from the land." It really pissed him off that I had a working-class background.

The death threats and boycotts obviously never achieved their intended goals of conjuring fear. After all, if someone really plans to kill you, why would they put in a phone call first? I managed to have some fun with the callers—I set up my outgoing voicemail message to instruct callers, "If you intend to issue a death threat, stay calm, and press one if you're a logger, press two if you're a rancher, press three if you're a motorhead."

The worst inconvenience of the boycott was when Morehead convinced the principal at Joseph High School to exclude me from the school gym. As it's a state-funded school, any pretense of discrimination wouldn't work. Instead, the principal instituted measures that applied to everyone who used the gym, but which made it especially difficult for me; for example, changing the times the gym would be open to the public and requiring a lifting partner.

I remained aware there was the possibility that some bloke, after oversudsing at the local grog shop, might decide it was a good idea to fire some rifle volleys through my living room window.

I had two acquaintances who covertly supported HCPC's work and were on speaking terms with some of my prominent detractors. I asked them to leak word that my house was under federal surveillance.

It made sense because in the minds of many of the more fervent locals, I was a well-financed agent of Commie insurgents, allied with the United Nations and the EPA. Such theorists would not have been surprised to see a black helicopter set down in my pasture. At any rate, my house and all occupants remained untouched.

I didn't hesitate to confront people who yelled from passing cars and/or flipped me off. I sometimes stopped and waved them back, and if they returned (which happened only twice), casually let them know that if anything happened to me, my friends, family, or property, my attorney was maintaining a record of those who expressed hostilities and thus, congratulations! They were now on the list of suspects.

On one particularly disturbing occasion, two people in an old Plymouth pulled up next to me as I rode my bike on East Street about two blocks from home. The driver rolled down his window and said, "You will burn in hell for what you've done." A woman stared coldly from the passenger seat.

My first inclination was to brush them off with a smart-aleck reply, like "I don't believe in hell." But that gave way to a hard look at the man. "Well, you're on the list now, buckaroo. I've got your license plate number. If anything happens, the cops will come to your door first." As I said it, my words felt hollow and vain.

The woman suddenly spoke with a shaking voice: "Why do you hate us?" A genuinely pained expression emphasized her words. The way she said it hit something in me. Suddenly, I was filled with guilt. These people actually believed I hated them and everyone like them and wanted to ruin their lives.

With sincerity, I said, "If you'd like, we can talk. I live right there," I said, pointing to my house. "I'd be happy to explain why we do what we do." They drove away.

I still harbor guilt for rarely initiating informal meetings with some of the people in the community, beyond the few I knew personally. It would have been helpful to look them in the eye and tell them my motivation was to protect the natural integrity of local federal land, there was still plenty of timber available, and my organization had some ideas to create new outdoor jobs.

The truth was, I had little time outside of managing my organization to become a missionary. I wasn't cut out for that role anyway. I am not a sociable glad-hander like Tim Lillebo. But of course, I hadn't fully learned yet that the integrity of the messenger is just as important as the message itself.

It struck me that the couple who approached me had probably been listening to Paul Morehead's conspiracy theories. Could I really have dispelled those fabrications? My frustration rode on the coattails of Morehead's oft-repeated epithet, "*You ain't no working man!*" Yes, you sorry son of a bitch, I am! And proud of it.

Still, I believe my refusal to back down, and facing my detractors after all the hostilities, fostered respect. Wallowa County is a bastion of independent hard-asses. I'm convinced refusing to leave and continuing HCPC's work was one reason I didn't experience worse than I did.

High Country News publisher Ed Marston once drew a parallel between me and Andy Kerr living in Wallowa County and a Black person living in Mississippi in the 1950s. I disagreed. Experiencing discrimination due to one's outspoken point of view is far less objectionable than the senseless poison of racial discrimination.

I was hated for what I believed in. The part of me that conjures self-loathing tells me I deserved what I got. Pride tells me I cannot claim to have been misunderstood. If I was, it was my fault.

Looking back with the long eyes of hindsight, I actually got used to being hated. In truth, it didn't bother me at the time because I'd never needed to be popular. What I hated was being misrepresented.

To counter my negative self-image, I would often fantasize about doing some small thing to help one of my political opponents. It would have felt really good.

CHAPTER 27
THE "SALT CREEK MASSACRE" AND YELLOW INK

When considering my experiences with media, a little devil pops up on my shoulder. Mini-Satan wants payback. All the times I got stabbed in the back by journalists with institutional and/or personal agendas accumulate like a flood of yellow pee.

However, I'm not going to use this book as payback with an accounting of all the incidents. Rather, I'll illustrate the power of controlling the ink in discussions over controversial issues and restrict myself to abbreviated editorializing: in fact, journalistic partisanship in northeast Oregon stoked the coals of hatred and misunderstanding.

I'll make my point by providing a comical example. It occurred in August 1990, back then flogging my consciousness with its ridiculousness. It involved a river trip on the Snake River through Hells Canyon, which featured an incident I call the "Salt Creek Massacre." All three primary media outlets in the area, the *Wallowa County Chieftain*, the *La Grande Observer*, and *The Oregonian* pounced on the "story." The contrived controversy eventually spread in a more objective way to a national audience.

I had organized the river trip, which included fifteen fellow activists and some of the politically influential of those times. Carole King joined us, as did fast-rising US Senate Democratic candidate Harry Lonsdale. Harry was engaged in a neck-and-neck duel for a Senate seat against Oregon's political icon, Republican Mark Hatfield.

During our second day on the water, our entourage of five rafts, a couple of kayaks, and my dory pulled into one of the largest camps on the river—Salt Creek. It was a large beach—actually designated as two camps by the Forest Service—before upriver dams starved it of sediment.

There was a jet-boat moored at the upper camp, but we didn't see any people. We pulled into the lower camp and did what campers in the backcountry always do—changed clothes out of doors and bathed in the river, as directed by the Forest Service river ranger, using soap only on shore below the river's high-water line, though a couple of the swimmers were (gasp!) naked.

We also complied with the ranger's instructions to pee in the river, a directive common to all recreationally popular rivers.

Only a couple of folks in our group eventually noticed the jet-boater. None of us realized we were being filmed. Turns out the cameraman was unlimited jet-boat-use advocate Dennis Gratton. He was ensconced among the hackberry trees.

Incidentally, he never saw fit to speak to us even though he knew me well, as we served together on the Forest Service river management plan consensus group.

Apparently, Gratton was fed up with floater depictions of jet-boaters ruining their Hells Canyon recreation experience. He seized an opportunity to illustrate that the reverse is also true. He captured—in the act—two people swimming in the buff, a few people changing out of their damp river clothes next to their tent, and one guy on the far end of the beach urinating into the river without adequate cover.

I didn't hear about Gratton's video until early in 1991, when a Wallowa County friend filled me in. As it turned out, during the previous months, there had been lots of gossip in Wallowa County about video footage depicting "environmentalists behaving badly."

The video eventually made it into the hands of Wallowa County sawmill manager Dave Shriner, one of the vocal critics of protecting public forests. After discovering I was on the trip, Shriner distributed the video to some fellow timber-industry lobbyists. He seemed determined to make a name for himself by exposing supposedly hypocritical forest advocates.

The gossip morphed into a rumor that Indiana Democratic Congressman Jim Jontz had been on the fateful river trip. Jontz had introduced legislation to protect ancient forests nationwide and was a prime target for timber industry character assassination. Actually, Jontz was not on the trip, but that didn't slow Shriner down.

I was racking my brain trying to remember something anyone had done wrong on the trip—like picking an endangered flower or leaving a footprint off an established trail. Motivated by concern over how the video could affect Lonsdale and King in particular, should it go public, I phoned Shriner.

Our conversation quickly leapt into a debate over forest practices. After all, Shriner had the local tree hugger on the phone and couldn't pass up the opportunity to offer some of his deep philosophical insights on forest management.

I listened patiently, unimpressed as Shriner offered several party-line quips, like how forests need to be "managed" (logged) or they're all going to die. I didn't see any reason to retort, although at one point I did retaliate: I asked about his company's recent logging on the face of Mount Howard that had left permanent scars on one of the most cherished viewsheds in the USA—Wallowa Lake. "So you want to responsibly 'manage' forests?" I inquired. "How do you explain trashing the Wallowa Lake viewshed?"

He curtly responded, "We only took the dead and dying."

Repulsed, I said, "I don't care what you took, it looks like shit!"

I moved on to the video. He tried to hit me with a clumsy sucker punch: one of the scenes the jet-boater captured shows me sitting on my dory with a cutting board, surrounded by a dozen people. According to the friend who first told me about the video, Shriner claimed I was "cutting coke or meth" and passing it out to the float trip participants.

Shriner confirmed this allusion during our conversation. When he did, I broke out laughing, after which he tried to distract with some choice quips about how I was trying to destroy the timber industry.

Actually, the contents of the cutting board were tiny curried shrimp, cream cheese, cilantro, and cocktail sauce. The dip was served with a variety of crackers.

The conversation with Shriner ended abruptly when I offered to provide him with the dip recipe and some cash in exchange for a copy of the video. For some strange reason, he agreed. I picked up the video the following day at his sawmill office. The receptionist asked for $10, which I gladly paid. Shriner was nowhere to be seen, so I left the recipe with her and carried the video to the house of a friend who had a VCR.

We couldn't find a darn thing any camper might be even mildly bothered by. The best depiction of the video came from *Outside* magazine, which picked up the story. Their writer described a boring production highlighted by some bad beach volleyball and the one guy relieving himself, his "lazy arc" showing no hint of confrontation.

After he gave me a copy of the video, Shriner gave another to *Wallowa County Chieftain* editor Rick Swart. After years of being a subject of

Swart's partisan reporting and smarmy attack editorials, I rebuke myself for ever speaking with him.

With the video in hand, Swart saw an opportunity to douse sinister local eco-radical Bailey with more toxic ink. But before he did, he obtained a list of trip participants from the Forest Service. After scanning the list, he got hold of a much larger fish.

Thus, he went after wilderness-friendly Senate candidate Lonsdale with his feisty claws bared. Wisely, the ever-clever Carole King had signed the Forest Service river manifest with her former married name, so it never went public that she was on the trip.

Actually, Lonsdale was nowhere to be seen on the videotape. But Swart, who was writing both news stories and editorials on the issue, endeavored to implicate Lonsdale with some of the most biased news stories and grasping attack editorials imaginable.

One editorial bore the headline "Harry Lies." That conclusion came after Swart asked one of Lonsdale's assistants whether Harry had been on a river trip where participants were taking drugs, howling at the moon, and pissing in the river. Of course, she answered, "No." Thus, in Swart's estimation, Harry was a liar. (Amusingly, the "howling" was Carole King's singing.)

Lonsdale later sued the albatross editor. I got a kick out of being deposed by Harry's attorney, with Swart sitting across the table. It provided an opportunity to describe the biased and factually flummoxed reporter and desperately grasping editorial writer whose dashing forays into journalistic irrelevance are the stuff of unsubscribing.

The Forest Service response to the controversy? Wallowa-Whitman National Forest Supervisor Bob Richmond issued a press release stating that his investigation of the Salt Creek incident revealed "no prosecutable violations of law."

I saw Richmond several weeks later at a department store in La Grande. I disregarded his averting eyes and approached him. After some cordial small talk, I jumped right into the subject. "How could there be a violation of law that couldn't be prosecuted?" It took him a moment, but when he got it, he just walked away.

The worst part of the Salt Creek Massacre was that I'd subjected my friends and colleagues to an addled universe of journalistic misrepresentation and contrived conflict. Most told me not to sweat it, anyone with any objectivity could care less. They were right.

It was a shame that with the *Chieftain*, most of my contact was with Swart. The paper had long employed a highly capable and objective reporter, Elaine Dickenson. Swart, who inherited his position as *Chieftain* editor from his father, the paper's owner, insisted on assigning himself to me. His agenda was at a very personal level.

I arrived in Wallowa County too late to work directly with Swart's grandfather, Gwen Coffin. By reputation, Mr. Coffin was a talented writer and courageous journalist who was not afraid to buck the local status quo.

I'll end this fateful recollection with an excerpt from a letter to Swart sent by trip participant, friend, and fellow logger/forest advocate George Atiyeh. After informing Swart that he was indeed *the* George Atiyeh, nephew of Oregon's former two-term Republican governor, co-owner of a mining company and a logging company, he hit him with this: "Not only do you feel we shouldn't have pissed in the river after the Forest Service told us to, you seem to think a guy hiding in the bushes filming us has more rights than my thirteen-year-old daughter's privacy at a backcountry campsite where privacy is universally expected."

* * *

Dick Cockle of La Grande was the *Oregonian* stringer. He was a factory of innumerable political and nonpolitical stories for his employer, which is somewhat of an enigma. The *Oregonian* is a decidedly Republican-leaning newspaper located in arguably the most liberal city in the United States. In fact, Bill Clinton is the first Democratic presidential candidate the *Oregonian* ever endorsed over its then-140-year existence.

The *Oregonian* editors perceived Cockle as a local voice from his perch in La Grande, with his finger on the pulse of conservative Northeast Oregon. Actually, Cockle was philosophically aligned with the most radical right-wing fringe in the region. In personal conversations, he expressed his adoration of Claude Dallas, who executed two unarmed Idaho game wardens after they caught him poaching deer, and Bo Gritz, the racist-appearing presidential candidate.

Cockle's political reporting fixated on the hope for some kind of revolution by cowboys and loggers. At each interview, I could feel him trying to yank a quote out of me that might lend credence to his hopeful theory.

Recognizing the importance of the regional audience of the *Oregonian*, I eventually protested to Cockle's editor about the reporter's consistent bias. I managed to set up a meeting with Cockle and the newspaper's designated environmental reporter, Kathie Durbin. With Durbin's articulation of how northeast Oregon environmental issues are important to Portland readers, the editor was convinced to assign stories on northeast Oregon environmental issues to Durbin. She was a stellar writer and objective reporter.

With the *La Grande Observer*, I struggled to find this newspaper's soul. Its reporters came and went with the wind. In 1993, the paper hired Brian White. I put my best foot forward with him, hoping only for some small hint of objectivity. I told White we knew the Boise Cascade timber spokespersons were going to get the majority of the *cookies*, a term White's editor Dave Stave used once in my presence to illustrate his alleged revulsion to journalistic favoritism. All we wanted, I explained to White, was to be accurately portrayed.

I had hope after White's first couple of stories on public land issues. He was a good writer, and he took the time to conduct research for his stories. But after one front-page article about the effigy hanging of me and Andy Kerr, all hopes crumbled like a stack of half-eaten Oreos.

When the paper hit the newsstand, White called me with profuse apologies. As it turned out, Stave had rewritten White's story, not only altering facts, but changing my quotes. One of his changes stood out—I had told White during the interview that I was not going to be intimidated by effigy hangings or death threats. Stave changed the quote to "Bailey *was being intimidated* (by local hostilities)."

I set up a meeting with Stave, White, and the paper's publisher, Bob Moody. I confronted Stave over the changed quote. But he gave no explanations and made no offer for correction. White disappeared a couple of months later. His replacement turned out to be a purveyor of the same old partisan junk I was used to. I was lucky there wasn't a television station within two hundred miles.

My local media adventures were a valuable lesson in not taking myself too seriously. I validate my mistakes in that I was the only "out" wilderness advocate in Wallowa County and thus compelled to try and provide the pro-wilderness point of view.

My outspokenness and emotional attachment to my cause often worked against me. Initially, while doing an interview, it was an assumption I was speaking to an objective person open to rational points of view. Bias was not something to be considered. And I never considered the full gravity of being presented as a person of repute to the thousands of people who read the local papers. My naiveté got me into hot water early on in the game.

I now look back down the barrel of the loose cannon I sometimes was, and see where I went wrong. On many occasions, I had lit the fuse of bad stories by being direct and colorful with my criticism of the Forest Service and my unbridled passion toward my cause.

Once the die of being a "radical environmentalist" was cast, trying to reshape the mold proved near impossible. It didn't take long to realize that with local press, letters to the editor won't compensate for misrepresentation in news stories and editorials. I stopped writing them.

In retrospect, I would gladly pay the price of bad local press with positive national press. HCPC rocked at the regional and national levels. Ironically, I exploited the story hook provided by the hostilities toward me from the rural populace, a hook baited by hostile local media.

It would have been wise to keep clips of all the stories published by Swart, Cockle, and the *Observer*. On the other hand, I can look at it as yellow water under the bridge, washed clean by time.

THE TROUT-FILLED MINAM RIVER

CHAPTER 28
SPEAKING OF SEMANTICS

Through exploits in media relations, and after experiencing the crafty manipulation of terminologies by the Forest Service, I came to recognize the importance of proper language. The Forest Service calls clearcuts "created meadows" and "wildlife openings." It calls soil erosion from those clearcuts "activity-generated soil-sediment output." Logging is "treatment" and "restoration." Many forest advocates have adopted those deceptively sanitized terms.

Brock Evans helped set me on a path to convince the forest-advocacy movement to speak to the general public rather than to itself. He began by encouraging forest defenders to stop using the term "timber harvest" to describe logging. "Harvest" doesn't articulate clearcutting giant, seven-hundred-year-old trees and ripping up the ground removing them.

By speaking only to ourselves, the movement allowed political adversaries to brand us, and we made no attempt to brand them. We were "extremist, radical environmentalists," while our detractors were "wise-use advocates." This false context doesn't just ferment in taverns, but also in religious institutions, workplaces, and homes.

My campaign began by explaining to anyone who would listen why I abhor the term "environmentalist." That label doesn't tell the general public who the respective champions of planetary causes are. The cultish-sounding term could apply to anyone—from organic gardeners to urban greenspace proponents, whale defenders, or supporters of renewable energy. Pro-nuclear-power interests in the northeastern United States used to refer to the "no-nukes" constituency as "tree huggers." Huh?

"Environmentalist" may be one of the most draconian and misused terms ever contrived. Virtually anyone could qualify if they claim to support anything that might loosely be considered pro-environment. My poker-playing friend-but-adversary Jerry Perren used to refer to me as a "pseudo-environmentalist." He was the true environmentalist, he said, because he supported "forest management," i.e., logging he claimed would help all the critters in the forest.

I was once in a La Grande pub with Nez Perce tribal ally and friend Levi Holt when, at the table next to us, four middle-aged men were engaged in deep talk. Eventually, we could hear the word in subtle undertones—"mumble, mumble, *environmentalist*"—as they tossed glances in our direction.

Finally, after additional grog, one of them turned to me and inquired in a mock-neutral tone, "Aren't you an environmentalist?"

Levi looked amused. I hesitated, then shot back, "You tell me what an environmentalist is, and I'll tell you whether I'm one of 'em or not."

* * *

Now we segue to the worst splat of slanderous excrement: "ecoterrorist" is by far the most egregious example of the wilderness movement's verbal self-immolation. It was invented by one of our most vitriolic detractors—Ron Arnold. Worshipper of the reverend Sun Myung Moon and advocate for murdering environmentalists, Arnold showed his verbal acumen by contriving the term "wise use" to describe fanatically anti-environmental mouth-breathers.

And yet, even when the ecoterrorist term was adopted by the media, the eco-movement failed to rebuke it—let alone counter-attack—for fear of appearing sympathetic to illegal acts in defense of the land. "Ecoterrorist" will be a festering carcass hanging from the neck of wilderness proponents until it is aggressively undressed.

I was shocked after finding an episode of *Real Time with Bill Maher* in 2018 where the allegedly liberal comedian used the word "ecoterrorism" as if it was a perfectly acceptable term to describe a person who had committed an illegal act in defense of nature. Bill Whitaker, a journalist on *60 Minutes*, referred to an "ecoterrorist" in his 2022 story about attacks against the US power grid.

"Ecoterrorism" is a sick hoax of a term. Placing people who pour sugar into bulldozer fuel tanks or pull up road survey stakes into the same class as people who fly airplanes into skyscrapers with the intent to kill as many people as possible, is the pinnacle of semantic abuse.

People who violate the law to protect land are not terrorists. They are, by literal definition, "saboteurs" and/or "vandals." Thus, the term "ecotage," that has been used by many people who espouse illegal means of defending land.

"Ecoterrorist" has stained the term *eco*, which in literal parlance comes from the Latin *oeco* (household) and from the Greek *oikos* (house). Is ambitiously protecting your home "terrorism?"

Using the conjunctive term *ecoterrorist* as a model, it would be more accurate to refer to the people responsible for 9/11 as *Muslimterrorists*. People who bomb abortion clinics are *pro-lifeterrorists*. The gun-slinging ranchers who occupied, shut down, and vandalized the Malheur National Wildlife Refuge are *rancherterrorists*. But if ranchers were so described, the ranching community would have screamed bloody murder. Why didn't wilderness advocates?

A federal law passed in 2001 requires stiffer penalties for "ecoterrorism" than other vandalism. Should eco-saboteurs face worse punishment because they are moved by principle rather than for personal gain, or amusement? If a company hires a pyromaniac to torch their warehouse in order to collect the insurance money, or someone engages in mindless property damage just for fun, how have they earned less severe consequences?

In Washington State, the person who shot and killed two endangered wolves was sentenced to probation and a $38,500 fine. Conversely, under the "ecoterrorism" statute, two people who torched unoccupied buildings at an invasive ski resort in Colorado were sentenced to twelve years in prison. Is that equal justice under law?

The legislators who were afraid to speak against the ecoterrorism law should be ashamed of themselves, as should the eco-advocates who should have lobbied them to oppose it. With strategic messaging, opposing the bill wouldn't have implied support for illegal activities, it would support fair treatment of all lawbreakers and prevent staining of the lovely word "eco."

I cannot stress too often that I am not an environmentalist or ecoterrorist. I am a wilderness advocate, just as those who want to restore native fisheries are salmon advocates. People endeavoring to protect species from extinction are wildlife advocates. "Advocate" presents an image of a caped hero coming to the rescue as opposed to elitist hypocrites wearing spandex, living in huge log homes, and haughtily trampling the working class, as "environmentalists" are viewed in the eyes of much of the general public.

Detractors of those who work to protect nature love to play the hypocrisy card: "*You oppose logging but you live in a wood house!*" It is imperative that eco-advocates explain that we do not oppose using wood, we work to minimize the need for it, seek ecologically responsible alternatives, and compel sustainable forestry. Society does not provide affordable alternatives to using wood, so we are working to change that.

As for hypocrisy, if the guilt card is being thrown down, let's play it on those who hunt the wildlife whose habitat we protect over their objections to wilderness protection. The double standard is best demonstrated by those who drink the clean water, breathe the clean air, and hike or pack in the wilderness areas environmental advocates protect over their objections.

One does not advance their cause by speaking only to their funders and members—the already-enlightened who cheer the "rah-rah" insider dialogue. The often flagrantly quotable Andy Kerr, the self-described "turd in the punch bowl," used to point to a survey that showed "environmentalists" to be among the most credible people in America. But a few years later, the same study showed environmentalists' credibility had tumbled dramatically.

That downfall may be partly attributed to Kerr's own characterization of a pro-timber, government-proposed northern spotted owl management plan as tantamount to "sending a drunk logger into the woods with a shotgun." This was the worst message that could have been sent to the general public. Not only did it unjustly disparage working people, it perpetuated the false conflict between loggers and "environmentalists" when the problem of public forest ecosystem collapse was the Forest Service.

I respect Kerr's impressive body of work to protect wilderness. Still, when he got hold of the microphone, including the cover of *Time* magazine, he clamped down on it like a praying mantis. And to keep it, he became abrasively quotable. One of the more dangerous places to be is between Kerr and a television camera.

Eco-advocates' poor use of words has left Middle America bewildered. Here are some examples of our deficiencies:

Most forest advocates use the word "roads" to describe logging roads in the national forests. In fact, these are bulldozer defacements ripping up slopes and causing hillsides to collapse into streams, ruining the habitat of native fish. Roads facilitate wildlife disturbance and benefit poachers. They're an artery for spreading invasive weeds via motor vehicles.

There are over 100,000 miles of logging roads on the national forests, and the damage they have done—and continue to do—is horrendous.

But in the minds of people not directly involved in forest advocacy, "roads" on the national forests conjures visions of placid country tracks fresh out of a John Denver song, leading to a nice fishing hole or beloved campsite. These portents of ecological ruination need to be described as "road cuts" or "incisions."

Opponents of livestock occupying federal land use the word "grazing" to refer to that general activity. But for most people, "grazing" doesn't equate to invasive cows defecating in once crystal-clear streams; on the contrary, the word conjures images of farmer McDonald's dairy cows in a lovely meadow surrounded by a white picket fence, or people at a party eating chips and salsa. "Livestock" comes nearer to the image of hordes of taxpayer-subsidized, invasive bovines, owned by industrial conglomerates, spreading weeds and trampling wildflower meadows under merciless hooves. "Razing" would be more accurate for what the livestock does to millions of acres of federal land. I have no problem with "grazing" so long as it's conducted by elk, deer, bighorn sheep, or antelope.

The misuse of language has also been applied to the artificially-created tubs of water behind dams. These are not, as dam proponents describe them, "lakes," nor "pools." Nature didn't form them. They are "impoundments," or "reservoirs." The dam builders try to make them seem attractive when they're really a once-living section of river that is now a dead, stagnant puddle.

I once asked a coalition of salmon advocates to consider an alternative to announcing they want to "breach" dams. *Breach* is a negative word; e.g., breach of contract, breech birth. People don't want to support "breach." The public should be encouraged to support something positive, so let's "retire" those ill-conceived fish-killing dams and "restore" the rivers.

I once met some Shoshone tribal elders before a Federal Energy Regulatory Commission (FERC) conference to discuss the relicensing of the three dams above Hells Canyon. Their candid insights inspired me to take a carefree leap. During my speech, I repeatedly referenced "retiring" the Hells Canyon dams. I then proceeded to explain how we could accomplish that. I proposed a way to finance the retirement of the salmon-killing dams—hold a lottery. The lottery winner gets to push the plunger that sets off the dynamite charges blowing up the dams. The Shoshones loved it. The FERC officials didn't.

Was I violating my own edict? Actually, I didn't feel espousing the legal dismantling of dams was at all harmful, it was a comical but serious proposal to fund dam removal.

I once sat on a panel to select a media consultant who would plan media strategy for a campaign to protect eastside Oregon and Washington forests. One of the consultants told us, "Poll after poll shows the vast majority of the American populace supports protecting public lands and ancient forests. Take those poll numbers to your senators and congresspeople!"

Really? Politicians do their own focus groups, and know which issues get them elected or defeated. When voters fill out their ballot, they don't cast their vote based on a candidate's position on wilderness or public land determinations. Those are not even in the top three for the voting majority. The ecological protection movement needs to make its cause a top three issue. To do so, we must address a broader audience, invoking the horrific specter of climate change and the role of intact forests in combating it. We must use language that eloquently produces the images, both positive and negative, that appeal to Middle Americans, particularly those who enjoy the outdoors and public land.

If advocates for our planet's health start speaking in illustratively favorable terms to the entire audience, we stand a chance of making respect for and love of our homeland an admirable quality. Heroes for the Earth can be found on every bike path, soccer field, hiking trail, and street corner—advocates for nature just need to learn how to talk to them.

SACAJAWEA PEAK, THE HIGHEST POINT IN THE WALLOWAS

CHAPTER 29

DEPARTURE, PHASE ONE

Despite my fixation over the accommodating use of semantics, I could never find the words to describe my dark feelings.

In July 2004, I experienced a mental collapse. The workload was oppressive—it included a critical lawsuit challenging the HCNRA regs and an attempted escalation of the national-preserve campaign, all confounded by two years of HCPC funding shortfalls brought on by the 2001 US economic downturn. I stayed away from everyone and practically everything but my bedroom for four days.

When I gathered up enough ambition to go outside, I pedaled up to Wallowa Lake, swam toward the middle, then dove down deep and let the air in my lungs alone take me back to the surface. My arms and legs seemed leaden. I slowly swam back to shore beset by confusion and fettered purpose.

Overwhelming thoughts of gloom and dejection translated to a rage against myself. I was convinced walking away from my organization would remove the cold, wet, black blanket that covered me.

I retreated to a friend's cabin in Montana and tried to make a decision. Thankfully, the refuge on the edge of the Bob Marshall Wilderness cleared my head. Objectivity and a sense of rational self-analysis ensued. The fear of leaving my organization and casting the fate of the Hells Canyon-Wallowa Ecosystem to others gave way to the painful recognition that I was no longer capable of carrying on.

In November 2004, I retired from HCPC. It didn't matter whether or not my accomplishments validated the decision. My sanity was at stake.

I wrote a letter of resignation to my board of directors and dismissed pleas that I remain. The board didn't fully understand the reasons for my exit; I shied away from providing any details.

I stayed on just long enough to help the board select my replacement. When I walked away in March of 2005, I did so completely, with no fanfare nor even notification of my departure outside the immediate HCPC circle. I didn't just leave HCPC, I abandoned all ties with the wilderness movement.

Tim Lillebo was the only person with whom I ever shared details of my reasons for departure. He was sympathetic, but concentrated on one question: "What will you do now to heal yourself?" He encouraged me to stay involved in the cause in some capacity. I think he feared—as much as I did—for HCPC's future. But he also seemed to recognize that without activism, I might lose my reasons for existing. He was correct; Tim was a very wise man.

After word of my retirement got out, calls for interviews from local and regional media flowed in. I ignored them all. I wanted complete anonymity and a clean departure.

But my vanishing act had unforeseen consequences. I should have more intensively mentored the new executive director, and more intimately shared with the HCPC board the intricacies of, and rationale for, our programs and strategies.

There was, however, one advantage to my abrupt departure. Now that I was no longer involved in activism and out of the spotlight, the overt hostility that had become a normal aspect of life in the Wallowa Valley noticeably subsided. The death threats disappeared and the angry glances and bird-flippings became infrequent. It came almost as a shock to realize the scenario of no hostilities was something I'd need to adapt to.

Life proceeded clumsily. I avoided intensively seeking work, only toying with ideas for a new career. I only half realized I was unfit for any job. I spent most of my time in the outback, on wild rivers and long hikes, or in the company of dear but distantly located friends. I was trying to bathe in the pleasant darkness of anonymity, but I was far removed from the prospect of healing.

I expected the depression to decrease with my departure. But I soon realized the darkness wasn't going to be tossed out along with the job. In fact, Tim was right—it got worse. Having lost the satisfaction of doing good works, I felt worthless.

But there was no turning back: I accepted that the activism stresses had pounded on my affliction like a self-wielded hammer. Amid the throes of self-loathing, the workload had cloned itself like tilted piles of madness, igniting despair.

I felt a terrible, consuming emptiness. The pursuit of joy and the myth of relaxation became unachievable flashes of faded recollections. I revisited every failure and indiscretion, and they overwhelmed every positive thought. I was stuck in an inescapable catch-22. Yet my revulsion to being weak and the despicable prospect of surrender to Dagloth triggered a pride that allowed me to stay on my feet.

I needed income, as I had no pension, only a few thousand dollars in a retirement account I had managed to set up after the HCPC board approved reimbursement of back pay at the end of the '90s, when HCPC was flush. I'd previously gone without pay for an accumulated total of almost a year.

I went back to the job I have loved more than any other—river guiding. But as much as I love guiding, it's still stressful work that demands intensive social interaction. My need to be alone was deepening.

I wasn't sure about financial survival by river guiding five months of the year. Plus, I had no health insurance amid deteriorating mental capacity. I searched for work less stressful than guiding. At the same time, I feared not having the energy and temperament to be a viable employee at any job.

I sought full-time employment outside activism, including driving a snowplow, working at a state park, and other jobs I thought would be relatively stress-free—but was never hired. Despite my meager lifestyle, after four years of doing nothing but occasional guiding, my savings were circling the drain. I rebuked myself for being overdependent on money.

I steered clear of any form of activism—paid or volunteer—for the first few years of my "retirement." I didn't want any news of the movement and its politics, and avoided any mention of it among my circle of friends. But with my job search outside the movement falling flat, I eventually saw no option but to seek work where I had the most experience.

I had used virtually none of the political capital I might have accumulated over my years of activism. Eventually, I convinced myself I might be able to handle an eco-based job that didn't involve leadership or too much responsibility. I had a solid resume, or so I thought.

I tried setting out a shingle as a consultant, and I applied for a variety of jobs in the advocacy sector. But I quickly discovered I had no political capital, as every attempt to get work in the eco-movement produced nothing. But that was probably a good thing.

I'd gotten to the point that I needed to address my condition or to just check out and call it a life. Enter the lab coats: in 2009, I got connected to local psychiatrist Joel Rice via a close friend who was seeing him. I already knew Joel from a common social connection, so there was some informality in our doctor/patient relationship. At an informal session, the doctor saw my affliction.

After some basic Q and A, Dr. Rice traced my history like a simple map. All my life I strove to be at arm's length from society, solitary in the wild, and wedded to the rural. This, he said, was a subconscious mechanism of self-protection. His observations made perfect sense. I was embarrassed I had never figured it out for myself.

My drive to be a recluse had increased upon arrival to Wallowa County at age twenty-five. But my desire to save wilderness dominated, and I wound up doing absolutely the worst thing possible—I leapt recklessly into the spotlight of public controversy, eventually becoming a harried figure, widely despised and regularly chastised, *exposed*, in the worst way.

Dr. Rice diagnosed me with clinical depression, the result of an innate imbalance of serotonin, endorphins, melatonin, dopamine, and other mood-regulating brain chemicals. He also confirmed I had post-traumatic stress syndrome—the consequence of being out of my element during my twenty-six years of activism, dealing with hostility and conflict every single day. It was startling, and humiliating. I considered PTSS to be the condition of assault victims and war veterans. I felt weak for the diagnosis.

I took on a philosophical outlook, and tried to convince myself the depression was as natural as the storms that beset the planet. "We're all part of the balance of life," I told myself. "Be like the mountain!" I would often shout to myself.

With Dr. Rice's help, I began to understand clinical depression—it's not cause-based; my experiences didn't cause the depression. I'd be depressed anyway, the stress only exacerbated it. I could have plenty of friends, a planet full of protected wilderness, my every wish granted, and I'd still be depressed on a regular basis.

Clinical depression is very different from the experiences of people who dive off the fourteenth floor because they lost their shirts in the stock market. I came to understand that the difficulties of my work life gave me reasons to explain the depression, and thus, I didn't recognize it as something inherent in my brain that could be treated.

I hearkened back to whispered family lore about the grandfather I never met, who left my grandmother and my mother when Mom was fifteen. He wound up in a mental institution. But I couldn't just blame it on DNA. That's a cop-out even to the tortured mind. I needed to believe it could be fixed.

I eventually agreed to things I'd never thought of doing—taking medication to change my brain chemistry, and beginning therapy. After experimenting with various anti-depressant medications for a year, we found a combination that seemed to help. My moods were evening out enough that handling a full-time job seemed possible. I had a tough time with the side effects, particularly a decrease in energy level and passion, but persevered.

In 2010, I hit what would in normal circumstances be an employment jackpot. I was a top candidate for a job overseeing the Dolores River protection campaign with the San Juan Citizens Alliance, a highly regarded eco-advocacy group in Southwest Colorado. Simultaneously, I was offered a job with Canyon Explorations, one of the premiere Grand Canyon river-outfitting companies, in a guide/managerial position. I took the Grand Canyon job because I felt it would be less stressful since it didn't involve activism. I moved to Flagstaff, Arizona.

Just before accepting the job, I made the common error of going off the medication because I wanted to be rid of the side effects. And besides, I figured I was on the road to being "healed." Big mistake.

Simple though the Canyon Explorations job was compared to the complicated tasks of being executive director of a nonprofit, its stresses were more intense than I could handle. I fumbled around in a fog, trying to hide my increasing mental anguish.

I decided to go back on the meds and was assisted by a psychiatrist at the Whale Foundation, which serves river guides who suffer with mental issues—for some reason, relatively common in the trade. The foundation is named for a guide who committed suicide.

The Whale psychiatrist coordinated with Dr. Rice, and soon I was re-committed to the antidepressants. But there was no immediate relief, and the outfitting job wasn't a good fit anyway. I enjoyed working with the clan of river guides, but being constantly micromanaged by the three company owners became nauseating. In November 2010, I returned to Joseph, feeling I was basically unfit to work at all.

New afflictions popped up out of nowhere—an auto-immune

disorder, spinal arthritis, and a bad case of West Nile virus, whose symptoms mysteriously persisted over several years. The mental and physical afflictions, and the side effects of the medications, became a potpourri of confused diagnoses and treatment. There seemed no way to pinpoint what condition or medication was causing the various symptoms. It felt like my feelings had been stuffed into a blender and cranked to puree. Still, in beleaguered progression, the march toward recovery continued.

I believe the physical issues that had developed were a direct result of the stresses of my activist work. At my retirement, I was as physically healthy as any fifty-three-year-old. It was frightening how quickly the downhill slide came on.

The self-termination urge arose again. But I began therapy, something I would have scoffed at even a few years earlier.

I financed medical treatment with money I saved working for Canyon Explorations. But I couldn't work and didn't know how I was going to support myself beyond the next few months. So, I filed for and received Social Security Disability. It's something I admit with great reluctance, as pride brooks no concession to weakness. All my life, strength had been my defining trait.

Languishing in Joseph, I didn't mind being the outcast so long as I was alone. The celebrity disgusted me more than the hostility anyway. I managed to do a good amount of hiking, and while I walked alone up those Wallowa Mountain trails, my favorite fantasy was that I'd remained a blue-collar guy with a simple life and maybe even a family. My successes as an activist were afterthoughts.

The truth is, despite my independent nature, being the hated outcast had chewed away patiently, like a determined stream on a sandstone wall. And now, even after being removed from activism, my guilt and self-consciousness lingered. People had called me evil. Even after leaving HCPC, I believed there was a grain of truth to that accusation.

My therapist tried to reassure, offering such comforts like "The majority of people who bear the misdirected brand 'mentally ill' are like you, neither irrational nor incoherent" or "They are not delusional or homicidal. Lots of people not diagnosed as depressed with PTSS are emotionally unstable. There are as wide a variety of afflictions and degrees of afflictions as there are people who are branded with the label. *You're not actually crazy.*"

It took a lot of time to crank up the gumption to tell anyone other than Tim about the diagnosis. Finally, I discussed it with the closest of friends and family. Subsequently, I learned the only people who will ever really understand clinical depression are those who have it. And if you're lucky enough not to be one of them, take comfort in not knowing what it's like.

Some friends asked, "Where did this come from? You never seemed sick to me."

I still occasionally riddled myself with guilt for discussing my affliction. Everyone deals with one medical condition or another. "Stop whining," I told myself. "Suck it up and regain your strength! That aspect of the psyche remains," I insisted. "It's just sleeping. Attend to yourself as you attended to the land."

I was constantly suppressing the consideration that even a slight imbalance in the treatment would allow the depression to leap up like a persistent weed in the garden of consciousness. Yet I found great comfort in knowing the demon could be caged, even if temporarily.

I still wonder whether my inherent love of wilderness has some connection with the depression. There's no question the eco-psyche instincts are far deeper than the desire to protect wilderness as a personal refuge from the ills of society, and to satisfy the desire for solitude. While comparing my own moods to the moods of the world, parallels emerged—there is no distinction between healing myself and healing the planet.

LAYERED ARROYOS NEAR THE IMNAHA RIVER

CHAPTER 30
THE SCOURGE OF QUID PRO QUO WILDERNESS

"Healing" became a mantra. Little did I know my compulsion for it would segue into the wilderness movement, the cause I'd dedicated my life to.

At my retirement from HCPC in 2005, the forest protection movement had been gravitating toward collaboration as a principle of activism. It began when reliable science was showing that logging and fire suppression had done serious damage to forest ecosystems, resulting in unnatural accumulations of slash and dense timber, subsequently increasing the risk of unnaturally large wildfires.

This equation was attractive to the timber industry and the Forest Service because one obvious solution to overly dense forests was to reduce fuel loading via logging. This created a climate where logging interests and forest advocates could come together to work toward win-win solutions. At first, I jumped on the bandwagon. But in the aftermath of my retirement, after further consideration of the issue, its causes, and the gravity of the response, I reconsidered.

I welcomed collaboration among forest advocates with timber workers. But I was skeptical of the involvement of timber companies, narrow-minded rural county commissioners, and the Forest Service. Yet the advocates, including some of the more prominent and dedicated organizations, were unconditionally embracing collaboration as the wave of the future.

In early 2011, with a measure of my mental stability restored, I cautiously began to monitor the activities of wilderness and forest-protection proponents from a safe distance. I was compelled. It wasn't enough to know I'd done good works. I needed to know the movement I'd dedicated the better part of my life to was standing tall, and that my organization's accomplishments would endure.

The first activities I began to monitor came after learning about wilderness bills that were being developed collaboratively, wherein wilderness proponents were agreeing to give away land to anti-wilderness constituencies in exchange for designating wilderness elsewhere.

The first one I focused on was an Idaho bill in the works. The pro-wilderness player was the Idaho Conservation League (ICL), a well-heeled statewide organization. ICL had been intent on passing a wilderness bill protecting the Boulder–White Cloud Mountains for decades. They found that recently elected Idaho Republican Congressman Mike Simpson, a far more reasonable member of the Idaho delegation than most, is a big fan of the Boulder–White Cloud Roadless Area.

Lying mostly within the Sawtooth National Recreation Area, Boulder–White Cloud is a half-million-acre intact block of wild country defined by stately mountains, and graced with idyllic alpine meadows and sparkling, trout-filled streams. It's one of the largest unfractured blocks of unprotected roadless land in the United States. To its credit, ICL convinced Simpson that wilderness designation was important to protect this incredible place.

But Simpson and ICL are not the only ones who covet the Boulder–White Cloud. Its secluded trails are used by members of a backcountry motorcyclists club. Just as sad, the roadless area is within Custer County, ruled by a rabidly anti-wilderness herd of county commissioners. In order to provide political cover for Simpson, ICL agreed to engage in collaborative discussions with commissioners and the motorcyclists' lobbying partner, led by the aforementioned Sandra Mitchell. They negotiated within the confines of the roadless area without consideration of the thousands of miles of motor-accommodating trails already open to motorized use, while there are so few large roadless areas left.

I would have begun discussions by convincing Simpson to dismiss the concerns of a handful of motorcycle riders, whose self-interest is nonsensical when compared to the opportunity to protect such a majestic place. What would be the bikers' irrevocable loss? They'd have to ride horses to see the Boulder–White Cloud? Motorbike somewhere else? I'd be willing to bet the total number of motorbikers who use the Boulder–White Cloud Roadless Area is well under a hundred. Are we now giving away hundreds of thousands of acres of primitive wild Earth so a few dozen people can invade it with motor bikes?

When ICL chose to negotiate a bill with the motorhead lobby, it conceded that pro-motor provisions would inevitably be included in the bill and that most or all of the roadless area that is used by motorcyclists would be left unprotected.

Eventually, the price ICL was willing to pay to accomplish the primarily organizational goal of designating a Boulder–White Cloud Wilderness was staggering: they first conceded to designating less than 300,000 acres of the 500,000-acre roadless area as wilderness and leaving the rest dedicated to motorbiking and whatever other wilderness-degrading activity might come along. They supported dividing the portion of the roadless area that would become wilderness into three pieces, pierced by dedicated motorized and mountain-bike trails. In addition, they would buy off local ranchers by precluding water rights for the new wilderness. That meant minimum stream flows could not be established in order to protect native fish.

The next item on the purchasing block was the giveaway of seven thousand acres of federal land within the Sawtooth National Recreation Area to Custer County, so it could gain a windfall by selling the land to resort developers. Finally, ICL supported diluting the Sawtooth National Recreation Area by overlaying it with another designation that would prioritize motorized use. What a price to pay for establishing a fractured wilderness area.

The impetus for designating the Sawtooth National Recreation Area in 1972 was a massive molybdenum mine proposed on Castle Peak within the Boulder–White Cloud Roadless Area. Yet ICL agreed to buy off its political opponents to pass a diluted Boulder–White Cloud bill when the only present threat was the motorheads.

Admittedly, ICL should not be blamed for trying to take advantage of a political opportunity. Since 1981, Idaho—the state with more roadless land than any outside Alaska—has been besieged by a congressional delegation that was for the most part vehemently opposed to protecting wilderness. Passing a wilderness bill in Idaho should be considered a stellar achievement. But therein lies the issue: at what cost would such a bill come? Does ICL deserve accolades for passing a wilderness bill in Idaho, arguably the most difficult state in which to do so, while setting a terrible legislative precedent?

ICL's justification for accepting the compromises in order to pass the bill was what I call "semantic accolades," self-congratulatory milestones like "passing the first wilderness bill for Idaho in twenty-five years" that benefitted the organization more than the cause of wilderness protection. This misplacement of priorities is deplorable on its face, but in the bigger picture it separates the protection of wilderness from the ultimate objective of restoring biodiversity and combating climate change.

I was distraught, and expressed my dismay to ICL executive director Rick Johnson, whom I'd considered a worthy ally.

After learning of Rick's unbending determination to pass a bill—any bill—I wound up joining with a good number of other noteworthy wilderness advocates in publicly opposing it. ICL's strategy to pass the bill became so internally controversial, they set up a chat room consisting of wilderness advocates, funders, and other allies. Unwisely, as it turns out, I joined in the discussions.

The concern I registered most firmly was that the dilution of an existing national recreation area by overlaying it with a less protective designation could simply not be allowed. It would set a legislative precedent for devious declassification of protected areas that could, and likely would, open the door to weakening protection to many cherished places, including the Hells Canyon National Recreation Area.

Oregon's Republican congressional representatives for the second district, which includes the HCNRA, had been looking to weaken the protection mandated by the HCNRA Act for years. But they had no legislative precedent for declassification.

With a legislative precedent set by the Boulder–White Cloud bill supported by a noteworthy pro-wilderness organization, Oregon's second-district congressional representatives could beckon HCPC and its allies to the table in a "collaborative" process with local resource interests and hostile county commissioners to "revisit" the HCNRA Act. It would make the dismantling of the act look neat and fair. HCPC would be compelled to participate, or be framed as "uncooperative" if it refused.

This made the Boulder–White Cloud issue personal for me, and it got even more personal. I began to lose my cool.

Wilderness advocates who were opposing the legislation were told by Rick Johnson that ICL was working to strengthen the bill by removing some of the negative provisions in committee. A week later, I learned via an ally who was lobbying in DC on a different bill that ICL lobbyists were actually making the rounds to committee members asking them to oppose all amendments.

Immersed in anger, I hastily wrote a two-page diatribe claiming ICL's motives were not pure, they could not be trusted, and the bill needed to be killed. I unwisely posted the letter in the chat room. I knew three minutes after clicking "send" I'd made a terrible mistake. In losing my composure, I also lost the respect of allies I deeply respect and to whom I owe a lot, most notably The Wilderness Society's Craig Gehrke. This might also have been the reason for Del Langbauer's scorn.

Still, I carry the banner of restoring the strength of the wilderness movement. There can be no fair negotiation over roadless areas. Notwithstanding other anti-ecosystem concessions to pass wilderness bills, it's not compromise to look only at the remaining roadless areas, slice them up, and pass them out to the vast "user constituencies." The reality that less than 20 percent of federal land remains untouched clearly shows to any objective mind that the compromise has already been made, and wilderness lost. When there's so little left, there's no logical reason, other than economic vanity, to protect all of it, with no conciliatory reciprocation to those who want to exploit it.

I do not regret my stark opposition to ICL's bill. Yet that brief foray told me that, even after several years of retirement, my anger and general emotional instability were far from healed. I was still obsessed with my cause, and obsession dilutes objectivity. My enemies weren't just the people who were destroying wilderness. They came to include the people on my team who didn't seem as dedicated as I was. Seeing the wilderness movement through the tainted glasses of a tortured mind blocked out everything good and expanded the bad.

When I decided to act in opposition to what I saw as untenable positions, I was relegated to standing on the sidelines throwing stones at the players on the field—a two-bit heckler.

I should have stayed out of all forms of activism, at least the public forums. Instead, I joined the lunatic fringe, a status to which I'd seen other advocates condemned. I recall my pity for the poor souls thus branded, but I had joined the club. What I'd be remembered for was not my contributions to the cause, but my ire toward my cohorts. But to sit by and, as I saw it then, allow the movement to deteriorate could not be borne. Yet I needed to heal myself before I could assume the hubris of trying to heal the wilderness movement.

HEATHER AT GLACIER LAKE, EAGLE CAP WILDERNESS

CHAPTER 31

DEPARTURE, PHASE TWO

About the time I returned to Joseph from my outfitting adventure in Flagstaff in 2010, the wolf issue was dominating local media. Wolves had established packs in the Wallowa territory. As a result, the more rabid anti-wolf forces needed a local demon toward whom they could vent their frustrations.

I caught wind of my name reappearing as one of the wolf-enablers. Rumors emerged that the radical Bailey, commonly known to still be haunting the streets of Joseph and remote trails in the outback, was really behind the "wolf conspiracy."

Local unaffiliated activist Wally Sykes took most of the heat, and gracefully. Still, it was widely known that HCPC had been the driving force behind protecting wolves. Thus, the local status-quo scuttlebutt factory once again spat out its cerebrally-challenged vitriol. My past was catching up with me.

There was no escape from my local reputation. It would endure as long as I was there, regardless of whether or not I was still involved in environmental politics. Self-loathing via that old-time feeling of being exposed and hated resurfaced. Once again, townie eyes glared. The pitiful routine of frequently getting flipped off returned, as did being ignored at some local business establishments.

I repudiated myself for believing all that hate had been rinsed away. With its renewal, I dug my heels in once again, and held fast to the principle of never allowing persecution to alter personal routines. Yet I was sick to death of the whole routine.

In assessing the situation, I considered my indictment on the Forest Service's phonied-up chainsaw theft charge back in 1982. I was vulnerable in a place where justice was based largely on which side of the political fence you inhabit.

It was in 2012 that I had my aforementioned monster truck encounter while on my bike ride up Hurricane Creek. That incident stirred a stark whirlwind of considerations, powered in part by the paranoia brought about by years of hostility. My mind conjured multiple scenarios of how I was vulnerable so long as I was residing in Wallowa County. There remained the possibility of assaults, but what about legal attacks from the local establishment?

There were two physical altercations during my activist years in Wallowa County: one was on a dance floor and the other at a campsite. I've never felt violence is a solution, but I also believe in defending myself and my friends via whatever means suits the occasion. Being unafraid to fight and doing so effectively when the need arose was an attribute in Wallowa County.

I frequently cruised the residential streets of Enterprise and Joseph hoping to find the beige behemoth that had run me off the road, but I never found it. Strangely enough, that was the only confrontation during my activist career that resulted in physical injury, and it came seven years after my departure from HCPC.

While pondering the ways my establishment detractors could attack again, I considered a recent local criminal case. The bizarre prosecution was brought by conservative Wallowa County District Attorney Mona Williams. It involved a nationally publicized double murder that occurred in a corral on a remote ranch at the edge of the Grande Ronde Canyon, thirty miles north of Joseph.

The incident involved four people—on one side were Donna Dunning and her boyfriend Shane Huntsman, on the other were Dennis Beach and his son Travis. Donna and Travis are cousins. During the confrontation in a corral, Dennis Beach and Huntsman were shot to death.

The incident began when Dennis and Travis went to the ranch belonging to Dennis's brother Tom, which was being caretaken by Huntsman and Dunning. The Beach boys had heard that Dunning and Huntsman had corralled some stray cows that apparently belonged to Dennis. An argument ensued when Huntsman and Dunning refused to allow the cattle to be removed. As the argument heated to a boil, Huntsman went into the ranch house and came out with a rifle and approached Dennis and Travis.

Dunning claimed Huntsman's rifle fired when Travis tackled him, the bullet hitting and killing Dennis. As Travis and Huntsman wrestled for control of the rifle, Travis emerged with the gun. He then shot and killed Huntsman as the latter tried to flee.

Travis, however, came up with a whale of a tale. The six-foot-five, 275-pound cowboy claimed Huntsman shot Dennis Beach out of the blue. He then jumped Huntsman and wrestled the rifle from him. After he had control of the weapon, he says Dunning and Huntsman remained in the corral and threw rocks at him. Fearing for his life, he ran away from the alleged rock-throwers, but fired wildly without aiming, and just happened to hit Huntsman straight through the heart.

After hearing the stories from both survivors of the incident, Mona Williams prosecuted Donna Dunning for the attempted murder of Travis Beach, alleging she handed a rock to Huntsman as he and Travis wrestled for control of the rifle. Williams claims a grand jury refused to indict Travis, so he was not prosecuted. (Absurdly, Travis followed up the incident with a short-lived career as an Enterprise police officer.)

The political leanings of the combatants probably explains Williams's abuse of prosecutorial discretion. Dunning and Huntsman were friends of the Nez Perce Tribe and supporters of wolf recovery. Dennis and Travis Beach were revered local ranchers, imbued in the local culture of wolf hatred and vehement opposition to protecting public land.

My review of the Dunning prosecution produced an epiphany of dread. If a fabricated criminal charge could be issued against Donna Dunning, what might reasonably happen to a locally hated activist?

Actually, it's likely I got lucky after Dan Ousley was elected Wallowa County District Attorney in 1995. Ousley, who was the DA until 2006, was an avid outdoorsperson and a fair-minded prosecutor.

Adding to the viability of the threat from DA Williams, I spent most of my personal and work time alone. I was the perfect patsy—a guy who rarely has an alibi. With a jury composed of the local status quo, the presumption of guilt would be a given.

Even if acquitted of an imaginary charge, I'd have to sell the house I purchased in Joseph in 1991, the only long-term home I'd ever known, to pay the legal fees. If convicted of any charge anyone could contrive, the eco-varmint would wind up in jail, emerging flat broke. I was a sitting duck.

After seeing what a prosecutor can get away with, and Mona Williams's allegiance to the local anti-environment status quo, my fear seemed rational. Even though I'd retired, bitter minds had not forgotten whom they held responsible for the closure of sawmills and the protection of wolves.

As I continued to dabble with outside-looking-in activist work, my perspective on "home" began to change. When considering raging pickup trucks and a biased prosecutor, Wallowa County just didn't feel right anymore. It came to me in almost an epiphany: relocate. And this time, permanently.

There was one other consideration that influenced the decision to leave my home of thirty-six years: I might instinctively associate depression with where I lived. Departure might remove the besieging antigen. My pride in refusing to be driven out was no longer an issue. I'd miss the Wallowa Mountains and Hells Canyon, but I was done with Wallowa County.

After convincing myself that relocating might remove some of the grist upon which my mental affliction fed, I began to relish the prospect of residing somewhere with a clean reputation—to live where no one would recognize me as an activist.

I have a strong family presence in the North Cascades of north central Washington. My second cousin had a ranch outside of Twisp, and my aunt and uncle owned a cabin on the Chewuch River. I'd visited the Methow Valley as a child and hiked the North Cascades as an adult, and retained fond memories of the place.

The prospect of returning to those frosty Cascade Mountains amid more than two million acres of protected backcountry ignited a spark of idyllic release. Besides the fact that no one there knew me, there was a strong conservation presence in the Methow Valley. The relief of anonymity and a cozy, isolated mountain town where most of the local folks actually support protecting wilderness was enticing.

MOONSET OVER THE WALLOWAS

CHAPTER 32
OF COLLABORATION

Even after I moved, my concern over the future of wilderness advocacy remained.

A secondary concern over organizations that used to be advocates but are now collaborators and compromisers is that they're vacuuming up millions of dollars from people who believe they are supporting advocacy. The list of organizations that have adopted collaboration at the expense of advocacy is long. And collaboration has gone far beyond horse-trading to pass wilderness bills.

Collaboration has since become a paradigm where those who embrace it dismiss those who don't, and those who don't embrace it wonder at the motivations of the faithful. Collaboration has ceased to be defined as speaking with people on the other side of issues, it means assembling sanctioned entities that wield tremendous influence over public policy.

As I learned more about the collaboratives, I realized that collaboration was being adopted as its own objective rather than a strategy to achieve ecosystem protection objectives.

I never saw collaboration and advocacy as a question of picking one or the other. There is room in the ecosystem movement for all forms of activism—science, political influence, litigation, collaboration, and education. All can be effective, and all are, in my opinion, necessary.

The false choice of going all in for collaboration and departing from advocacy seems the contrivance of those who fail to understand the principles by which ecosystem advocates operate, and the urgency of their cause. I see adherence to science and defense of environmental laws as the duty of forest advocates. They would be negligent in honoring their mission and their constituencies by allowing science to be only selectively applied and lawbreaking to proceed. Law is all we have to defend public land.

Today, collaboratives are partly composed of select forest protection groups, all of whom accepted federal money to fund their involvement. They also include timber industry trade associations, timber companies, and ecologically-challenged county governments. Forest advocates that cling to the collaboration principle are enabling binding decisions toward federal land management policy that focuses on logging. They're also providing valuable political cover for the Forest Service. All the collaboratives do is design massive logging projects.

Forest protection groups who remain advocates are finding themselves outside the circle. On the Okanogan-Wenatchee National Forest, the Forest Service has virtually excluded forest advocacy groups who have asked to be involved in the inception of projects, in favor of the North Central Washington Forest Health Collaborative (NCWFHC), where it finds almost unhindered support for its agenda of logging our way back to "healthy" forests—the forests that existed before the Forest Service's timber sale program fractured them.

Maybe I'm out of fashion, but I'd always been a meat-and-potatoes activist who sees protecting land as a social and ecological imperative, not a compromisable principle to be used in negotiations. There is an urgency in the cause that does not lend itself to vast discussions over how we can ramp up logging in the national forests to solve a problem that was caused by logging.

* * *

I have tremendous respect for the publisher of *High Country News*, the late Ed Marston. He was a strong proponent of collaboration as the primary principle of activism. But he criticized litigation, something I still don't understand. Failure to enforce environmental laws renders all the work that went into passing legislation like the Endangered Species Act, the Wilderness Act, and the National Environmental Policy Act meaningless. Once again, law is all we have to protect wilderness and ecosystems.

After monitoring collaborative processes, particularly the NCWFHC, I became concerned the forest protection policies that had been gained, particularly the Northwest Forest Plan, would be negotiated away. This plan was devised to prevent the extinction of the Northern Spotted Owl and a wide variety of other ancient forest-dependent species that have been driven close to extinction by the Forest Service's breakneck logging programs.

It is with regret that I offer an example of how a forest advocacy organization is defeating its own interests by dedicating itself to collaboration as an objective and an achievement, rather than a means of pursuing science-based ecosystem goals.

I do not presume to judge how organizations fashion their programs and set their missions and program priorities. But I do reserve judgment for those who claim to be protecting ecosystems when they are not.

My example involves Conservation Northwest (CNW), based in Seattle, a member of the NCWFHC. CNW's executive director is the aforementioned Mitch Friedman, once a close friend. Mitch was always a stellar activist with a keen wit, lots of unique ideas, and a dedication to science. He began his eco-career as a protestor, climbing giant trees to prevent them from being felled.

In 1999, Mitch founded the ingenious and successful Loomis Forest Fund, which raised money to buy out the timber rights on twenty-five thousand acres of state-owned land in Washington to permanently protect critical Canada lynx habitat in the North Cascades from impending logging.

But in his latter days, Mitch experienced an abrupt, 180-degree turnaround. In one recent missive, he dismissed the North Cascades Conservation Council (NCCC), which remains a strong advocate for protecting the North Cascades Ecosystem, as "a group of grumpy old men pacing the floor and shaking their fists at the government."

Through the Collaborative, CNW participated in the development of the Mission "Restoration" Project, a timber sale billed as a fuels reduction project in the Libby Creek and Twisp River watersheds.

The Mission Project was opposed by landowners whose property adjoined the federal land proposed for intensive logging. Some of them pursued litigation against it. In cooperation with an organization not involved in the collaborative, Alliance for the Wild Rockies, they filed suit in federal court to stop the project.

In response, CNW and two other former forest advocacy representatives involved with the Collaborative submitted amicus briefs to the federal court, opposing the lawsuit and supporting the Mission Project. Ultimately, the judge ruled against the litigants. Supposed forest advocates' support for the logging project unquestionably influenced the judge's decision.

On the heels of the Mission Project, the Forest Service developed two additional "restoration" logging projects adjacent to Mission, called Twisp Restoration and Midnight Restoration. Together, these would impact seventy-seven thousand acres, essentially a chainsaw and bulldozer reconstruction of the entire Twisp River forest ecosystem.

The Forest Service fast-tracked these timber feasts with an expedited and grossly inadequate environmental analysis. The agency was madly rushing timber sales through the administrative process to take advantage of the Trump Administration dismemberment of environmental rules before the Biden Administration could restore them. The Midnight Project proposed to log areas supposedly protected by the Northwest Forest Plan, a hard-won victory for forest advocates.

The Forest Service saw fit to inform the Collaborative of its plans, yet obstinately refused to disclose the information, nor provide the same opportunities for influence, to the rest of the public. The Collaborative coyly kept its insider relationship with the Forest Service to itself. In addition to Conservation Northwest, the other forest conservation groups in the Collaborative, The Wilderness Society, Trout Unlimited, The Nature Conservancy, and the Methow Valley Citizen's Council, refused to share any information with its supposed allies.

The NCWFHC spent 20 months working to develop the logging prescriptions for the Midnight Project before existence of the proposal was publicly disclosed. After it was disclosed, concerned citizens got only 24 hours notice of a Forest Service "open house" to discuss the project, and twenty-three days to comment on the more than 800 pages of technical documents cited in the project prospectus. Both the Forest Service and the NCWFHC refused multiple requests by NCCC to be involved.

The former forest protection advocates in the Collaborative eventually cut off all communication with other advocacy organizations outside its circle. They joyfully proceeded to help the Forest Service devise the massive timber sales as they continued to rake in the dough from federal grants. Their arrogance was akin to a group of jurors who had fixed the trial of an axe murderer. They followed the Forest Service around like a faithful puppy, nonchalantly betraying everything they claimed to stand for.

I agonized over renewed involvement in activism, fearing the added stress. But the threat of losing the wild forests of the Twisp, anger toward the Forest Service, and disappointment with forest advocacy organizations compelled me. My new home was threatened, and reacting was instinctive. I joined forces with NCCC. In November 2022, we sued the Forest Service to stop the Twisp project.

Many forest advocacy groups that were initially involved in collaboratives have pointedly criticized them, particularly Oregon Wild. Unfortunately, CNW has shown no propensity to object to Forest Service corruption or insist on equitable treatment of publics. Their cozy seat at the feeding table and access to hundreds of thousands of dollars in federal grants, remain secure. As I worked against this former ally, I could feel the wrecking ball of past frustration and depression re-emerging.

I asked Mitch Friedman what his motivation was for supporting these law-violating, ecosystem-dismantling projects, but did not receive an answer. Were there federal grants at stake? According to IRS 990 form for 2020, Conservation Northwest received $441,000 in government grants, but I couldn't locate the grant proposals that would reveal the conditions of the awards.

Certainly, some of these grants could include stipulations that the grantee must maintain a cooperative relationship with the Forest Service. In an article published in the newsletter of the Association of Forest Service Employees for Environmental Ethics, executive director Andy Stahl says: "Collaborative groups grew like invasive weeds. The Forest Service deftly sidestepped the Federal Advisory Committee Act, which mandates openness and representative participation, by outsourcing the formal convening of collaboratives to its trusted confederates, especially the National Forest Foundation, which incentivized participation by passing along federal dollars to environmental groups willing to take the bait."

The NCWFHC and its member companies and organizations continue to engage in closed meetings with the Forest Service—where all other publics are excluded. Former forest advocates have become privileged insiders, taking advantage of their special status to assist in returning the national forests to the status of "log banks" at the service of the timber industry, all under the unholy mantle of protecting people from wildfires.

It's no surprise the conservation members of the Collaborative do not seem willing to give proper deference to new studies, even some endorsed by former high-ranking Forest Service officials like Jim Furnish, which contradict the claim that logging reduces the risk of unnaturally large wildfires.

* * *

I would be remiss if I failed to note that CNW's dedication to collaboration that compromises environmental principles is not limited to timber sales. The organization supported construction of a dam on the Bumping River in an undesignated sliver within the William O. Douglas Wilderness. That was such a radical proposal, no one with even a slight understanding of conservation principles should fail to vigorously oppose it. As Mitch explained it to me, CNW's support of the dam was a concession to some irrigators CNW was working with, who were reciprocally supporting one of its campaigns to purchase land.

Just as incomprehensibly, CNW supported the killing of a wolf pack in Northeast Washington. This was rationalized as a means of protecting the organization's collaborative relationship with a group of eastern Washington ranchers.

Unless I've gone completely mad, protecting wolves as they struggle to repopulate their former ranges is more important than protecting relationships, particularly with adversaries who vehemently oppose wolf protection. I still await news of ranchers making concessions to protect wolves.

CNW is still involved in good works, particularly in the area of land exchanges for conservation purposes. Those campaigns, however, do not mitigate their emphasis on collaboration at the expense of self-proclaimed ecosystem advocacy. I would suggest that if an organization is no longer involved in advocacy to protect federal lands, it needs to be honest about its program priorities. However, CNW is still proclaiming it is "Keeping the Northwest Wild."

I take no pleasure in airing my disagreements with allies—doing it got me into hot water during my career. But illustration of the dubious path of collaboration as an objective requires exposure.

* * *

As for establishing objective parameters for compromise, forest biologist Rick Brown once debated a timber industry lobbyist. During the discussion, he noted that only 1.5 million acres of intact ancient forest remains in the Pacific Northwest. The lobbyist countered that, actually, three million acres remains. Brown offered to agree with the lobbyist's figure if he'd agree to split the acreage in half—and let forest advocates decide which half gets protected. The lobbyist declined the offer.

There is nothing wrong with compromise when it involves discussing the fate of the entire public land pie. But now, the compromisers discuss how to divide up the last tiny slice of forest ecosystem integrity with the parties that already devoured the rest of the pie.

I would support collaboration as a principle if the discussion involved how to eliminate degradation of forest ecosystems rather than redefining it. If it involves decommissioning logging roads, eradicating weeds, and planting riparian areas, count me in.

The collaborators brag to their members and funders about their success in restoring the national forests to "desired conditions" and "helping prevent large wildfires." It allows them to report a "win" to their financiers. These "partners," as the Forest Service likes to call them (though the agency doesn't disclose how one gets to become a "partner"), decline to take on tough issues because there's a chance they might not win.

We live in an unsavory age when enforcing America's hard-won environmental laws has been branded by collaboration groups as "confrontational." Ignoring, or even encouraging Forest Service lawbreaking, has become commonplace with the collaborators.

This has left the task of advocacy to all-volunteer, or limited-budget organizations, for example the North Cascades Conservation Council, League of Wilderness Defenders, and Cascadia Wildlands. But sometimes, the enlightened groups face the prospect of the well-heeled groups providing political and judicial cover for the feds when the latter intervene in legal proceedings on behalf of the Forest Service.

We are dealing with a dying planet, and in this scenario, collaboration and compromise must be redefined, and advocacy must not be allowed to perish.

* * *

My thoughts have gone to every decision I've made, every fight I picked, and every place where I found peace. I've looked at where the movement to protect ecosystems is going. I cannot indulge in past accomplishments while fighting the same fight all over again, this time dueling with former allies.

Before my readers give money to an organization, I hope they will support the kind of activism they really want to see.

Will we live to see the reciprocal day when timber companies and industry trade groups are helping ecosystem defenders develop wilderness legislation, and helping fund road decommissioning on public lands? I'm not holding my breath waiting for such an (im)possibility, but I am holding my nose while witnessing the shameful abandonment of advocacy.

SHEEP DIVIDE AND THE DISTANT WALLOWAS

CHAPTER 33
THE LIMITS OF COMPROMISE

Of all the wrong moves the wilderness movement ever made, using collaboration to determine the fate of what remains of roadless areas gets the gold. With such a process, wilderness advocates resign to the sacrifice and likely eventual destruction of precious wildlands and ecological integrity.

The vast majority of federal lands have been incised with roads, logged, dammed, and mined. Quid pro quo wilderness is a losing process—an unequal compromise favoring irreversible industrial exploitation has already been made. Wilderness protection always had the moral high ground because so little is left.

The starting point for negotiations determines the equity of compromise. It should not be limited to roadless areas, but should include all public land, whereby opportunities for rehabilitation of degraded land is also the subject of discussion.

I dream of the day wilderness proponents are marshaling the collective strength of the movement toward a new paradigm—roadless areas are not fodder to sacrifice in negotiations, but the salvation of the planet in the age of climate change. The internationally accepted reality of climate change has provided an opportunity to make wilderness a banner issue that touches all people. Wild areas have the best remaining biodiversity. The stronger the biodiversity, the better the resilience to climate change. All that remains must be protected.

The distracting motivations of many of my cohorts has undermined my faith that the movement will stand by strong principles based on ecological necessity. If habitat protection and restoring biodiversity are the overarching objectives of protecting wilderness, creeping toward them with the occasional protection of bits and pieces while giving away other pieces to the consumptionists achieves nothing. The solution is to make wilderness a national issue, as occurred with passage of the Alaska National Interest Lands Conservation Act of 1980, which designated tens of millions of acres of wilderness and national parks in Alaska.

Over my long career, every time I brought this up among allies, the suggestion was met with scorn. I became sick of hearing about how politically impossible it is to pursue a national, or even regional bill, when in fact it had already occurred.

The strength of the standard-bearers of the wilderness cause was once passionate defense of land using the sword of science. But with roadless area compromise, science is discarded—protecting wildlands becomes a political gambit, blind to ecological necessity. It becomes a zero-sum game where every step forward requires at least one step backward.

As a rural activist, I have a deeper concern over the collective wilderness movement's gravitation toward negotiated wilderness protection—it has left rural organizations that cannot compete with "local opposition" out in the cold. For them, ceding the future of wilderness to local politics renders their cause all but hopeless.

The local congressional delegation and the county commissioners representing most rural municipalities would sooner cut off their arms than work with "enviros," and if they do, it's because they know they have the advantage. The only way to designate significant wilderness around rural communities in the West without making huge sacrifices is to roll the local delegation by making wilderness a national issue, and with climate change headlining, it can be done. Protecting wilderness in Oregon and Idaho benefits people in New York and Texas.

Wilderness protection is an international necessity, not a political favor. I still believe the wilderness movement is at its best when it discloses the urgency of protecting vanishing wildlands that can never be replaced in the context of a dying planet.

I've even seen the aversion to pursuing large, ecosystem-based wilderness proposals even among the stronger organizations. Oregon Wild (OW) is one of the most deservedly popular statewide organizations in the United States. I have a long history with OW, having sat on its board of directors for seven years. I remain a strong supporter of OW for many reasons.

Still, I believe their effectiveness has been diluted because they've been held in thrall by the wilderness-moderate Oregon congressional delegation. Oregon, allegedly the greenest state in the Union, ranks next to last among the thirteen Western states in the percentage of federal land protected. OW has not used that fact to generate support for a large statewide bill. It could promote an ecosystem vision to protect what's left of the original Oregon.

Since the passage of wilderness bills on a state-by-state basis in 1984, OW has favored opportunistic campaigns to protect individual roadless areas where they can impress the delegation with local community support.

OW could employ some powerful tools in leading the state's delegation toward supporting a visionary ecosystem protection campaign, which could be an integral component of a national or regional bill. The power of Oregon's state pride cannot be understated. Oregon could be the first state to recognize and act on the value of protecting wilderness and restoring biodiversity as a means of combating climate change. Oregon's remaining intact forests represent a critical biodiversity component.

I once sat on a steering committee organized by OW to pursue legislation to designate an Ochoco National Recreation Area. Oregon Wild's effort was initiated not only to protect an important keystone ecosystem, but to honor Tim Lillebo, as the Ochoco Mountains was the first place Tim worked to protect.

At the beginning of our discussion to design a bill and a strategy to promote it, the steering committee was informed by Oregon Wild staff it had already drawn a boundary for the proposed Lookout Mountain Wilderness Area inside our proposed national recreation area. I was stunned to find it protected only half of the small nineteen-thousand-acre roadless area.

Oregon Wild staffer Erik Fernandez, a very worthy activist, explained that this was a concession he'd negotiated with the local mountain-biking association. This allowed them to bike a couple of trails that run through part of the roadless area. In exchange, they'd concede to "give up" a trail that would be included in the proposed wilderness area. Without the mountain-bike association's support, Erik told the steering committee, an Ochoco bill would be DOA.

I was shocked that Oregon Wild accepted the sordid principle that once a motorized/mechanized user group establishes use of a place, that use is thereby permanently memorialized. Just as objectionable, Tim Lillebo is not honored by cutting a roadless area in half. Tim would have found a way to protect all of it while maintaining a positive relationship with the mountain-bike lobby.

Along with seasoned wilderness veteran James Monteith, the former executive director of Oregon Wild, and highly respected activist Dave Willis, I expressed dismay at the preemptive compromise. Our concerns were brushed aside.

I asked what support we would get from the mountain bikers to pass the bill in exchange for our concession. We were told the bikers would not be lobbying on behalf of the bill; their contribution is that they would not publicly oppose it. I remain dumbfounded. Is there not a time when going to bat for wilderness means opposing the politically powerful?

Another perplexing aspect was that there had only been a mountain-bike lobby in Oregon for about fifteen years. These people came out of nowhere and now they have veto power over wilderness bills? And what paltry payment, I thought, for our ten-thousand-acre giveaway. We wouldn't get half a roadless area, we would lose half a roadless area to a handful of mountain bikers.

If the biking constituency is going to prioritize protecting its unfettered use of every trail it likes over wilderness protection, it has my contempt, and my desire to roll them. Their selfish use arguments hold no more water than the motorhead's piddling claims of near-death consequences due to their exclusion from a single place.

Soon after we had drawn up our preemptively compromised bill, Oregon Wild learned that the mountain-bike association was going through some internal discussion that might bring an end to their involvement in legislation. So, I suggested we redraw the boundary for Lookout Mountain to include the entire roadless area. The reaction from Oregon Wild staff was what I might have expected if I'd suggested we burn down the mountain bikers' clubhouse.

I cannot tolerate political wheeling and dealing while trying to protect the last shreds of dying ecosystems. Yet I reproach myself for criticizing Oregon Wild given its many accomplishments. I cringe at my insistence on being the storm crow, the chronic complainer. I only hope the criticism was accepted as constructive.

* * *

I still fear for the future of wilderness advocacy. There's a big difference between passing wilderness bills and protecting ecosystems. The former is an organizational objective, while the latter is a scientific objective. I worry that the urgency of the cause of ecological protection has been forgotten by its very defenders. Or maybe it's just me, being the crazy man on fire once again, overreacting with anger and failing to accept change. Perhaps I should melt back into the mountains and keep trying to forget about activism.

But I won't. I can never be content to watch activism inspired by vision and dedicated to principle be sterilized by the toxic Clorox of politics. It suggests that the leaders of the forest and wilderness protection movement cannot effectively deliver an articulate, impassioned, science-backed plea for the protection of all wildlands, they must offer concessions to their detractors to accomplish anything.

Wilderness advocates should not accept the political paradigms created by wilderness detractors—they should be creating their own. The once-bold defenders should emerge from the shadow of being scavenging gleaners, gathering handfuls of acres enabled by payments the ecosystems cannot afford, and pretending something profound has been accomplished.

There will always be space in the world for divergent strategies for protecting wilderness. Regardless, my respect is reserved for people who lead organizations that refuse to capitulate in the face of ecological collapse.

Wilderness icon David Brower once said, "Polite conservationists leave no mark, save scars upon the Earth that could have been avoided had they stood their ground." He was right.

LARCH TREES PRECEDE REDMONT PEAK

CHAPTER 34

THE ORGANIZATION VERSUS THE CAUSE?

I take no pleasure in exposing the mysterious retreat of my former allies. Still, I will never apologize for sticking to my principles, rejecting all other political or financial considerations. Seeing so many organizations go "all in" for collaboration and quid pro quo wilderness, I see the collaborative paradigm as the demise of advocacy. I fear for the future of the movement when upcoming activists are indoctrinated into "principles" that emphasize negotiating with adversaries over the last vestiges of deteriorating ecosystems.

The compromise of principles is common with organizations in every worthy cause. Yet I urge all my readers to consider that activists dilute their principles if they serve an organization that places self-interest before the cause they're supposed to be fighting for. I cannot define the fine line that should not be crossed, just let your conscience guide you.

I've mentored volunteer activists, including many from environmental studies departments at colleges. Students are going into that field not due to the prospects of a lucrative career, but due to their convictions to protect land. They are willing to make sacrifices in salary and benefits compared to what they could be making in the for-profit world.

I advise the newcomers who are the future of the wilderness movement to be conscious of the missions and organizational plans of prospective employers to determine whether their strategies fit with your convictions. I am all for financially stable organizations so long as they honor why they exist.

I know of only one forum where activists are schooled in the intricacies of nonprofit leadership. In the early 2000s, the Wilburforce Foundation invested in Training Resources for the Environmental Community (TREC), an entity designed to educate existing and aspiring activists. It was a wise move by Wilburforce, as there is strong concern over the future of leadership in the wilderness movement.

TREC was a good idea in principle, led by dedicated staff. But having sampled the organization's programs and paradigms, I found it to be all about the business end. Its curriculum followed corporate-based principles designed more to create prosperous companies, rather than dedicated NGOs led by activists whose goal is to protect and restore wildlands over maximizing income at any cost to the land.

Just prior to my 2005 retirement from activism, I attended a 2004 TREC seminar designed to train and recruit executive directors. Its intention was to fill a growing gap in NGO leadership by educating people already employed by environmental nonprofits to assume leadership roles. The "training" involved five week-long sessions at lavish retreat facilities throughout the West. I found it incredibly unhelpful, as did most of the other attendees.

The information provided was designed not for experienced executive directors, but for aspiring leaders. Yet it was attended by twenty people who were already long-time executive directors and only two who were not. My advice, in retrospect, is that TREC should recruit from college environmental studies programs, small, all-volunteer NGOs, and volunteer pools recommended by the organizations the volunteers work for.

The curriculum drew almost exclusively from corporate leadership training models. There was no time dedicated to allowing participants to share with each other what had and had not worked for them. The time I spent with my fellow EDs between sessions was far more helpful than the curriculum.

The "trainees" were given literature produced by for-profit motivational institutions, and speakers from the for-profit sector promoted the message "Run your organization like a business and you'll be successful."

But successful at what? Raising money and writing good budgets? There was never a hint of discussion on predominant land protection issues or politics. Nothing on how to focus organizational growth around mission, how to articulate to the public the urgency of the mission, how to attract and empower volunteers, or how to inspire others to be leaders.

The information was one-size-fits-all, with no recognition of the distinctions between organizations. There are education-based groups, collaborators, science providers, and advocacy groups specializing in law and/or legislation, to name a few. There are small, medium, and large organizations, rural-based and urban, all-volunteer and paid-staff organizations. All of these have needs distinct from the others.

That shortcoming was exhibited by TREC's curriculum surrounding fundraising, especially membership management. The instruction was cherry-picked from the generic templates of fundraising "experts." For example, the organization is advised to excise people from their membership list who don't donate regularly. HCPC's 1,900-person membership was unique in that many were clients from my river trips and names from old HCPC mailing lists. We were supported by loyal people, many of whom were not members of other organizations. HCPC's staff and board knew many personally and kept in touch.

I had an enlightening experience that exposed the lack of wisdom of the "cut and add" membership management philosophy—two members we hadn't heard a peep from, one for five years, another for six, were re-inspired by articles in our newsletter, which we had continued to send them even though they hadn't paid up. One evolved into a consistent $1,000-per-year donor. The second gave us a one-time gift of $7,000 and remained a regular paying member. Had we followed the TREC template, removing those two folks and saving pennies would have cost us well over $15,000.

It costs only a few cents per mailing to send a household your promotional materials. So if you have 500,000 members, it might make sense to trim some long-time nonpayers. But for groups with 1,900 members, particularly "exclusive" members, it doesn't make sense to excommunicate someone when they might rejoin.

The mantra of the professional fundraisers brought in by TREC was to do mailing-list purchases and swaps with other organizations to add members. After the TREC seminar, I tried it once, and it flopped. We signed up a few new members, but I got notes from several existing members asking why their name was being sold to other organizations. It was embarrassing trying to assure our membership that they weren't just wallets being shuffled between bureaucracies, but valued members of a tight-knit and successful group.

During one TREC session, I had a one-to-one discussion with TREC executive director Dyan Oldenburg. The conversation touched on HCPC's financial outlook. I tried to convey to Diane the special challenges in fundraising that are unique to rural organizations. I disclosed that it was always a challenge to achieve consistent non-grant income. I added that at present, due to the economic downturn, we were on pretty shaky long-term financial footing.

"Do you have a trust fund?" she unexpectedly asked. I hesitated. After a few seconds, I realized she meant me personally, not HCPC. I was too flabbergasted to respond.

I developed a saying I unwisely kept to myself: "*The cause does not exist to serve the organization; the organization exists to serve the cause.*" The same holds true for the individual—the organization does not exist to serve them. My standard is simple—when the mission becomes secondary to personal or organizational prosperity, the organization has not only lost touch with its purpose, it is betraying its members.

* * *

In light of the limited teaching forums for present and upcoming activists, it is stunning that opportunities to cultivate vision and knowledge by sharing the experience of veterans are ignored. Knowledgeable wilderness advocates wind up "out to pasture" when their experiences and ideas should be shared.

The most profound example is Brock Evans, whose wealth of knowledge of how to run an organization, how your organization can succeed in its mission, and how to be a successful activist has been all but forgotten. Brock still serves wilderness, but only as a volunteer resource for those who already know him. He's written two books, *Fight & Win* and *Endless Pressure, Endlessly Applied*, but they're not being promoted by organizations, colleges, or environmental funders.

I'd cherish the opportunity to get an audience with funders and leaders within the wilderness movement to discuss the establishment of an Institute for Wilderness Vision and Knowledge. It would set up a collective of experienced advocates to visit environmental studies departments at colleges, be available to small nonprofits who need advice, and sit in roundtable discussions with the present leaders of environmental nonprofits.

Those involved should include people who support different approaches and strategies. Participants would provide a variety of viewpoints on everything from developing public land protection proposals to garnering political support and targeting funders who support an organization's goals.

I once had a conversation with highly respected wilderness advocate Ken Rait in his Portland office, just after he took a lucrative job with the well-endowed Pew Wilderness Center. My respect for Ken makes me refuse to believe one of his statements was anything but satirical, but it stoked a deep chord of concern.

Laughing, Ken addressed my contention that it's wiser to mobilize the strength of the movement to support regional and national wilderness bills rather than to support piecemeal, opportunistic wilderness designations year after year. "Hey," he cautioned, "we've got to think about our careers."

The logic is, if we protected all the roadless areas in one fell swoop, what purpose would there be for wilderness activists if there was nothing left to protect? I know that kind of narrow thinking does exist.

There's plenty to be done even after all roadless areas are protected, and Ken of course knows this full well—rehabilitating logged-over federal land, improving laws like the Wilderness Act, removing laws like the Multiple Use Sustained Yield Act and the Mining Law of 1872, and reforming the Forest Service. Monitoring of federal agency activities and guarding against attempts to declassify wilderness and national parks will always be imperative.

As for careers, I cannot fault anyone for making a big salary so long as their dedication to support strong wilderness advocacy sustains. As for me, I took my $37,500 annual salary and continued to live my usual and accustomed lifestyle. I also enjoyed the second paycheck of rich fulfillment in being on the front lines in the battle to rescue the Earth.

I don't begrudge Ken his six-figure salary. He's earned it. I could never sit in the chair he now occupies, even if it were offered (which is highly unlikely as I'm not known as a "team player"). The truth is, I'm proud of never having made any money during my activist career beyond immediate minimal financial survival.

Many high-profile former advocates have devolved into fundraising bureaucracies. I remain shocked at where the vast majority of contributions from individuals go, from annual donations to bequests. It stands to reason that organizations that build the strongest fundraising infrastructures will raise more money. But it also speaks to their priorities. I only wish there were a way to scrutinize every organization to show what success they have to show in protecting land versus their success in raising money, and to share that information with their members and donors.

Many huge organizations have, as far as I can see, completely departed from advocacy, like the National Audubon Society. I'd love to see protecting avian habitat, which was the initial objective of Audubon, take precedence over programs that attract the most funding. I have no idea what the National Audubon Society does these days, nor the enigmatic National Wildlife Federation, which claims to be "America's largest and most trusted conservation organization." Its promotional quips are long on rhetoric and short on details.

The best example of the money-first phenomenon is The Nature Conservancy (TNC). The reality is that this organization has devolved into a multibillion-dollar, tax-exempt real-estate conglomerate. It has leased some of its "conserved" land for cattle grazing in Oregon and Idaho, and oil and gas drilling in Texas. The *Washington Post* caught the Conservancy making shady deals with landowners to get them tax breaks, and using its developed properties as wine-and-dine resorts for donors.

When I think of all the money and land TNC receives through donations and bequests from people who really believe they're saving nature, and what that capital could do for dedicated local activists, I get sick to my stomach. With its devious creativity in maximizing profits, TNC epitomizes the principle of the cause serving the organization.

I'm not big on disclaimers, so in saying I know many Nature Conservancy employees who are fine and dedicated people, I'm not trying to sugarcoat my critique. Yet from the standpoint of institutional philosophy, I do not regard TNC as a fellow "advocate"; I view them as a collection of businesspeople rather than activists.

Incongruously, TNC deviated from its mission of buying land to protect it and got into the business of influencing federal land management. Their public-lands work is primarily geared toward helping federal agencies increase logging and livestock grazing behind the facade of "enlightened resource management."

I was always bothered by the fact that during my HCPC tenure, the Conservancy's "CEO" enjoyed a salary nearly double HCPC's total annual budget. But I was even more upset when TNC's Northeast Oregon coordinator Berta Youtie joined in a brutal attack against one of the most respected wilderness advocates in the Pacific Northwest—Tim Lillebo.

Tim and his wife Karen built a house on the Middle Fork John Day River, a designated State Scenic Waterway under Oregon law. Their house was lauded by the State of Oregon's coordinator of compliance with the Scenic Waterways Act as a statewide model for exceptional adherence to the law's standards.

Enter Youtie, former Malheur National Forest Supervisor Ken Evans, and the Grant County commissioners. They decided to teach Tim and Karen a lesson in "regulations." The honorable commissioners withdrew Tim and Karen's building permit after the house was almost completed, citing violations of the Scenic Waterways Act. The Lillebos faced having to tear the house down. To curry political favors, Youtie wrote a letter in support of the commissioners' action.

Tim and Karen finally "won" when they hired an attorney who made it clear the commissioners' action was a loser in court, not that the commissioners, Evans, and Youtie intended to go that far. What they did do was cost the Lillebos around $40,000 in legal fees, not to mention innumerable headaches.

The Conservancy has also been involved in a number of illegal shenanigans in Idaho, including trespassing on federal land. But the most ironic incident was when TNC allowed a group of jet-boaters with a track hoe access across its Garden Creek Preserve in lower Hells Canyon to remove a troublesome rock in the Snake River. A few jet-boats had some unfortunate encounters with the rock when it refused to budge. Upon their departure, the track hoe set off a spark, igniting a fire that burned the entire preserve, which had been purchased to protect an endemic plant.

* * *

Internal whistleblowers are important. I learned that there are few or none within TNC. But I never imagined there would be one inside HCPC who came after me in a very personal way. Nonprofits are driven by their members, and the more people that know which organizations are still advocates, and which are not, the better. I'm willing to accept scorn as an infighter so long as it strengthens the principles of the movement.

Reputation is something I unwisely didn't give a lot of thought to. Maybe it's because my reputation was so completely trashed among most of the people in my home community of Wallowa County, I disregarded defending my integrity anywhere. My reputation among my peers took some shots when I was willing to publicly question them.

I learned the hard way that, toward the protection of your own and your organization's effectiveness, it's wise to dedicate whatever effort is needed to defend your reputation. Assassination of your character is an assassination of your organization, and subsequently your cause.

The most destructive sniper shots can be friendly fire. Long since my short-lived retirement from activism, I developed a desire to clarify my own record. This evolved from my weariness in always being the bad guy, the evil infighter, and the accused taker of jobs from working-class people. It also came from one particularly egregious personal attack.

The assault came from a former employee—an impeccable activist who had enough credibility to be heard by a sizable audience among our peers.

I share this story in part because it serves to convey the importance of establishing the line between a person's benefit and their liability. It shows how important it is for an organization to place the cause above the comfort and personal interest of the individual. Of course, there will always be personality conflicts with personnel in any company or organization that must be managed. But in this case, I looked the other way when I should have defended myself from a terrible smear that infected me.

I'm going to refer to this former HCPC employee as "Kelly," whose knowledge, dedication, and energy were astounding, but the negatives were equally impressive. Kelly's instances of rage were punitive, and overwhelmingly disruptive. They occurred in one-to-one conversations, at staff meetings, board meetings, and even external meetings with people outside HCPC.

This behavior was driven in large part by their frustration over my disinterest in a specific personal relationship. I am partly at fault for pretending to fulfill a lesser role in this person's life to retain an excellent activist.

Several of my board members advised that I should dismiss Kelly sooner than I finally did. They were right. But I was torn by the prospect of losing the positives and was willing to sacrifice organizational and personal comfort for excellent work on behalf of the cause.

Kelly was a person inclined to speak with anyone about anything. Conversely, I have a compulsion for privacy and discretion in airing internal laundry. After Kelly's dismissal, he/she approached important people in the wilderness movement and described my alleged unfair behavior—fabrications of bullying and discrimination.

One can usually defend oneself by finding credible people to come to your defense when it becomes personal. But I never wanted to ask anyone to become involved in a civil war. In the realm of the stalked, objectivity is often the first casualty.

I learned there are times when taking the moral high ground—refusing to give credibility to one engaging in personal attacks by not responding—doesn't always work. It seemed that attempting to lay the thread bare and fix it would appear vain, so I declined, even though the attacks continued after my retirement. I now believe that defending oneself is not vanity.

Besides, when I left the movement, the gleaming light of salvation in being out of the public eye was so enticing, I ignored every distraction. I still muse on whether HCPC might have been less impacted if I had chased down the perpetrator and showed the "audience" the cards I had (handwritten notes I still possess), which would have been incontrovertibly damning to Kelly's crusade.

All of us want our legacy to be presented accurately. My wish is to be remembered not as much for who I was, but for what I accomplished.

Still, I am loath to see my legacy as the smoldering carnage of bridges burned by the confrontational warrior. I only hope to have contributed to the conscience of the movement.

"Angry idealist," some of my former cohorts might be saying. But despite my occasional recklessness, all I ever wanted was to protect the land. I never expected to get popular doing it.

PONDEROSAS MINGLE WITH LARCHES

CHAPTER 35
YOU CAN NEVER GO HOME

Anxiety is an entrenched beast—next to impossible to purge. In considering what seemed like the fall of wilderness advocacy, I perceived the movement's successes to be in jeopardy, and the prospect of more wins was nil. Worse yet, I worried over how my personal achievements would endure in the new passive climate.

When I left HCPC, I had assumed the programs I'd initiated and the knowledge I'd gained would carry on with the next generation of HCPC's leadership. I assumed our campaigns and means of coordinating and funding them were self-evident and had a life of their own. I was wrong. The program I developed was hanging by a thread.

Immediately after my departure, HCPC abandoned the Hells Canyon–Chief Joseph National Preserve campaign. Soon after, it departed from wolf advocacy, falling from being the go-to organization on wolf issues in Oregon. Also biting the dust was the effort to restore Imnaha River salmon runs, including continuing legal action to force the Forest Service to write the HCNRA regulations after four decades of defiance. The ongoing endeavors to close the Lord Flat Trail to motorized use also fizzled.

That didn't mean HCPC would not be doing positive things. I'm not so arrogant as to think my ideas and campaigns are the only good ones. But the loss of all the work HCPC had invested in was agonizing. The suddenness of my complete departure was mostly to blame for the demise of those campaigns. But I continued to observe HCPC from a distance and didn't make any effort to influence the new direction.

My first year in the Methow was difficult. I was bombarded by an intensifying of my physical and mental health issues, exacerbated by the stresses of building my house. But by the summer of 2015, I'd managed to get back on my feet. After having been absent from any meaningful association with HCPC since my retirement, I was nudged back into the HCPC loop by Brock Evans and Jennifer Schemm, both of whom sat on the HCPC board. They convinced me to give the keynote address at HCPC's 2015 fall gala, their primary member event. By this time, HCPC had been renamed the Greater Hells Canyon Council (GHCC).

A few days before the October 15 gala, I joined Brock and GHCC board member Marina Richie on a camping excursion to the magnificent upper Imnaha River corridor, which Brock had never seen. It was my first trip to the HCNRA in nearly nine years. The three of us were giddy with anticipation.

With ferocious diligence, HCPC had prevented the Forest Service from conducting any more logging in the spectacular Imnaha River corridor after the disastrous Skook Timber Sale of 1986. In 1999, we'd secured a promise from HCNRA Ranger Ed Cole that there would be no commercial logging in the Imnaha corridor. In 2003, we inspired the HCNRA comprehensive management plan that discouraged commercial logging in the HCNRA, deferring to protecting its ecological uniqueness. Upon my retirement, I felt the Imnaha was safe.

Visiting the Imnaha for the first time in several years seemed a great way to spend the days before my reacquaintance with my former organization. Why was I so optimistic?

The trip quickly became a toxic flashback. From the moment the three of us crossed Lonesome Saddle and descended into the Imnaha Canyon, we were assaulted by fresh scars incised by the Forest Service. The ten-mile drive from Ollokot Campground to Indian Crossing was riddled with logging scars. The officially designated "scenic" road was pocked with slash piles, log decks, clearcuts, stumps, and ripped-up ground. It was so shocking I could barely breathe.

Indian Crossing Campground was being logged, including dozens of trees well over the legal limit of twenty-one inches diameter. A log deck—with trees piled askew—languished next to the interpretive sign telling visitors about the endangered salmon in the river. The campers would—like it or not—stomach the experience of camping in a logging operation.

Posterity escaped me. It took several hours before I could entertain objective thought, like how important constant vigilance is in protecting land that is always vulnerable. If one cannot enjoy a pristine recreational experience in one of the most popular camping areas within a congressionally designated national recreation area, where can one go? But then, the Forest Service always claimed camping amid logging debris was enjoyable for all.

Thoughts of hatred for the Forest Service were insurmountable. But with Brock's help, I managed to level my mood.

Deflated, the three of us departed. We drove up the narrow road toward PO Saddle Trailhead on the west rim of Hells Canyon. On the way, we tangled precariously with two loaded log trucks driving down. My heart sank. Upon arrival at the trailhead, we gazed in dismay at the incision of new roads and heavy logging. Fresh clearcuts reached up to the west rim of the canyon to the very edge of the Hells Canyon Wilderness boundary.

Our encounters with logging occurred in two once-beautiful parts of the place Brock thought he had "saved" back in 1975. He maintained his usual cool demeanor, but was clearly shaken. Politely, he asked me, "Can we find someplace to camp that isn't being logged?" Seeking refuge, we solemnly drove up the Lick Creek/Coverdale Road toward Skookum Creek.

Driving toward Lick Creek Campground, thankfully, we found no fresh logging. But what we did find were cows and heaps of cow shit. Disgusted, we stepped out of our vehicle, circumvented the feces, and walked down the slope toward the Imnaha River amid the stumps left from the Skook Timber Sale thirty years earlier. The dual degradation of the old timber sale and the cow defacement represented a perpetual legacy of abuse.

"This is supposed to be a protected place," I muttered to myself. The anger boiled once again. All HCPC had done to "re-save" the HCNRA was to temporarily stave off inevitable doom.

All the deception and destruction I had experienced in my time as a Hells Canyon advocate came roaring back like a recurring nightmare on eternal repeat. All the work HCPC had invested in the new CMP appeared to have gained us nothing.

At last, the three of us found a place to spend the night—one of the few spots that wasn't completely scarred by logging or cattle—a campsite in what used to be Evergreen Campground. The Forest Service had closed the campground a few years earlier because they claimed they didn't have the funding to maintain it. But they sure had the money to log. That night, we sat around our campfire, where our conversations focused on how we could once again save the HCNRA.

The next day, we returned to La Grande. Brock and I met with a number of GHCC staff and board members prior to the gala. News from GHCC was as grim as our camp tour's revelations. I learned with utter dismay that the Wallowa-Whitman National Forest had recently lumped the HCNRA into a single ranger district with the Wallowa Valley Ranger District. And when GHCC conservation director Veronica Warnock met with Kris Stein, the new district ranger, Stein accused GHCC of being extreme obstructionists. This apparently meant that it was no one else's business what Stein did with the HCNRA. The Forest Service's logging of the HCNRA isn't just corrupt, it's vindictive.

It was another sucker punch that landed on my addled chin like a sledgehammer. The mantra we used to repeat over and over in the 1990s was that to the Forest Service, the HCNRA is just another ranger district. It's nothing special to them at all.

With the merger of the HCNRA with standard national forest land not recognized by special legislative protection, the HCNRA has few staff versed in recreation management, and none in ecosystem science. It has sawlog foresters who roam the woods of the HCNRA looking for trees to cut, and "range technicians" searching for more cow playgrounds.

The Forest Service thus has no viable budget for recreation or ecological restoration in the HCNRA, just slop from its general budget from which it "manages" (read, *logs*) standard national forest lands. The move was no different than if the Department of the Interior had merged Grand Canyon National Park into an adjoining Bureau of Land Management district.

I gave my speech at the GHCC gala on October 22. But I was so angry it felt like someone else was speaking. Then I went home to the Methow, far from the place I had adopted as my contribution to a better world. I tried with all my might to forget.

* * *

In 2016, a year after my camping trip with Brock, my love of the place pulled me back to see what other demonic things the Forest Service might have initiated. I nervously returned to the Imnaha. Predictably, I was greeted with more fresh logging, resurrected by the newly appointed HCNRA ranger, Chris Stein. In response to my subsequent letter and accompanying photographs to the Wallowa-Whitman National Forest supervisor, I learned the agency considered those big old trees to be "danger trees." The claim was insultingly ludicrous, since the trees were nowhere near a campground or even a trail. I terminated the irrational discussion, but tried to encourage GHCC to launch a campaign to stop the Imnaha logging.

It was as if the Forest Service brass were telling me and GHCC they could log whatever they wanted in the HCNRA and there wasn't a damn thing we could do about it.

A couple months later, after finding what the Forest Service called "beetle-prevention" logging, GHCC Board President Marina Richie consulted an entomologist who wrote a letter to the Wallowa-Whitman National Forest supervisor telling him that the logging of the pines would likely do more to help the beetles spread than to eliminate them. But the loyalty of the Forest Service doesn't lie in science, and the supervisor virtually ignored the scientists' observations.

During my tenure, fighting when collaboration didn't work was the only way HCPC achieved anything. If we're now in the age of collaboration, and being confrontational is seen as undesirable, does that mean we forget the lessons of the past? Does it mean we should trust the people who compulsively stab us in the back? Does it mean we forget the urgency of our work, and that we allow the Forest Service to ignore the law?

Even though GHCC became a collaboration-based organization, they eventually pulled out of the Wallowa-Whitman National Forest Collaborative after their contributions to the discussions were meaningless as the group merrily concocted old-style timber sales. I found that heartening, but I still lament that so much of what HCPC had been is now gone, and it's mostly my fault.

Backward glances at my career have become a colorless dusk splashed with the cold emotion of a languid sunset. I revisit the campaign to remove the HCNRA from Forest Service jurisdiction and remain mystified that so few seemed to understand the logic. Our successful litigation didn't change policy. Additional lawsuits stopped some individual projects, but the Forest Service could simply serve up more, and force us to sue again. There was no means to hold the agency accountable to the law over the long term. Stunningly, at the time this book was going to publication, the Forest Service had still failed to comply with a 2004 court order—inspired by our fourth lawsuit challenging the content of the regulations—to rewrite them to define the compatibility requirement.

Hoping for the Forest Service to change after nearly fifty years of neurotically pissing on a national treasure is nothing more than an irrational fantasy. Banging one's head against a titanium wall has to end at some point.

They say you can't go home unless you're ready for disappointment. Maybe I should have stayed away from Hells Canyon and fed my complacency with the false assumption of security.

MOUTH OF THE IMNAHA RIVER

CHAPTER 36

HONORING LIFE

Life. That's what wilderness is. Experiencing the purity of life as it originally came to be on Earth is the pinnacle of the wilderness experience. The spontaneity of moments, the involuntary progression of existence, and the essence of spirituality are exhilarating to the unbarred mind.

As I wandered along the Zigzag River in the wonder of my youth, the subtle revelations amid childhood's innocent perceptions stuck with me. In the damp rain forest, I was at home. For some of us, such a feeling reaches beyond connection to a place. We're part of the land, not an entity experiencing it from a separate plane of awareness. Our actions to defend the connection are instinctive. Our ground is our home. Stand your ground, and let the enemies defeat themselves. We are all druids, defending our green.

With each revelation, humanity is revealed as reasoning beings contemplating the rich detritus of life, and embracing its perpetual entropy as we fashion our survival in tune with it. We're modules of perception that bring consciousness to the magic; vessels of humble explanation where mystery reigns.

Experiencing near-death, as occurred to me twice in the wild—once via a very large bear and once on a cliff—was just as fulfilling as living in peace. One of those experiences stands out. In May 2001, I was invited to speak at a conference in Anchorage, Alaska, on river management. I accepted, and decided to hang around an extra couple of days for some hiking on the fringes of the Alaska wilds.

My presentation on how river managers can prevent motorized watercraft from ruining their river's natural quality went well. That evening, I felt as expected in a sterile hotel room—sleeplessness was highlighted by moods that churned in my head like a pot of melting caramel. As I struggled to sleep, I was oppressed by the fear of continuing activism, and the fear of leaving it—perplexed by the paradox of defending life, yet wanting to die.

I finally drifted off with the assistance of my preferred sleep aid, Benadryl. I awoke feeling a hike might distract the dark thoughts.

I chose the Eagle River Trail in Chugach State Park, about fifty miles north of Anchorage. It was May 2, cold and overcast. Flecks of snow flitted through the thick air at the trailhead. My plan was to hike ten miles to a frozen lake, then return.

Still, the Alaska spring was coming on strong and the land was waking up. Hoisting my day pack, I took off at a good clip, invigorated. The mountains of Alaska were grand, glacier-draped peaks glinting in the sun streaks that shot earthward between strips of determined cloud.

Five miles in, I came to a rotting sign on a tree that read "Twin Falls." I saw the falls on the opposite side of Eagle River and admired its changing trajectory and spray pattern as the flow increased with the warming of the day. About a half mile up the trail from the falls, movement teased the corner of my left eye.

Turning and focusing my gaze, I caught a glimpse of a wolf at the top of a rock outcrop, about fifty yards away. Showing a coat of mottled beige and black, the tall, slender canid looked at me with stinging yellow eyes. I reveled in the glory of the first wolf I'd seen in the wild. It paused as I watched, but as I took out my camera, it darted over the lee side of the ridge.

A few steps later, I caught the scent of death. I soon found the carcass of an adult moose. The wolf, likely hungry after a winter of survival jeopardy, had been snacking. I assumed it hadn't killed the moose on its own, a very tall order for a lone wolf. I photographed the moose's hooves, as large as my heavily booted feet.

I thought to myself in a moment of primal lust that this is how I'd like to go—having my flesh and bones honored by returning to the great organic cycle via random chance—life's organic inevitability.

I marked the location in my mind. Two and a half hours later, I got to the frozen lake and slid along its edges close to shore. I conjured up enough gumption to venture thirty feet toward the center. I challenged the solidity of water while flirting with the panoply of life surrounding me. I scurried around the lake for hours, topping rock outcrops and investigating knotted groups of spruce trees.

My hike afforded the privilege of seeing lots of critters, from a badger to what I thought was a marten. In Alaska's wild country, where humans are relatively scarce, it almost seems as if the critters are as curious as they are afraid.

My mind reluctantly reverted back to time counting. I figured three hours to cover the mostly downhill ten miles back to the trailhead before nightfall. I began a waltz of satisfaction amid the wild Eagle River, thanking aloud the people who had dedicated themselves to protecting the wildlands of Alaska.

In a trance of contentment, I re-approached the place where I'd seen the dead moose from the opposite direction. At that moment, my proximity to it was the furthest thing from my mind. I'd forgotten the mental markers I made while striding unthinking along the trail.

The wind had wheeled around from the north to the west. Reaching a point when the trail required the hiker to take a few steps onto a rock outcrop, the scent of the moose hit me.

With a startling suddenness, the sound of cracking branches spun my head toward the riparian bushes to my left between the trail and the river. In that frozen instant, I saw one of the most beautiful things my eyes have beheld—a huge grizzly bear boar.

The reddish-brown fur around his neck was like a mane. It seemed to gleam. The textured twirl of his hair was rich and beautiful. Transfixed, I began to stare at it. Then I remembered my grizzly bear education, taken from griz ally Doug Peacock—don't make eye contact, as that might be construed as a challenge, and **do not run.**

My bear pal was balanced on his haunches about forty feet from me, the vegetation around him like a picture frame. Very little vegetation lay between us. I averted my eyes, and stood still. Involuntarily, I began to softly hum a song, Led Zeppelin's "Battle of Evermore."

I had brought no bear spray. That's always seemed like cheating the communion with nature. Risk is part of the fulfillment. As I slowly bowed my head for a few anxious seconds, I knew either I was dead, or he'd leave me alone. Then, I suddenly realized I stood between him and the dead moose. Oops. I stood silent with my head bowed, humming the song aloud.

In a lingering instant, I heard crashing in the vegetation. As I braced myself and looked right toward him, all I could see was the grizzly's huge rump and swollen balls retreating. I was happy not to be another statistic in the annals of grizzly attacks, and grateful for his gift.

What I remember most about my thoughts in the moments just before he retreated, is that my only fear was of being left half-dead, and the discomfort of the mauling. But the prospect of dying brought no fear.

Walking back to the trailhead and appreciating my continued consciousness, I pondered the human tendency to eliminate all threats or even inconveniences to us—wolves, bears, mosquitoes. And yet, we all but ignore the extinction event we're perpetrating toward a slow and painful demise—climate change and ecological collapse.

We humans have talents. We have emotion, ingenuity, wisdom, and can contemplate life's structure and meaning. Life's great fulfillment is that it is mysterious.

If life is to continue to flourish on Earth, we must use our wisdom and our passion to pull ourselves out of the track we have been on since the industrial revolution—the unconstrained consumption of natural resources; the unravelling of ecosystems; the dumping of poison into the air, soil, and water. Protecting wilderness is an act of securing the completeness of life and, ultimately, facilitating our own survival.

I plead to everyone, whatever your religion, whatever your philosophy, culture, or social status, as long as humanity exists, our progeny will need a clean and healthy planet to live on. Land filled with grizzly bears, wolves, mosquitoes, buzzards, snakes, and scorpions.

Our history as a species, and our biological legacy, can only be assured by surviving here on Earth. I deplore those who speak of saving humanity by populating other planets, while we show insufficient willingness to stop killing our own.

In late 2022, a panel of esteemed scientists released a report published by the National Academy of Science that found we are on a direct path to the Earth's sixth extinction event. We are losing one species at a time, many species every day. We may be facing the sixth extinction, but it will be the first caused by the activities of one of Earth's inhabitants.

I suggest the thinking among us consider the choices of combating climate change and ecological collapse—on one hand, if we assume neither is true, do nothing, and wind up being wrong, the Earth dies and us with it. If we assume it's true and work to reverse it, no life will be lost. There are no adverse consequences to aggressively combating climate change, other than greedy billionaires losing the opportunity for a few more billion before they dissolve into gasping dust.

To advocate for the continued course of depletion and pollution is worse than denying science. It's opposing progress. As humanity continues to accumulate knowledge, we will continue to find better ways to live before life comes to the end of living, and the beginning of survival.

Biodiversity is what gives life strength and resilience. Protecting wilderness upholds the original complexity of life and provides us with a baseline of what the planetary ecosystem is supposed to look like should we finally endeavor to restore our planet's living systems.

* * *

If you see the wisdom of protecting nature, here's a humble suggestion—consider defending life even beyond protecting yourself and those you love; consider protecting or restoring a part of your/our homeland. It can be done without much effort, yet you'll still be in the same league as the medievals who defended their homeland from marauding hordes with swords. It's akin to immortality, as these places we protect and restore will always exist beyond each of us.

How about establishing a city park? Restoring a plant or animal that used to exist where you reside? Reinstating native vegetation where crops failed? Maybe you could prevent the construction of tract homes on open space, a proposed water diversion along a nearby creek, or save a vacant lot in the inner city that has some grass and a tree.

Wherever you call home, consider studying up on the plants and animals that are native to where you live. Consider consulting with federal, state, and university scientists, and your local advocacy group to help you learn what it would take to bring nature back.

However large or small, every place and every species is a thread of the interconnected tapestry of life. We do not need to dam every river, mine every stone, and cut down every tree. Nor do we need to drive species to extinction, poison the soil and water, and dump billions of tons of garbage into the ocean in order to be comfortable.

We do not need to be helpless before seemingly invincible economic forces and the lawmakers that serve them. The life you protect will endure. It will be your legacy, a gracious salute to life when most of humanity recognizes there is nothing more important than a healthy planetary life-support system.

Whether urban or rural, conservative or liberal, this culture and ethnicity or that, standing in mock helplessness is not living. It's postponing disaster and handing off the solutions to our children, who will bear the brunt of the previous generation's denial.

* * *

I believe the defense of life itself—not humanity in false isolation—is instinctive for those who possess the eco-psyche. But instinct blends with the spectrum of emotion. My obsession to save wilderness fed the anxiety, and vice versa. Both fed the depression. They were fanned by cynicism and teased by the desert of hope. I was a blind elk tortured by the rut, chasing the desire for contentment amid the chaos of Earth's agony.

Yet healing comes with acceptance: I sit beside the Methow River and ask the mountain whether my work meant anything. The answer is, once again, that I do not wish to be remembered for who I was, but for what I left behind. I certainly didn't do it for fame, which is good because upon my departure, there was none. I walked away from my organization quietly, ensuring my unimpeded exit.

It is a fragile contentment, yet I believe my retirement—walking the woods in peace, biking the back roads, paddling the living streams, and basking in solitude—was earned. I still enjoy dreaming about how the world could be if we humans respected nature. I did my best, and the reinforcement of good deeds done is now a means to cast off the cold wet blanket of depression when it rises.

* * *

My path of activism taught me that our minds are ecosystems, and wilderness can be a refuge for the most tortured of them: a living Valhalla where we go to find our true selves, where freedom is unconditional and expressed in physical form. Wilderness is where the anguish of recognizing our culture's misdirection is assuaged. It's the place where the scalding eye of surveillance is shut, and where the turmoil of the brain is not judged. It is where seemingly random color and form blend into perception's miracle, and our own moods reflect those of the world. It is where our existence is embraced without condition.

I now take comfort in recognizing the inseparable parallel between the internal and external ecosystems. My internal ecosystem was cursed with the dire composition of Dagloth. But it was graced with the eco-psyche, just as calm complements the storm. Even though I don't know how either got there, or why each is so extreme, I beg for the salvation of the eco-psyche more than for the defeat of Dagloth.

In my frantic pursuit to save wilderness, I was endeavoring to illuminate that innocent aspect of oneself that sometimes glows forth—like a wolf pup peering out from the den with wide yellow eyes after a raging storm. Wilderness is the uncorrupted slice of our psyche that the social collective endeavors to usurp.

I take heart. There is so much good in so many of us. The constituency of humans who respect and understand life is growing. It is composed of those who believe in evolution, and those who believe in creation, and those who believe in both. At their root, both philosophies honor life. I have the deepest gratitude for folks of all persuasions who embrace the eco-psyche—the instinctive love of nature. Therein lies our collective hope.

We all fit into the equation. As for me, despite the curse of depression, I think I'll stay alive for now. I'd really like to see if a few of my dreams might yet come true.

THE END

SUNSET FROM PETE'S PEAK, WALLOWA MOUNTAINS

Manuscript Counsel

Lois Barry
Michael Beaudoin
Mary McCombs
Lynn Post
Suzanne Sherman

* * *

Inspiring Allies

Kathleen Ackley
Karen Anspacher-Meyer
Lori Aschenbrenner
Mike Bader
Jim Baker
John Barker
Amy Barnouw
Jack Barry
Claudia Beausoleil
Adam Berger
June Bombaci
Jim Bradley
Susan Jane Brown
Will Brown
Brett Brownscombe
Harriet Bullitt
Emory Bundy
David Carle
Shelly Cimon
Vic Coggins
Joel Connoly
Sue Coleman
Tim Coleman
Juanette Cremin
Marnie Criley
Marilyn Cripe
Kate Crockett
Tom Derry
Jennier Devlin
Louie Dick, Jr.
Lisa Dix
Barbara Dugelby
Greg Dyson
Alice Elshoff
Brock Evans
Kevin Everhart
Dave Foreman
Mitch Friedman
Paul Fritz
Pete Frost
Craig Gehrke
Esack Grueskin
Judy Guse Noritake
Jessica Hamilton
Mike Hammar
Doug Heiken
Dick Hentze
Mike Higgins
Levi Holt
Loren Hughes
Mike Jakubal
Denise Joines
Chas Jones
Jim Jontz
Carole King
Min Lee
Charlotte Levinson
Karen Lillebo
Tim Lillebo
Martin Litton
Gilly Lyons
Mary McCracken
Al McGlinsky
Ralf Meyer
James Monteith
Mary Beth Nearing
Jonathan Nicholas
Julie Norman
Mary O'Brien
Bob Packwood
Darilyn Parry-Brown
Karen Pickett
Laurel Reuben
Mike Rozelle
Dave Rusk
Jennifer Schemm
David Sears
Vic Sher
Liam Sherlock
Dave Simon
Tony Sowers
Randi Spivak
Andy Stahl
Valerie Wade
Bethanie Walder
Veronica Warnock
Paul Watson
Cathy Wiggins
Ross Wiggins
Dave Willis
Marcy Willow
Ken Witty
Tara Wolfson
Howie Wolke

All apologies to those I missed

* * *

Honest U.S. Forest Service Officers

Ed Cole
Woody Fine
Jim Furnish
Mike Liu
John Lowe
Meg Mitchell
Kurt Wiedenmann
Karyn Wood

RIC BAILEY: WORKER AND ACTIVIST

While growing up in the suburbs of Portland, Oregon, Ric Bailey irrepressibly gravitated toward wanderlust, and was besieged by a craving for the wild outdoors. He was quiet and independent, yet a somewhat rebellious kid.

After high school, he migrated to rural enclaves and eventually resided in many small mountain towns throughout the Pacific Northwest, beckoned by nearby backcountry.

Ric's work history began as a jack of many blue collar trades. He worked as a timber faller, long haul trucker, wildland firefighter, and river guide. He became a self-taught wilderness activist after the shock of realizing the irreplaceable wild places he loved were being dismantled by runaway industrial exploitation.

In 1984 he resurrected the dormant Hells Canyon Preservation Council after being struck by federal mismanagement of the public lands embracing his new homeland: The Hells Canyon–Wallowa Mountain Ecosystem of northeast Oregon and western Idaho.

During his activist career, Ric faced off with a corrupt federal agency, and dealt with overt hostility from logging and ranching proponents in the rural community of Joseph, Oregon. He faced down death threats, was shut out of local businesses, and was hung in effigy by local political opponents.

In his memoir, Ric describes his unconventional transition from a blue collar worker with no college education to a white collar executive director of a formidable local conservation organization. He graphically describes his liaisons with wild places, and draws a deeply personal parallel between the need for respite from clinical depression and the healing power of the natural world.

Ric now resides in the rural enclave of the Methow Valley in the North Cascades of Washington, and has risen from retirement to combat the same threats to his new home he faced in the Hells Canyon–Wallowa Country. I'm proud of his dedication to his cause, and his principles. After all, I'm his mother.

—Wilma Bailey

photo credit: Cynthia Hunter

www.lonedruidchronicles.com

For this and other titles available from Wake-Robin Press, please visit:
www.wakerobinpress.com

Also available through Ingram, Amazon.com, Barnesandnoble.com, Powells.com and by special order through your local bookstore.

www.ingramcontent.com/pod-product-compliance
Lightning Source LLC
Chambersburg PA
CBHW050930240426
43671CB00020B/2975